SHARE

SHARE

DELICIOUS AND SURPRISING RECIPES TO PASS AROUND YOUR TABLE

CHRIS SANTOS

WITH RICK RODGERS

Photography by Quentin Bacon

GRAND CENTRAL
Life & Style
NEW YORK • BOSTON

Copyright © 2017 by Chris Santos

Cover design by Gary Tooth / Empire Design Studio.
Cover photography by Quentin Bacon.
Cover copyright © 2017 by Hachette Book Group, Inc.

Hachette Book Group supports the right to free expression and the value of copyright. The purpose of copyright is to encourage writers and artists to produce the creative works that enrich our culture.

The scanning, uploading, and distribution of this book without permission is a theft of the author's intellectual property. If you would like permission to use material from the book (other than for review purposes), please contact permissions@hbgusa.com. Thank you for your support of the author's rights.

Grand Central Life & Style
Hachette Book Group
1290 Avenue of the Americas, New York, NY 10104

grandcentrallifeandstyle.com

twitter.com/grandcentralpub

First Edition: February 2017

Grand Central Life & Style is an imprint of Grand Central Publishing. The Grand Central Life & Style name and logo are trademarks of Hachette Book Group, Inc.

The publisher is not responsible for websites (or their content) that are not owned by the publisher.

The Hachette Speakers Bureau provides a wide range of authors for speaking events. To find out more, go to www.hachettespeakersbureau.com or call (866) 376-6591.

Photography copyright © 2017 by Quentin Bacon

Print book interior design by Gary Tooth / Empire Design Studio.
Food Stylist: Suzanne Lenzer
Food Stylist Assistants: Erica Clark, Kate Schmidt

Library of Congress Cataloging-in-Publication Data

Names: Santos, Chris, 1971- | Rodgers, Rick, 1953-
Title: Share : Delicious and Surprising Recipes to Pass Around Your Table / Chris Santos with Rick Rodgers ; photographs by Quentin Bacon.
Description: New York : Grand Central Life & Style, [2017] | Includes index.
Identifiers: LCCN 2016029295 | ISBN 9781455538430 (hardcover) | ISBN 9781455538423 (e-book)
Subjects: LCSH: Cooking. | LCGFT: Cookbooks.
Classification: LCC TX714 .S2833 2017 | DDC 641.5—dc23 LC record available at https://lccn.loc.gov/2016029295

ISBNs: 978-1-4555-3843-0 (hardcover); 978-1-4555-3842-3 (ebook)

Printed in the United States of America

Q-MA

10 9 8 7 6 5 4 3 2 1

THIS BOOK IS DEDICATED TO
MARY LOU
(MY SIBLINGS CALL HER MOM, BUT SHE'LL
ALWAYS BE MARY LOU TO ME), WITHOUT
WHOM NEITHER THIS BOOK, NOR MY
AMAZING LIFE AS A CHEF, WOULD HAVE
BEEN POSSIBLE.

VIII   INTRODUCTION: SHARING AS A WAY OF LIFE

2   SHARE YOUR COOKING

12   COCKTAILS

32   STARTERS

64   SALADS AND A SOUP

84   CHICKEN

104   SEAFOOD

INTRODUCTION

SHARING AS A WAY OF LIFE

For over 20 years, day in and day out (or, I should say, night in and night out), I have watched people socialize over my signature dishes at my restaurants. I've always created food that is designed to be passed around the table, where forks and knives are often left untouched because much of the meal is comprised of fun finger foods. My vibrant dining rooms are filled with people creating memories over their shared dining experience.

Share: Delicious and Surprising Recipes to Pass Around Your Table extols the idea that communal eating is the best way to enjoy an amazing dinner while catching up with friends, celebrating a special occasion with family, or simply bringing people together for the sake of a party!

At-home entertaining is an even more intimate experience than dining out. The effort and love that go into hosting a dinner party or brunch are most clearly felt through the dishes you serve. For that reason, when it comes time to play host, I want to think you will use this book to impress your guests—and have fun—with some of my favorite recipes.

I am one of four siblings. When I was growing up, both of my parents worked long hours at night and I was often left to fend for myself in the kitchen while my mom delivered babies at the nearby hospital. (That's a true story.) But, when we did manage to have the rare family dinner, not sharing was *not* an option. Six sets of arms were reaching in every direction, clamoring for my mom's famous Chouriço and Pepper Sloppy Joes (page 158), among many other dishes.

When I think of my life as an adult, I realize that I've done a lot of laughing with my mouth full, and rarely at a "fancy" restaurant. My best memories have been of meals where the food was exciting and fun to eat, and was enjoyed with beloved company. Years ago, my business partner Rich Wolf and I started forgoing the entrées when we ate out. Instead, we started ordering every appetizer on the menu. The appetizers were always our favorite part of the meal because they were much easier to share and we were able to taste a bunch of different flavors as opposed to the typical three-course format. We were always passing around a copious amount of dishes, yelling things like "You have to try this! It's incredible!" I realized that the flexibility and camaraderie of this shared style of dining was adding to my overall dining (and tasting) experience, and I embraced this communal format as the best way to serve my guests, both in my restaurants and in my home.

Share is about how to entertain your friends and family with creative food in the comfort of *your* home. When people think about entertaining, they often consider the drinks they are going to serve or the music they are going to play as the pivotal elements. For me, the food always comes first. I like my food to do the entertaining, and that's why I serve dishes that are delicious but that are also innovative enough to start conversations among my guests—about the food and also about just how much they are enjoying every bite.

At the end of the day, life is too short for boring food. It sounds so simplistic, but it's true! People come to my restaurants and to my home because they know that they are going to have a great meal *and* a good time. I hope *Share* will help you re-create a perennial party in your own kitchen.

And because brunch has become such a popular time for people to socialize, I am concluding this book with my brunch recipes, ranging from savory delights like baked eggs (page 247) and breakfast tacos (page 251) to sweeter offerings like the over-the-top French toast bread pudding (page 263).

While I have tweaked many of the recipes for easier home cooking, in some cases I have kept the original, restaurant version intact. These items are marked *Santos Signature*. You'll also find notes, dubbed *Chef Talk*, with some of my thoughts on various ingredients and culinary techniques.

These are the dishes that I come back to time and time again when I am hosting a party because I know that they are the ones everyone at the table is going to love. From the simplest of dishes to the most complex, you can be assured that all of the recipes in this book have been road tested as guaranteed crowd pleasers. My hope is that some of these recipes become incorporated into your go-to menu when it comes time to entertain.

My main goal for *Share* is to, well, share with you a different way of cooking for your friends and family by sharing (there's that word again) my favorite recipes with new twists on old favorites along the way.

—*Chris Santos*

SHARE

YOUR COOKING

Eating is only partly about sustaining your body. It is also about *dining*, sustaining and developing relationships among the people at the table and one of the most important ways that people come together.

Over time, the dining experience transformed from a crowded table of family or friends into a ritual of eating alone. Even when people are sitting together, each person kept his or her own plate and did not share. In fact, it is often considered rude to reach across the table and dig into another diner's plate. Not at my table!

Too many meals follow a format, a carved-in-stone approach to eating. I would rather have the experience be full of surprises, a kind of potluck where guests don't have to bring anything and never quite know what is going to be served next. My best meals have been the ones that have been intimate and communal at the same time: intimate because I was with close friends, yet communal because of the elements of sharing and community.

In a perfect world, people would spend more time enjoying weeknight dinners together at home. But, realistically, most of the people I know reserve their "special" cooking for the weekends when they have more time. While there are recipes in this book that you can make on a school night, I prefer to plan my more complex cooking for leisurely meals with friends and family.

Here are some details on how to have the *Share* experience with your friends and family.

MAKE IT SPECIAL

In addition to great food, I have two huge passions: boxing and rock music (especially drumming). Like chefs, boxers and drummers need very specific skills, and there is a big instant-gratification component of the jobs. In all three professions, if you want to be a star, you have to be unique—a lethal uppercut, a cutting staccato riff, a talent for mixing flavors.

When you cook, you want people to walk away from the table saying, "Wow, I couldn't have had a better meal anywhere else." Give your guests food to talk about on their way home. That said, my time is important to me, so when I cook at home, I want it well spent to make a memorable meal, not just food on the table. And I want the same for you.

In the pages that follow, I include some special favorites that are right out of my family's recipe box, including my mom's spicy Chouriço and Pepper Sloppy Joes (page 158) and my grandmother's melt-in-your-mouth meatballs (page 142). But for the most part, I like to create dishes that are whimsical and irreverent twists on well-known favorites. I am inspired by the comfort foods of Americana, such as Twinkies, chicken wings, corn dogs, and crab cakes (I've even combined these last two in the same dish on page 48), as much as I am inspired by international street foods like dumplings, tacos, and arepas. Mix all of these inspirations together, and the results include dishes like my spicy mac 'n' cheese (page 169), a traditional American baked macaroni spiked with a Mexican spin of sausage and chiles.

In selecting the rest of the recipes for this book, I concentrated on the flavorful ingredients that can make home cooking more adventuresome with the goal of expanding your culinary repertoire.

MAKING YOUR MENU

The majority of these recipes are self-contained and don't require side dishes—they are small bites to savor in a mouthful or two. I rarely serve plated dishes as individual servings (unless it is for dramatic effect like the Individual Beef Wellingtons on page 130). Instead, I love to offer up large platters of finger food, generous bowls of heaping pastas and salads, beautiful sliced steaks, and smaller dishes of starches and vegetables to round out the meal.

Do not be scared by long ingredients lists! I have been sure to break each recipe down into its individual components, many of which are no more complicated than stirring the listed ingredients together. There are no recipes where you cook all of the way through from start to finish. Instead, each element can be prepared separately, and beforehand, so it is just a matter of putting together each dish before serving.

This is the secret to my success in my restaurants, and it can be applied to create a perfect party at home. Our restaurant guests marvel at how we can serve hundreds of people every night with such delicious consistency. The answer is that it is all in the planning. When the various components are prepped ahead of time, not only will you be relaxed before your guests arrive, but you'll be able to get brunch or dinner on the table while enjoying the pleasure of their company.

Most of all, I want you to break loose of the expected course progression. I always begin my parties with cocktails and I always end them with dessert (and perhaps some more cocktails), but everything that happens in between is a parade of dishes dictated by what's ready first. Mix up your planned menu with dishes that are finished and those that need some last-minute finishing touches so you can enjoy the party, too.

STOCK THE PERFECT PANTRY

Every chef has not-so-secret ingredients (condiments, seasonings, and other foods) that deliver huge bang-for-the-buck flavor.

The pantry is a great place to start upping your game. Get to know the ethnic markets in your area. Latino and Asian markets are terrific places to find interesting ingredients to use in your everyday and special occasion cooking. So often I'll hear a home cook say, "I can't find such-and-such at my market." When I explore the issue, I find out that it is more a case of "I have never *looked* for such-and-such at my market." Recently, I was at a commonplace suburban market looking for canned chipotles and found arepa flour on the shelves!

Many of these not-so-secret ingredients are loaded with umami, the "fifth flavor" that adds dimension to dishes. Fermented ingredients (such as miso, Korean seasoning pastes, and fish sauce) are famous for ratcheting up flavors in a just a spoonful.

Take a trip to an ethnic market, if you have one in your neighborhood, and load up. Or hop on the internet and buy them online. (If you do the latter, buy a few items at once to save on delivery costs. I am not providing individual sources for shopping because a simple Google search will uncover countless options.)

Most of these ingredients are cheap and keep forever. Only a couple of items in the boxed list of must-haves even need refrigeration.

Asian

Chunjang: A thick, fermented Korean black bean paste.

Fish sauce: Either Vietnamese (nam pla) or Thai (nuoc mam) fish sauce, with a salty profile similar to soy sauce; skip the less flavorful Indonesian variety (pastis).

Furikake: A Japanese seasoning to sprinkle on top of cooked rice; can be very colorful with green wasabi or pink dried salmon.

Gochujang: A brick-red Korean chili paste with the consistency of peanut butter.

Green papaya: One of the most refreshing salad ingredients on the planet, this is a specific variety of fruit (not just unripe standard papaya) with a firm texture and neutral flavor, perfect for soaking up tasty dressings.

Miso (white or mild): A salty paste made from fermented grains; the mild white (shiromiso) version is the most versatile.

Sambal oelek: Indonesian ground chili paste, one of my favorite spicy condiments.

Soy sauce: Kikkoman is a reliable Japanese brand that always tastes the same, which cannot be said for the many varieties of Chinese soy sauce, so I have specifically called for it in the recipes.

Sriracha: Similar to sambal oelek, but this hot sauce has a distinct vinegar flavor.

Thai basil: A fresh herb with an entirely different flavor than Italian basil (some think it has an anise-like taste), although it is equally delicious.

GET YOUR ACT TOGETHER

Latino

Ancho chile (pure ground): A very useful chile powder with a mild, sweet heat. It is now available at supermarkets in the spice section, although it is most economically purchased in larger quantities online or at Latino markets.

Chipotles (canned, in adobo): Smoked jalapeños, packed in a vinegar sauce. They are a perfect example of a foreign food that has mainstreamed. After you open a can, the remaining chiles can be refrigerated in a small covered container for months.

Smoked paprika: A product of Spain, and sometimes called pimentón de la Vera. Buy the sweet variety (meaning only that it is not very spicy), which is more useful than the hot version.

Miscellaneous

Grating cheeses: Parmigiano-Reggiano is the king of Italian grating cheeses—accept no substitutes. Save the rinds to simmer in sauces. I also like the sharpness of Pecorino Romano and the nutty tang of Asiago.

Harissa: Hailing from Morocco and North Africa, a complex mix of spices and ground chile. The moist paste is sold in cans and very convenient tubes. Don't confuse it with the dry harissa spice seasoning. If you buy the canned version, transfer any leftovers to a small jar, and it will keep in the refrigerator for weeks.

Merguez: Spicy coarse lamb sausage seasoned with harissa—and my favorite sausage. When you find it (try specialty butchers and halal markets), buy extra to freeze.

Smoked peppercorns: I like adding these to rubs for extra smoky flavor.

Vinegars: A commonplace ingredient not to be underestimated—it is an important flavoring, and you should have a few different kinds. Supermarket-variety balsamic is OK, but for the best flavor, use the more pricey aged balsamic. Champagne and white wine vinegars bring a lighter, but distinct, flavor to dressings and more.

White truffle oil: An intensely perfumed oil that should be used sparingly, or the funky flavor and aroma of truffle will take over.

In my restaurants, customers are often surprised at how my staff can serve hundreds of people so effortlessly (or so it may seem). The answer is: Almost every part of a dish is made ahead and pulled together at the last minute. You should apply this "secret" to how you entertain at home, too.

When I cook at home, I think of the Rolling Stones' "Time Is on My Side": I let time do its job to enhance the food. Marinating and brining bring incredible flavor and extra moisture to meats and poultry; sauces that have been made a few hours (or even days) ahead get a chance to bloom and develop. Use this make-ahead technique to your advantage because quickly made food often comes with a trade-off in the overall flavor.

When you are unfamiliar with a recipe, read it through a few times to be sure you understand the game plan. I am a big proponent of *mise en place*— "setting in place," or having all your ingredients ready before you start cooking. This used to be entirely unfamiliar to American home cooks, but TV shows like *Chopped* have changed that. Prep every single item, no matter how mundane, right down to mincing the parsley garnish.

I also provide make-ahead instructions for every component of a recipe, so when you are ready for the final assembly, it is often just a matter of putting the various parts together. Don't let long ingredients lists turn you off. Very often the same ingredients are repeated a few times, and it all melds to give the dish the depth of flavor that will set your cooking apart from the rest of the pack.

Very useful, if not essential, is a stack of small and medium bowls, again just like on TV, to hold your prepped ingredients. (Plastic delicatessen containers are also good and are unbreakable.) If you cover them, do so loosely with plastic wrap so the covering is easy to remove when you are ready for action.

When the food requires hands-on attention (say, folding dumplings and pierogi), ask your friends to jump in. It is another way to get people to share the dining experience. Set out a bowl of the filling, the wrappers, and a couple of brushes (some dumplings are sealed with a brushed-on liquid), and you will have a mountain of dumplings in no time.

Speaking of action, write down a schedule for cooking each dish of the meal. You won't believe how helpful this is when you are cooking a number of recipes for the first time. You might also want to make a prep list, too. It feels very satisfying when you cross a chore off that to-do list.

Perhaps the most important aspect of making a multi-course meal is choosing the right recipes. Combine dishes that need last-minute attention with those that can simply be put out on the table, such as the pickled vegetables (page 61). Know your strengths—if you like making dessert, spend a little extra time on that part of the meal. If you hate baking, purchase a stunning dessert and feel no shame. The important thing is that you, as the cook, enjoy the party, too.

Party Playlists

I love music. When I have a party, I carefully choose the sounds to go with the mood. After all, not every gathering is the same. Mellow, hyper, daytime, nighttime—each has its own soundtrack. There are so many ways for you to get music for your party—mainly music-streaming services—that you don't need me to tell you how to manage it. Some streaming services even have party-ready playlists. Just search for them within the service, and play away.

MAKE IT A PARTY

I love throwing parties! Because I like to cook for my friends at home, I am prepared for cooking for a crowd. But nothing is more frustrating than trying to cook for a group when you have a tiny skillet and are short on platters and other serving implements. Plan ahead!

AT THE TABLE

Cocktail napkins: You can never have too many small paper napkins to act as coasters, to serve with starters, and for quickly sopping up little spills (which are actually the hallmark of a great party).

Big napkins: At my meals, there is a lot of eating with fingers, so big cotton napkins (some of the polyester ones just aren't absorbent) are essential items. White works here, as you won't have to worry about clashing colors, and you can usually bleach out stains.

Tablecloths: Here is an instance when I like dark colors to camouflage spills, crumbs, and so forth.

Glasses: The "right wine in the right glass" frame of mind works at formal dinners, but for more casual parties, don't get finicky. Those stemless glasses do double duty for both wine and cocktails and are much harder to knock over... especially when there is the amount of reaching and passing that I like to see. Let's just pretend that plastic glasses don't exist. I don't care if the glasses are cheap, as long as they are made of glass.

Plates: You can't lose with white plates, both for their versatility and to set off the food well. For a meal where food is going to be shared, a tall stack of smaller plates might be more useful than a smaller number of dinner plates, especially if you like to provide fresh dishes after serving something with a lot of sauce.

Serving utensils: Always count and be sure that you have enough spoons, large forks, and short-handled tongs to serve up the food.

Cake stands: Decorative cake stands can be used for more than cakes. Height is important in serving food—lifting a serving platter off the table will give a sense of drama to the proceedings. Put a platter on a cake stand to make a bit more room on the table and allow for easier serving.

Platters and bowls: Long (over 14 inches) and oval platters are very useful, especially when serving individual pieces of food, such as my open-faced arepas (page 96) or shrimp and "grits" (page 119). Solid colors work best because they allow the food to be showcased. Avoid platters that have busy patterns that will clash with your cooking, unless you are sure designs match up with the food.

KITCHEN ESSENTIALS

Large baking dishes and gratins: Have a few sizes of these oven-to-table serving pieces. And be sure to have fresh, clean potholders or kitchen towels on hand for passing the hot dishes.

Big skillets: By big, I mean 14 inches across and at least 2 inches deep. With a truly large skillet, you can brown meats properly (if crowded, the meat will steam and not brown). I really like cast iron skillets because they can be used as serving vessels, too (see my baked eggs on page 247). Sometimes, you'll serve right from the skillet, so don't forget to have a trivet (or two) already waiting at the table.

Half-sheet pans: Measuring 18 by 13 inches, these shallow aluminum pans are the workhorse of the kitchen. It's another item that you really can't have too many of. Sure, they're great for baking and roasting, but they are also good to hold your mise en place for a recipe, or to store the individual bases for finger food like my avocado or chicken liver focaccia (pages 47 and 44). Quarter-sheet pans, which are 13 by 9 inches, are also useful.

COCKTAILS

In many cookbooks, beverages are placed at the end of the book, sometimes as a kind of afterthought. That is not the way I roll! I always offer my guests something to drink as soon as they walk through my door. Like my cooking, my cocktails have to have something extra and unexpected. A house drink—something made especially for the gathering at hand—is a great way to demonstrate hospitality. I offer recipes for individual portions, but also pitcher-sized batches, in order to save time when pouring out multiple servings. And don't forget to always have something interesting for the non-drinkers, be it fresh-squeezed juice or a booze-free punch—be sure everyone gets the true beverage of their choice!

BEAUTY
Elixir
—
The
CORONADO
—
Emerald
GIMLET
—
Ginger Rogers
—
PINK
GRAPEFRUIT–
Mint Martini
—
La Presa
—
The
Woodsman

Red Tequila
SANGRIA
—
The Best
BLOODY MARY
—
GARNET
Gimlet
—
WHITE SANGRIA
with
Cranberry and
Cucumber
—
Ruby Red
Punch
—
SHERRY-CITRUS
PUNCH

Beauty Elixir

Gin brings its herbaceous flavor to this pink drink, a favorite at Beauty & Essex, one of my restaurants on the Lower East Side of Manhattan. If you are looking for the perfect drink for a Sunday ladies' brunch, look no further than this fruit-forward drink splashed with a bit of bubbly.

2 (¼-inch) slices Kirby cucumber, unpeeled, plus more for garnish

¾ ounce (1½ tablespoons) strawberry puree (see Note)

1½ ounces London dry gin

¼ ounce fresh lemon juice

¼ ounce Lemon Simple Syrup (page 25)

½ ounce rosé sparkling wine or Champagne, as needed

Muddle the cucumber and strawberry puree well in a cocktail shaker. Add ice and the gin, lemon juice, and lemon syrup; shake well. Strain into a chilled martini glass. Top with the sparkling wine. Garnish with a cucumber slice and serve.

Note: *To make strawberry puree, process hulled strawberries as needed (3 large strawberries make about 1½ tablespoons puree) in a mini–food processor until smooth.*

Party-Sized Beauty Elixir: Pulse 8 slices cucumber and 3 ounces (6 tablespoons) strawberry puree in a blender to mince them. Add 6 ounces (¾ cup) gin, 1 ounce (2 tablespoons) fresh lemon juice, and 1 ounce (2 tablespoons) lemon syrup and pulse just to combine. Strain the gin mixture through a wire sieve into a small pitcher. (The mixture can be covered and stored at room temperature for up to 3 hours.) For each drink, pour about 3 ounces (a generous ⅓ cup) into an ice-filled cocktail shaker. Strain into a martini glass, top with the sparkling wine, and garnish with a cucumber slice.

Makes 4 cocktails

DRIED CITRUS CHIPS

Makes about 30 chips (10 chips of each fruit)

When I throw a party, I try to make every single element a bit more special than my guests expect. This even includes the citrus garnishes for my cocktails. Yes, you can cut round slices (sometimes called wheels) from lemons, limes, and oranges to perch on the edge of your glass. But, with a little extra effort, you can candy and then dry them to create dried citrus chips. You can make more than one kind of fruit at a time, and they keep for months.

1 cup sugar

1 cup water

1 navel orange, ends discarded, cut into ⅛-inch rounds

1 large lemon, ends discarded, cut into ⅛-inch rounds

1 large lime, ends discarded, cut into ⅛-inch rounds

1. Bring the sugar and water to a boil in a small saucepan over high heat, stirring constantly until the sugar is dissolved. Boil for 2 minutes. Let cool until warm.

2. Place the orange, lemon, and lime slices in separate small bowls (such as cereal bowls). Pour enough syrup over each fruit to cover it well. Let the fruit soak for 30 minutes.

3. Position racks in the top third and center of the oven and preheat to 200°F. (If you have a convection oven, use the convection bake setting and reduce the temperature to 175°F.) Line large rimmed baking sheets with wire cake racks.

4. Drain each fruit well and arrange the rounds in separate groupings on the racks. Bake, flipping the rounds over after 30 minutes, until they are firm, about 1 hour total. The large orange rounds may take about 20 minutes longer. If possible, let the chips cool completely in the turned-off oven overnight. (The chips can be stored in airtight containers at room temperature for up to 3 months.)

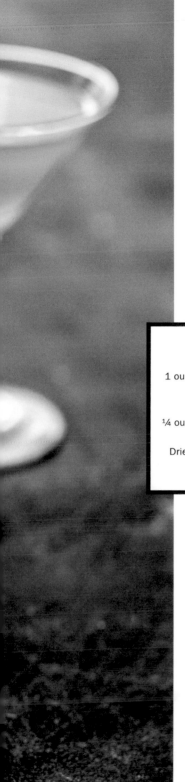

The Coronado

MAKES

1 *or* 4

COCKTAILS

Margarita, move over… there's a new tequila drink in town! With tropical flavors from passion fruit and coconut water, the Coronado also gets a slightly bitter edge from Aperol. Although it is almost a century old, the orange-based Italian aperitif has established itself as a new favorite with mixologists.

2 ounces coconut water

1½ ounces silver tequila

1 ounce passion fruit juice (available frozen at Latino markets)

1 ounce Aperol

¼ ounce fresh lemon juice, preferably Meyer lemon

Dried orange chip (see page 16) or orange wheel, for garnish

Combine the coconut water, tequila, passion fruit juice, Aperol, and lemon juice in an ice-filled cocktail shaker. Shake and strain into a tall, ice-filled glass. Garnish with the orange chip.

Party-Sized Coronado: Combine 8 ounces (1 cup) coconut water, 6 ounces (¾ cup) silver tequila, 4 ounces (½ cup) passion fruit juice, 4 ounces (½ cup) Aperol, and 1 ounce (2 tablespoons) fresh lemon juice in a small pitcher. (The mixture can be stored at room temperature for up to 3 hours.) For each serving, pour a scant 6 ounces (about ¾ cup) into a tall, ice-filled glass and garnish with an orange chip.

Makes 4 cocktails

Emerald GIMLET

MAKES

1 *or* 4

COCKTAILS

The Emerald Gimlet looks like something the Wizard of Oz might order and drink down in a couple of gulps. Bright green from a muddle of fresh basil and lime juice, it is equally suited for a sophisticated nighttime soiree and a casual backyard summer cookout.

---

5 large basil leaves

¾ ounce fresh lime juice

2 ounces vodka

¼ ounce Lemon Simple Syrup (page 25)

Dried lime chip (see page 16) or lime wheel, for garnish

Muddle the basil and lime juice together well in a cocktail shaker, extracting as much green basil juice as reasonably possible. Add ice, and pour in the vodka and lemon syrup. Shake well and strain into a martini glass. Float a lime chip on the cocktail surface and serve.

Party-Sized Emerald Gimlet: It is best to serve this cocktail within an hour of making, before the basil oxidizes. Pulse 20 large basil leaves and 3 ounces (6 tablespoons) fresh lime juice in a blender to just crush the basil. Add 8 ounces (1 cup) vodka and 1 ounce (2 tablespoons) lemon syrup and pulse to combine. Strain the vodka mixture through a fine wire sieve into a small pitcher, discarding the solids. (The mixture can be covered and stored at room temperature for up to 1 hour.) For each drink, pour about 3 ounces (6 tablespoons) of the vodka mixture into an ice-filled cocktail shaker. Shake and strain into a martini glass. Garnish with a lime chip.

Makes 4 cocktails

BAR ESSENTIALS

Of course, any die-hard whiskey or tequila drinker wants his or her standard drink, so I always stock a bar for people to help themselves in addition to serving my specialty drinks. To be sure that you have all of your options covered, where appropriate I give recipes for both single servings and larger batches. But some drinks, such as punches and sangrias, are always best served in one large portion to accommodate your entire party. (Having a second batch waiting in the fridge is never a bad idea either.)

Great cocktails do require a few inexpensive tools. First, the best bartenders always measure their ingredients for reliable results. For accurate measuring, use a **jigger**, a small cup with markings for fluid ounces, the standard measurement for making cocktails. (A jigger is also the name of the outdated measurement used to make cocktails—one jigger equaled 1½ ounces or 3 tablespoons. No bartender I know uses that term anymore, although you will still find 1½-ounce-capacity metal jiggers for sale.) For some large-batch recipes, you'll need a transparent **liquid measuring cup**. (For your convenience, I also give the larger measurements in cups so you won't have to do any math. Use your jigger for the smaller amounts.)

A **cocktail shaker (aka cobbler shaker)** is used to mix "straight up" cocktails, the ones served chilled and not over ice. This shaker has a perforated lid so you won't have to purchase separate strainers to keep the ice cubes at bay when pouring out the drink. The average home bartender with limited bar space will prefer this kind of shaker to the large **Boston shaker**, comprised of a large mixing glass and even larger metal container that acts as the lid during shaking. Yes, it is the professional's favorite shaker, but it takes some practice to learn how to use it, and a cobbler shaker is a no-brainer right out of the box. A Boston shaker also uses either the perforated **julep strainer** or the spring-lined **Hawthorne strainer** to top the mixing glass when pouring a drink into the glass. But my recommendation is to get a cobbler shaker and be done with it!

Other cocktails are stirred because shaking makes them foamy. A metal long-handled **bar spoon** is optional (as an iced-tea spoon would work just as well), but it's sometimes good to have one stashed at the bar, easy to find when you need it.

Some cocktails get extra flavor from fruit, herbs, or other ingredients *muddled* (that is, crushed) into the shaker glass. Sure, you can use a long-handled spoon, but a blunt-nosed **muddler** is much more efficient. There are many models, but the heavier, wider ones are best. When making a large batch of drinks, a blender works well too, but take care to crush the solid ingredients without pulverizing them.

Ginger Rogers

MAKES
1 *or* 4
COCKTAILS

Even people who aren't old movie fans know the name Ginger Rogers, and associate her with the musicals of Hollywood's Golden Age. After a sip or two of this drink, you may start singing and dancing, too. Fresh ginger juice is the secret ingredient, and gives the drink real kick.

> 2 quarter-sized slices fresh ginger
> (no need to peel)
>
> 2 ounces orange-flavored vodka
>
> 1 ounce Lemon Simple Syrup
> (page 25)
>
> 1 ounce fresh orange juice
>
> About 1 ounce lemon-lime soda,
> as needed for serving

Using a garlic press, squeeze the juice from the ginger into a cocktail shaker. Add ice with the orange vodka, lemon syrup, and orange juice. Shake well and strain into an ice-filled tall glass, leaving 1 inch of headroom. Fill the glass with the lemon-lime soda and stir gently.

Party-Sized Ginger Rogers: Pulse 8 quarter-sized slices of fresh ginger and 8 ounces (1 cup) orange-flavored vodka in a blender to chop the ginger. Add 4 ounces (½ cup) lemon syrup and 4 ounces (½ cup) orange juice and stir well. Strain the mixture through a wire sieve into a container, pressing hard on the solids. (The cocktail base can be stored at room temperature for up to 3 hours.) For each drink, pour about 4 ounces (½ cup) of the orange mixture over ice in a glass, leaving 1 inch of headroom. Pour about 1 ounce (2 tablespoons) lemon-lime soda into the glass, stir gently, and serve.

Makes 4 cocktails

PINK GRAPEFRUIT–MINT
MARTINI

You'll have to pace yourself when drinking this smooth and tart martini. If you think of a martini as an evening drink, preferably sipped in black tie with a cocktail piano tinkling in the background—think again. This is a great drink for any hour, especially when the sun is shining.

1 large sprig fresh mint
¼ ounce Lemon Simple Syrup (page 25)
2 ounces pink grapefruit juice
1½ ounces lemon-flavored vodka
1 fresh mint leaf, for garnish

MAKES

1 or 4

COCKTAILS

Muddle the mint sprig and lemon syrup in a cocktail shaker. Add ice with the grapefruit juice and lemon vodka. Shake well and strain into a martini glass. Float the mint leaf on the surface of the cocktail as a garnish.

Party-Sized Pink Grapefruit–Mint Martini: Pulse 4 large sprigs mint with 1 ounce (2 tablespoons) lemon syrup in a blender to chop the mint. Pour in 8 ounces (1 cup) pink grapefruit juice and 6 ounces (¾ cup) lemon-flavored vodka and pulse to combine. Strain through a fine-mesh sieve into a small pitcher, discarding the solids. (The mixture can be covered and stored at room temperature for up to 2 hours.) For each drink, shake about 4 ounces (½ cup) of the vodka mixture in an ice-filled cocktail shaker. Strain into a martini glass and garnish with a mint leaf floating on the surface.

Makes 4 cocktails

La Presa

MAKES

1 *or* 4

COCKTAILS

The only way to (slightly) improve on an icy shot of Jägermeister is to employ its incredible mix of spices and herbs in an even more complex cocktail. Smoky mescal can hold its own against the liqueur's complex flavors. Quick linguistics lesson: *Jägermeister* means "master hunter" in German, and *la presa* has a similar translation in Spanish.

---

3 sprigs fresh mint

¾ ounce Lemon Simple Syrup (page 25)

1½ ounces mescal

¾ ounce Jägermeister

¾ ounce fresh lime juice

1 dash Angostura bitters

Muddle the mint and lemon syrup well in a cocktail shaker. Add ice with the mescal, Jägermeister, lime juice, and bitters. Shake well. Strain into a tall, ice-filled glass.

Party-Sized La Presa: This is another drink that shouldn't linger too long before serving, or else the mint could turn brown. Pulse 12 sprigs fresh mint with 3 ounces (6 tablespoons) lemon syrup in a blender to coarsely chop the mint. Add 6 ounces (¾ cup) mescal, 3 ounces (6 tablespoons) Jägermeister, 3 ounces (6 tablespoons) lime juice, and 4 dashes of bitters and pulse just to combine. Strain the mescal mixture into a small pitcher. (The mixture can be covered and stored at room temperature for up to 1 hour.) For each drink, pour a scant 4 ounces (scant ½ cup) into an ice-filled glass.

Makes 4 *cocktails*

The WOODSMAN

MAKES

1 *or* 4

COCKTAILS

The Woodsman uses bourbon as its base liquor, a spirit that is aged in oak casks. But that's not where the wood connection ends, as all of the other ingredients come from trees—pear, maple, lemon, and allspice. This slightly spicy drink is best made with a very ripe and juicy pear.

¼ ripe pear, such as Bosc, unpeeled, cored and coarsely chopped

1½ ounces bourbon

½ ounce fresh lemon juice

¼ ounce pure maple syrup

¼ ounce allspice (pimento) dram (see Note)

Muddle the chopped pear well in a cocktail shaker. Add ice with the bourbon, lemon juice, maple syrup, and allspice dram. Shake very well. Strain into an ice-filled rocks glass.

Party-Sized Woodsman: Pulse 1 ripe pear (cored and thinly sliced), 6 ounces (¾ cup) bourbon, 2 ounces (¼ cup) fresh lemon juice, 1 ounce (2 tablespoons) maple syrup, and 1 ounce (2 tablespoons) allspice dram together in a blender to coarsely chop the pear. Strain the mixture through a fine-mesh sieve into a small pitcher and discard the solids. (The mixture can be covered and stored at room temperature for up to 4 hours.) For each drink, pour a scant 3 ounces (about ⅓ cup) into an ice-filled rocks glass.

Makes 4 cocktails

Note: *Allspice dram is a spice-flavored liqueur from Jamaica (where allspice is better known as pimento). If you can't find it at your local liquor store (St. Elizabeth and Bitter Truth are the most common brands), it can be ordered online, or make some according to one of the recipes on the internet.*

RED TEQUILA
SANGRIA

MAKES ABOUT **12** DRINKS

The best sangria recipes are more than red wine and fruit—they are fortified with spirits, too. In Spain, brandy is common, but I like this combination of American bourbon and Mexican tequila for a multi-national twist. For the best results, make the sangria the night before serving so the ingredients have time to really blend together.

18 ounces (about 2¼ cups, three-fourths of a 750-ml bottle) medium-bodied red wine, such as Rioja or Pinot Noir

10 ounces (1¼ cups) fresh orange juice, preferably blood orange

5 ounces (⅔ cup) reposado tequila

5 ounces (⅔ cup) bourbon

4 ounces (½ cup) fresh lime juice

4 ounces (½ cup) Simple Syrup (this page)

2 navel oranges, cut into thin wheels, for garnish

2 limes, cut into thin wheels, for garnish

Stir all of the ingredients except the garnishes together in a large pitcher. Cover and refrigerate for at least 2 hours or overnight. For each drink, pour about 4 ounces (½ cup) into an ice-filled wineglass, adding some of the fruit.

COCKTAIL SYRUPS

Many cocktail recipes use syrups to add sweetness and to balance the strength of the alcohol. Syrups are easy to make in small batches at home, but refrigerate them for storage, as they don't last forever. Here are the three syrups used in this book.

Simple Syrup
Makes about 6 ounces (¾ cup)

An easy mix of sugar and water, this is a common syrup for when the cocktail requires sweetness without any other flavors.

½ cup sugar

½ cup water

Bring the sugar and water to a boil in a small saucepan over high heat, stirring constantly to dissolve the sugar. Let cool. (The syrup can be refrigerated in a covered container for up to 2 weeks.)

Lemon Simple Syrup
Makes about 4 ounces (½ cup)

This citrusy syrup is used as a sweet-and-sour ingredient in many of our cocktails.

⅓ cup plus 1 tablespoon sugar

3 tablespoons water

1 tablespoon fresh lemon juice

Bring the sugar and water to a boil in a small saucepan over high heat, stirring constantly to dissolve the sugar. Remove from the heat and add the lemon juice. Let cool. (The syrup can be refrigerated in a covered container for up to 2 weeks.)

Cinnamon-Pear Syrup
Makes about 5 ounces (⅔ cup)

Used in Ruby Red Punch (page 30), this cinnamon-y syrup can also be added to hot cider for a warming nonalcoholic drink.

1 cup water

½ cup sugar

2 (3-inch) cinnamon sticks

½ ripe pear, such as Bosc, quartered (no need to peel or core)

Combine the water with the sugar, cinnamon sticks, and pear in a small saucepan. Bring to a boil over medium heat, stirring to dissolve the sugar. Reduce the heat to very low and simmer until the pear is soft, about 10 minutes. Remove from the heat. Using a wooden spoon, mash the pear in the liquid to extract as much juice as possible. Let cool. Strain through a fine-mesh sieve and discard the solids. (The syrup can be refrigerated in a covered container for up to 1 week.)

THE BEST
Bloody Mary

MAKES
ABOUT
12
DRINKS

If there's one thing I can't stand, it is wimpy Bloody Mary mix! If it is only a notch or two away from tomato juice, what's the point? My mix is full of some of my favorite seasonings, including Old Bay and Maggi. Between the horseradish, pepper sauce, and sriracha, I can guarantee that this Bloody Mary will have you feeling the heat.

1 (46-ounce) can tomato juice

¼ cup prepared horseradish

¼ cup brine from bottled olives

¼ cup Old Bay seasoning

1 tablespoon Maggi seasoning sauce (see Note)

1 tablespoon Worcestershire sauce

2 teaspoons hot red pepper sauce, such as Tabasco

2 teaspoons sriracha

2 teaspoons Dijon mustard

24 ounces (3 cups) vodka

Lime wedges, celery or carrot sticks, and/or pimiento-stuffed olives, for garnish

To make the base: Whisk all of the ingredients except the vodka and garnishes together in a large pitcher. For each drink, pour 2 ounces (¼ cup) vodka into a tall, ice-filled glass. Add about 4 ounces (½ cup) of the tomato juice mixture and stir. Add a garnish or two and serve.

Note: *Maggi seasoning sauce, with its base of hydrolyzed vegetable protein, is similar to, but not the same as, soy sauce. As such, this rich and salty condiment is packed with umami. It is considered an essential ingredient in Mexican and Southeast Asian kitchens.*

GARNET GIMLET

MAKES

1 *or* 4

MOCKTAILS

I am always sure to have something interesting to serve people who don't drink alcohol. The drink can be a cool soda pop, or freshly squeezed fruit juice, or a homemade beverage like this one with berries, basil, and ginger ale. It's a true mocktail because it is served straight up in a martini glass.

1½ ounces fresh strawberry puree, (see Note, page 15)

3 large fresh basil leaves, cut into fine shreds

2 ounces white cranberry juice

1 ounce fresh lime juice

¾ ounce fresh lemon juice

Splash of ginger ale

Dried lime chip (see page 16) or twist (see page 31), for garnish

Muddle the strawberry puree and basil together in a cocktail shaker. Add ice and the cranberry juice, lime juice, and lemon juice; shake well. Strain into a chilled martini glass and finish with a splash of ginger ale. Add the lime chip and serve.

Party-Sized Garnet Gimlet: Mix 6 ounces (¾ cup) strawberry puree, 12 shredded fresh basil leaves, 8 ounces (1 cup) white cranberry juice, 4 ounces (½ cup) fresh lime juice, and 3 ounces (6 tablespoons) fresh lemon juice in a large pitcher. For each drink, shake 4 ounces (½ cup) of the mixture in an ice-filled cocktail shaker. Strain into a chilled martini glass, garnish with a lime chip, and serve.

Makes 4 mocktails

WHITE SANGRIA *with*
Cranberry and Cucumber

MAKES
ABOUT
9
DRINKS

White sangria, with all the fruity wine flavor of the magenta version without the threat of staining your upholstery, is deliciously refreshing. The cranberry juice (pressed from the white cranberries that you'll occasionally see in the bag of red ones) makes this an especially great choice for a winter holiday bash.

18 ounces (about 2¼ cups, three-fourths of a 750-ml bottle) dry white wine, such as Pinot Grigio

4 ounces (½ cup) sweet white wine, such as Moscato

4 ounces (½ cup) white cranberry juice

6 ounces (¾ cup) fresh lemon juice

3 ounces (6 tablespoons) Simple Syrup (page 25)

1 medium Kirby cucumber, unpeeled, cut into thin rounds

18 ounces (about 2¼ cups) chilled seltzer water, as needed

Fresh mint sprigs, for garnish

Stir the dry white wine, sweet white wine, cranberry juice, lemon juice, and syrup together in a large pitcher. Add the cucumber, cover, and refrigerate for at least 2 hours or overnight. For each drink, pour about 4 ounces (½ cup) into a tall ice-filled glass, leaving about 1 inch of headspace. Fill with about 2 ounces (¼ cup) seltzer and stir gently. Garnish with a slice of soaked cucumber and a mint sprig. Serve immediately.

Ruby Red
PUNCH

This is a fantastic punch for a holiday party, with a warm festive-red color, toasty cinnamon-pear flavor… and slightly elevated alcohol content to get the party started. A punch bowl is entirely optional, but if you want to go that route, float an ice block in the bowl for dramatic effect. To keep the punch from being diluted by plain water, freeze a combination of half water and half pineapple juice or pear nectar in a loaf pan, and add a few orange slices for a splash of color.

---

1 (750-ml) bottle ruby port

12 ounces (1½ cups) pineapple juice, preferably freshly prepared (see sidebar)

6 ounces (¾ cup) Cinnamon-Pear Syrup (page 25)

6 ounces (¾ cup) fresh lemon juice

8 dried orange chips (see page 16) or thin orange wheels, for garnish

4 ounces (½ cup) cognac, as needed, for serving

Mix the port, pineapple juice, syrup, and lemon juice together in a punch bowl or large pitcher. Float the orange chips in the punch. For each drink, pour the punch in a punch glass or short rocks glass. Gently pour about ½ ounce (1 tablespoon) cognac onto the punch surface, and add one of the orange chips.

PINEAPPLE JUICE

Fresh pineapple juice is a wonderful ingredient for cocktails, but I realize it may not be practical for some people. If you have a centrifugal juice extractor, you are home free—just top, pare, and core the pineapple, and process the flesh. If you don't… you can still get the job done without too much trouble. You will need a blender, though. (A blender works better than a food processor because the juice tends to run out of the center stem of the processor.)

For simplicity's sake, purchase a peeled and cored pineapple, a product that just about every supermarket sells these days. If you have the time, grill the peeled pineapple before juicing to add incredible caramelized flavor. To do this, quarter the pineapple lengthwise, and grill it over direct high heat (500°F or more), with the lid closed, turning occasionally, until the fruit is seared all over with brown grate marks, 7 to 10 minutes. Let the pineapple cool.

Coarsely chop the (grilled or ungrilled) pineapple flesh. In batches, process the flesh in a blender until it is pulverized. Strain the minced pineapple through a fine-mesh wire sieve set over a tall bowl, pressing hard on the flesh to extract as much juice as possible. You're done!

SHERRY-CITRUS
Punch

**MAKES
ABOUT
12
DRINKS**

Unfortunately, sherry has pretty much been relegated to the kitchen, and not too many people drink it as an aperitif anymore. That's a shame, because sherry is one of the world's great beverages and is made in a variety of styles. *Fino* ("refined" in Spanish) is the driest of the lot; I combine it with citrus flavors for a remarkably special punch.

18 ounces (2¼ cups) fino sherry

9 ounces (1 cup plus 2 tablespoons) fresh grapefruit juice

9 ounces (1 cup plus 2 tablespoons) fresh lemon juice

4 ounces (½ cup) Aperol

4 ounces (½ cup) Simple Syrup (page 25)

6 ounces (¾ cup) dry sparkling wine, as needed

Grapefruit twists (see sidebar), for garnish

Stir the sherry, grapefruit juice, lemon juice, Aperol, and syrup together in a large pitcher or small punch bowl. Serve in ice-filled rocks glasses, leaving about ½ inch of headroom. Float about 1 ounce (2 tablespoons) sparkling wine on top of each drink and garnish with a grapefruit twist.

CITRUS TWISTS

A strip of fresh citrus peel, twisted just before serving to release a spritz of its essential oils into a drink, is a popular cocktail garnish. To make a twist—lemon, grapefruit, orange, or lime—use a swivel or harp-shaped vegetable peeler to remove a strip of zest (just the colored part) from the fruit. The zest should be about 2 inches long and ½ inch wide. Just before serving, hold both ends of the zest and give it a sharp twist in opposite directions to squirt a fine spray of oil into the drink. You might see the spray, or you might not… but you will smell a burst of citrus.

STARTERS

I like chips and dip as much as the next guy, but when I'm throwing a party I like to go the extra mile to impress my friends and family. Put one of these truly extraordinary dishes in front of your guests and you are guaranteed rave reviews (even if their mouths are full). These dishes—mostly small plates or finger food—feature new flavors, interesting textures, and beautiful colors to set the mood for the rest of the meal. I usually like to have a few platters sitting out on the counter when guests arrive. And if I can use some extra hands-on help folding or stuffing an appetizer, I encourage people to join me in the kitchen and jump in.

WARM STUFFED
PIQUILLO
PEPPER BRUSCHETTA

—

"Grilled Cheese"
DUMPLINGS
in TOMATO SOUP

—

The Famous
FRENCH ONION SOUP DUMPLINGS

—

Chile Relleno
EMPANADAS

—

Pizza **Bianca**

Crab Corn Dogs
with OLD BAY AIOLI

—

NORI-SPICED
Tuna Poke
CRISPS

—

Potato *and* Goat Cheese
PIEROGI
with Caramelized Onions

—

Tomato "Tartare"
on Brioche Crostini

—

Spicy Wok-Seared
Edamame

—

CITRUS-PICKLED
VEGETABLES

CHEF TALK

Balsamic Glaze

This near-black condiment is used to garnish food with a drizzle of sweet-tart syrup that holds its shape on the plate. If you wish, you can reduce the average vinegar to a similar viscosity. Bring ½ cup supermarket-quality balsamic vinegar and 2 teaspoons light brown sugar to a boil in a small saucepan over high heat. Reduce the heat to low and simmer until it is reduced by about one-third, about 5 minutes. Let cool—it should be syrupy and easy to drizzle. If it is too thick, adjust the viscosity with more vinegar (or, if it is too thin, boil it down a bit more).

Warm Stuffed
PIQUILLO PEPPER
BRUSCHETTA

MAKES

8

SERVINGS

I started my love affair with piquillo peppers—the full-flavored Spanish red peppers—when I first traveled in Europe as a very young chef. Every time I saw them on a menu, stuffed with tuna, potatoes, or cheese, I ordered them. The trick here is to simply warm the stuffed piquillos—if they are overheated, the cheese filling will ooze out.

6 ounces goat cheese,
at room temperature

1 tablespoon mashed Roasted Garlic
(page 134)

2 tablespoons julienned fresh basil

½ teaspoon finely chopped
fresh thyme leaves

Kosher salt and freshly ground
black pepper

8 small canned piquillo peppers
(see Chef Talk, this page),
drained and patted dry with
paper towels

8 (½-inch-thick) slices
baguette bread

½ teaspoon balsamic glaze
(see Chef Talk, page 34)

CHEF TALK

Piquillo Peppers

In the U.S., piquillo peppers are often sold in bulk in the olive bars at supermarkets and specialty food stores. You find them in cans or jars, in the international foods aisle of markets with Mediterranean products and online. In the rare chance that you happen to come across fresh piquillos at a farmers' market, they are notoriously difficult to skin, and you will probably just wish you had bought the prepared variety.

1. Mix the goat cheese, roasted garlic, 1 tablespoon of the basil, and the thyme together in a small bowl with a rubber spatula until well combined. Season to taste with salt and pepper.

2. Snip the corner from a 1-quart plastic bag to make a ½-inch-wide opening. Transfer the goat cheese mixture to the bag. Pipe equal amounts of the cheese mixture into the peppers. (The peppers can be covered and refrigerated for up to 1 day. Bring to room temperature before heating.)

3. Position the broiler rack about 8 inches from the source of heat and preheat the broiler on high.

4. Put the bread slices on a broiler pan and toast them in the broiler, turning occasionally, until golden, about 3 minutes. Transfer the toast to a serving platter. Turn off the broiler.

5. Put the stuffed peppers in a flameproof baking pan (such as a metal cake or pie pan) and transfer to the turned-off broiler. Heat the peppers just until they are warm and plump, about 3 minutes.

6. Arrange the toast on a platter. Using kitchen tongs, carefully top each with a pepper (taking care not to squeeze the filling out of the pepper). Sprinkle with the remaining 1 tablespoon basil, and add a few grinds of fresh pepper. Finish with a drizzle of the balsamic glaze and serve immediately.

"Grilled Cheese" DUMPLINGS in TOMATO SOUP

MAKES 6 to 8 SERVINGS

Grilled cheese and tomato soup is an iconic American diner staple. I'm all about turning the classics inside out, so here's my version— an incredible tomato soup topped with plump, cheesy fried dumplings. I worked very hard to come up with the correct mixture of six cheeses for the filling, but you could experiment on your own with other combinations. I finish the dish with chopped bacon bits, since my grilled cheese order always includes bacon.

½ cup (2 ounces) shredded aged Vermont white Cheddar cheese

¼ cup (2 ounces) packed chopped pasteurized cheese product, such as Velveeta

¼ cup (1 ounce) shredded Fontina cheese, preferably imported Fontina d'Aosta

¼ cup (1 ounce) shredded sharp provolone cheese

2 tablespoons goat cheese, preferably smoked goat cheese, at room temperature

2 tablespoons cream cheese, at room temperature

1 ripe Roma (plum) tomato, seeded, minced, and drained

1 tablespoon finely chopped fresh basil

1 tablespoon finely chopped fresh chives, plus more for serving (optional)

24 gyoza or round dumpling wrappers, cut into 2¾-inch rounds with a cookie cutter

1 large egg, beaten well

Vegetable oil, for frying

Cream of Tomato Soup (page 83), heated

2 strips bacon, cooked until crisp, drained, and very finely chopped, for serving

Special Equipment: 2¾-inch round cookie cutter; kitchen torch (optional)

1. Beat the Cheddar, pasteurized cheese product, Fontina, provolone, goat cheese, and cream cheese together in a medium bowl with an electric hand mixer until combined. Beat in the tomato, basil, and chives. Cover with plastic wrap and refrigerate until the mixture is chilled, at least 1 hour, or up to 1 day.

2. Using about 1 teaspoon for each (a #100 portion scoop works perfectly), scoop the cheese mixture into 24 equal balls and transfer to a plate. For each dumpling, place a wrapper on the work surface and brush lightly with the beaten egg. Place a cheese ball in the center and fold in the wrapper at 12, 3, 6, and 9 o'clock, letting the sides touch the cheese ball. Pinch the four resulting points closed. Fold two points together to meet and overlap on each side of the dumpling, adhering the points together with a dab of the beaten egg. Plump the dumpling so the filling barely peeks over the top of the wrapper. The dumpling top will be open and the filling exposed. Transfer the dumplings to a waxed paper–lined baking sheet. (The dumplings can be loosely covered with plastic wrap and refrigerated for up to 4 hours.)

3. Pour enough oil to come about ½ inch up the sides of a large skillet and heat over high heat until the oil is shimmering. Using kitchen tongs, carefully stand half of the dumplings in the skillet, being sure that the oil does not cover the cheese filling—only the bottom and sides of the wrappers should touch the oil. (It is a good idea to fry a single dumpling as a test run to check the oil height.) Fry until the sides of the dumplings are golden brown, about 1 minute. Using the tongs, carefully transfer the dumplings to a wire rack to drain, taking care not to squeeze out the filling. If you wish, using a kitchen torch, lightly brown the exposed filling.

4. Divide the hot soup equally among six to eight soup bowls. Using kitchen tongs, transfer three or four dumplings to each soup bowl. Sprinkle with the bacon and chives (optional) and serve immediately. (Warn your guests that the cheese dumplings are very hot and should be cooled slightly before eating.)

The Famous
FRENCH ONION SOUP
DUMPLINGS

MAKES
6 to 12
SERVINGS

ONION-SHALLOT FILLING

½ cup (1 stick) unsalted butter

½ medium yellow onion, thinly sliced (1 cup)

2 medium shallots, thinly sliced (½ cup)

1 cup hearty red wine, such as Shiraz

1 cup reduced-sodium beef broth

1 cup reduced-sodium chicken broth

2 tablespoons minced fresh thyme

1 tablespoon balsamic vinegar, preferably aged

Kosher salt and freshly ground black pepper

CROUTONS

1 tablespoon extra-virgin olive oil

1 small garlic clove, minced

¼ teaspoon minced fresh thyme

Kosher salt and freshly ground black pepper

12 (¾-inch) cubes trimmed artisan bread

SOUP DUMPLINGS

36 square wonton wrappers

1 large egg, lightly beaten

ASSEMBLY

Vegetable oil, for deep-frying

2 cups (8 ounces) shredded Gruyère cheese

Softened butter, for the baking dish

Kosher salt and freshly ground black pepper

Special Equipment: 2 ovenproof escargot dishes, each with 6 indentations, or 1 large gratin dish without indentations; 12 (4-inch) wooden or bamboo skewers, for serving

The best bite of French onion soup includes the beefy broth, caramelized onions, a bit of the soaked bread, and, of course, the bubbling cheese that oozes over the edges of the bowl. I wanted to re-create that perfect bite with these soup dumplings, which contain a condensed version of the soup and are baked with a generous serving of gooey Gruyère on top. This dish is one of my proudest culinary accomplishments, and you can now make it at home for your guests.

Note that the recipe makes 36 dumplings, but only 12 of them are used here. Unless you're having a big party, I suggest freezing the full batch of dumplings and cooking them as needed. For a quick soup, the leftover dumplings can be added to hot chicken broth and simmered until cooked through, about 5 minutes. Or they can be steamed on an oiled rack over boiling water for about 6 minutes and served with a drizzle of balsamic vinegar.

1. To make the filling: At least 6 hours (but preferably at least 12 hours) before making the dumplings, melt the butter in a large skillet over medium heat. Add the onion and shallots and reduce the heat to medium-low. Cook, stirring often, until they are deep golden brown and very tender, about 30 minutes.

2. Add the wine, increase the heat to high, and cook, stirring often, until the wine has evaporated to a glaze, about 7 minutes. Stir in the beef and chicken broths, bring to a boil, and cook until the liquid has evaporated by half, about 10 minutes. You want to make sure that your soup has a thick texture—more onion than liquid. Stir in the thyme and vinegar and season to taste with salt and pepper. Let cool completely.

3. Line the bottom and sides of an 8-by-4-inch loaf pan with plastic wrap. Pour the filling into the pan and loosely cover the top with the wrap. Freeze until the filling is solid, at least 4 hours, or up to 1 day.

4. To make the croutons: Position a rack in the center of the oven and preheat the oven to 400°F. Stir the oil, garlic, thyme, salt, and pepper together in a small bowl. Add the bread cubes and toss well to coat the bread. Spread the mixture on a large rimmed baking sheet. Bake, stirring occasionally, until the croutons are golden brown, about 15 minutes.

→

5. To make the dumplings: Invert and unmold the frozen soup mixture onto a cutting board. Using a heavy knife, cut the mixture equally lengthwise into 4 long strips, then vertically into 9 sections to make 36 cubes. Keep the cubes frozen until ready to wrap.

6. Working with about 9 wonton wrappers at a time, place the wrappers on a work surface. Lightly brush the edges of the wrappers with the beaten egg. Place one cube in the center of a wrapper. Bring up the edges and tightly pinch them closed to create a small packet that resembles a purse. Transfer to a baking sheet. Repeat with the remaining cubes and wrappers. Cover tightly and freeze for at least 2 hours. (To freeze longer, transfer the frozen dumplings, separating the layers with waxed paper, to an airtight container, and freeze for up to 1 month.)

7. Pour enough oil to come about 2 inches up the sides of a large, deep saucepan and heat over high heat until the oil reaches 350°F on a deep-frying thermometer. Place a large cake rack over a large rimmed baking sheet to drain the fried dumplings.

8. Remove 12 dumplings from the freezer, reserving the remaining dumplings for another use. In batches, without crowding, carefully add the dumplings to the oil (the oil will bubble up) and cook until golden brown, about 2 minutes. Using a wire spider or slotted spoon, being careful not to pierce the dumplings, transfer them to the wire rack to drain. (The dumplings can stand at room temperature for up to 30 minutes.)

9. Position the broiler rack about 8 inches from the source of heat and preheat the broiler on high. Lightly butter 2 escargot dishes (including the tops) or a large oval baking dish.

10. Place each dumpling in its own indentation in the escargot dishes. Cover the entire dish with the shredded Gruyère. Broil until the cheese is melted and bubbling brown, 4 to 6 minutes. Meanwhile, spear each crouton onto a skewer.

11. Insert a crouton-speared skewer into the top of each dumpling, being sure not to poke the bottom of the wrapper, or the dumpling will leak. Sprinkle the dumplings with salt and pepper and serve immediately.

Chile Relleno
EMPANADAS

When I go to a Mexican restaurant, I always order the chile relleno, with its irresistible melted cheese filling. These addictive little pies embrace the same combination of roasted poblanos and gooey cheese. A bit of ancho chile in the dough adds a hint of spice and gives the empanadas a nice orange color.

EMPANADA DOUGH

2¾ cups (385 grams) unbleached all-purpose flour, plus more for rolling the dough

2½ teaspoons pure ground ancho chile

2½ teaspoons ground cumin

2½ teaspoons sugar

¾ teaspoon kosher salt

4 tablespoons (½ stick) cold unsalted butter, cut into ½-inch cubes

¾ cup ice water

1 large egg yolk

JALAPEÑO LIME CREMA

½ cup sour cream

1 jalapeño, roasted (page 42), peeled, seeded, and minced

2 teaspoons minced fresh cilantro

2 teaspoons fresh lime juice

Pinch of sugar

POBLANO FILLING

1 large poblano (fresh ancho) chile, roasted (page 42), peeled, and seeded

⅔ cup (about 2½ ounces) shredded Fontina Val d'Aosta cheese

¼ cup (1 ounce) shredded Manchego cheese, or more Fontina cheese

1 tablespoon freshly grated Parmigiano-Reggiano cheese

———

1 large egg yolk beaten with 1 teaspoon water, for an egg wash

Vegetable oil, for deep-frying

2 radishes, cut into thin strips, for serving (optional)

———

Special Equipment: 3½-inch round cookie cutter

1. To make the dough: Put the flour, ground ancho, cumin, sugar, and salt in a food processor and pulse to combine. Add the butter and pulse a few times until the mixture resembles coarse meal with some pea-sized pieces of butter. Transfer to a medium bowl. (Or whisk the dry ingredients together in a medium bowl. Add the butter and cut it in with a pastry blender or two knives.) Mix the ice water and egg yolk together. Stir in enough of the egg mixture until the dough clumps together. Gather the dough together and shape into a thick disk. Wrap in plastic wrap and refrigerate until chilled, 1 to 4 hours.

2. To make the crema: Mix the ingredients together in a small bowl. Cover and set aside.

3. To make the filling: Coarsely puree the poblano in a blender or food processor and transfer to a medium bowl. Add the Fontina, Manchego, and Parmigiano and stir well. Using about 1 teaspoon for each (a #100 food portion scoop works well), shape the mixture into 24 equal balls.

4. To make the empanadas: Cut the dough in half. Working with one half at a time on a lightly floured surface, roll out the dough to about ¹⁄₁₆-inch thickness. (This dough is rolled thinner than dough for piecrust to compensate for the empanadas' double-thick edges.) Using a 3½-inch-diameter cookie cutter, cut out rounds of the dough. Transfer the rounds to a baking sheet, overlapping them as needed and separating the layers with waxed or parchment paper. Gather up the scraps and repeat once more to make a total of 24 rounds. Discard the remaining dough. Refrigerate the rounds until chilled, 10 to 20 minutes.

➤

MEASURING FLOUR

Most chefs weigh their ingredients and don't bother with measuring cups. Believe me, it is a lot easier to scale out 5 pounds of flour than it is to scoop out its American measurement equivalent of 16¼ cups! Many, but not all, home cooks like to weigh ingredients, too, especially flour, whose weight can fluctuate according to how it is measured. Yet I didn't want the readers of this book to feel that they absolutely must own a kitchen scale. (I recommend one, but it just isn't imperative. There are many reliable and inexpensive models.)

If you like to weigh flour for baking, I provide the flour measurements in grams. The metric system is just easier to manage, especially when dealing in fractions, than the American pounds and ounces. And if you have an electric scale, they always provide both grams and ounces. Other dry ingredients, such as sugar, aren't as powdery as flour, and their weight is pretty stable.

Also, when I have observed my friends in their kitchens, most people use the dip-and-sweep measuring method when working with flour. Dip a squat measuring cup for dry ingredients (not a glass one, which is for liquid) into the flour bag or container, filling the cup without packing it. Sweep the flour off with a knife or your finger so it is level with the lip of the cup. Measured this way, a cup of flour weighs 140 grams.

5. Place a round on the work surface and brush the edges with the egg wash. Place a cheese ball on the lower half of the round and fold the dough in half to enclose the filling. Press the open edge closed with a fork, being sure it is completely sealed. Return to the baking sheet. (The empanadas can be covered and refrigerated for up to 4 hours.)

6. Position a rack in the center of the oven and preheat the oven to 200°F. Line an 18-by-13-inch half-sheet pan with a wire rack. Pour enough oil to come 2 inches up the sides of a large deep saucepan and heat over high heat until it registers 350°F on a deep-frying thermometer.

7. In batches, without crowding, deep-fry the empanadas, turning as needed, until they are golden brown, about 3 minutes. Using a wire spider or a slotted spoon, transfer the empanadas to the wire rack and keep warm in the oven while frying the remaining empanadas.

8. To serve, place the empanadas on a platter. Top each with a small dollop of the crema and sprinkle with the radishes, if using. Serve immediately, with the remaining crema passed on the side.

ROASTING PEPPERS AND CHILES

Most bell peppers and chiles have a thin, bitter skin that should be removed before eating. The best way to do this is to char the chile under a broiler (or over high heat on a grill) so the skin can be lifted off with a small knife.

Position the broiler rack about 6 inches from the source of heat and preheat the broiler on high. Arrange the chiles on the broiler rack. Broil, turning occasionally, until the skins are blackened and blistered, 5 to 8 minutes, depending on the size of the chile. Transfer to a bowl, cover with plastic wrap, and let stand for 10 to 15 minutes to cool the chiles and loosen the skins. Using a small knife, cut off and discard the skin, ribs, and seeds.

Pizza **Bianca**

MAKES ONE

9 x 13-inch

FOCACCIA

Pizza bianca ("white pizza" in Italian) is similar to plain focaccia. While you can find fresh focaccia at some stores and bakeries, it is very easy to make the flatbread at home. I am not a big fan of serving bread on the side at meals, but I use this often as a base for toppings like avocado focaccia (page 47) or chicken livers (page 44).

FOCACCIA DOUGH

3 cups (420 g) unbleached all-purpose flour

1½ teaspoons instant (also called bread-machine or quick-rise) yeast

1 teaspoon kosher salt

1 cup cold tap water

2 tablespoons extra-virgin olive oil, plus more for the bowl

TOPPING

1 teaspoon extra-virgin olive oil, plus more for the pan and brushing

½ teaspoon kosher salt

---

1. **To make the dough in a food processor:** Add the flour, yeast, and salt to a food processor. Combine the water and oil in a liquid measuring cup. With the machine running, pour the water mixture through the feed tube and process until the dough forms a ball that rides on top of the blade. Feel the dough— it should be moist and tacky. If it is wet and sticky, add flour, 1 tablespoon at a time, and process until the dough feels right. Let the machine run for 45 seconds to knead the ball of dough.

To make the dough in a stand mixer: Combine the water with the oil, yeast, and salt in the bowl of a heavy-duty stand mixer fitted with the paddle. With the machine on low speed, gradually add enough of the flour to make a dough that pulls away from the sides of the bowl. Change to the dough hook and knead on medium-low speed, adding more flour as necessary, until the dough is smooth, elastic, and slightly tacky, about 8 minutes.

To make the dough by hand: Combine the water with the oil, yeast, and salt in a large bowl. Using a sturdy spoon, gradually stir in enough of the flour to make a stiff dough that can't be stirred. Transfer the dough to a floured work surface. Knead, adding just enough flour to keep the dough from sticking to the work surface and your hands (but keeping the dough moist and slightly tacky), until the dough is smooth and elastic, about 10 minutes.

2. Generously oil a medium bowl. Turn out the dough onto a lightly floured work surface and shape it into a ball. Add the ball to the bowl and turn to coat it with oil. Cover the bowl tightly with plastic wrap and let stand in a warm place until the dough has doubled in volume, about 1¼ hours. (Or refrigerate the dough for 18 to 24 hours.) ➤——➤

3. Lightly oil a 9-by-13-inch quarter-sheet pan. Punch your fist into the dough to deflate it. On a lightly floured work surface, pat the dough into a thick rectangle. Using a rolling pin, roll out the dough into a 10-by-14-inch rectangle. Fit the dough into the pan, being sure to reach the corners. Cover the pan with plastic wrap and let stand for 5 minutes. If the dough has retracted, press it into the corners of the pan again. Cover again, and let stand in a warm place until the dough looks puffy but not doubled, about 30 minutes (or about 1½ hours for refrigerated dough).

4. Meanwhile, position a rack in the center of the oven and preheat the oven to 400°F.

5. Dimple the dough with your fingertips. Drizzle the oil over the top of the dough and sprinkle with the salt. Bake until the pizza is golden brown, 20 to 25 minutes. Lightly brush the top of the pizza with oil (this keeps the top tender). Let the pizza cool completely in the pan. (The pizza can be covered with aluminum foil and stored at room temperature for up to 12 hours.)

CHICKEN LIVER
FOCACCIA
with Braised Shallot–Rioja Marmalade

I lived on the Lower East Side for many, many years, surrounded by the likes of Katz's Delicatessen and Sammy's Roumanian Steakhouse—institutions in the art of perfect chopped liver. I like my chicken livers pureed smooth, spread over toasted focaccia (aka pizza bianca), and topped with wine-braised shallots. The portions are fairly big, so you can cut them in half again to make 24 pieces, if you wish. Or, instead of making the pizza, spread the mousse over 24 crostini (see page 55).

1. To make the mousse: Melt 2 tablespoons of the duck fat in a large skillet over medium-high heat and then heat until the fat is very hot but not smoking. Add the chicken livers and cook until the undersides are browned, about 3 minutes. Flip the livers and sprinkle in the shallots and thyme. Cook until the livers are browned and medium-rare and the shallots are softened, about 2 minutes.

2. Using a slotted spoon, transfer the solids to a medium bowl. Return the skillet to high heat and cook until the cooking juices are reduced to a few tablespoons. Pour in the Madeira and carefully ignite it with a long match. (Don't worry if it doesn't ignite.) Boil for 15 seconds. Add to the liver mixture and let cool until warm, about 15 minutes.

3. Process the warm liver mixture, the remaining 2 tablespoons duck fat, the cream, and the nutmeg in a food processor until smooth. Season to taste with salt and pepper. Transfer to a bowl and let cool. Cover with plastic wrap and refrigerate until chilled, at least 2 hours or up to 1 day.

CHICKEN LIVER MOUSSE

4 tablespoons rendered duck fat
(see Note) or unsalted butter

1¼ pounds chicken livers, trimmed

2 tablespoons coarsely
chopped shallots

½ teaspoon fresh thyme leaves

¼ cup Madeira wine

2 tablespoons heavy cream

Pinch of freshly grated nutmeg

Kosher salt and freshly ground
black pepper

SHALLOT MARMALADE

2 tablespoons unsalted butter

5 shallots, thinly sliced lengthwise
(about 1¼ cups)

1 small garlic clove, minced

¼ cup hearty red wine, such as Rioja

½ cup reduced-sodium chicken broth

2½ tablespoons balsamic vinegar

2 tablespoons honey

¼ teaspoon finely chopped
fresh thyme leaves

Kosher salt and freshly ground
black pepper

———

Pizza Bianca (page 43)

Olive oil, for brushing

4. To make the shallot marmalade: Melt the butter in a medium skillet over medium heat. Add the shallots and garlic and cover. Cook, stirring occasionally, until the shallots soften, about 3 minutes. Reduce the heat to medium-low. Uncover and cook, stirring often, until the shallots are browned and tender, about 10 minutes. Increase the heat to high. Add the red wine and bring to a boil, scraping up any browned bits in the skillet. Stir in the broth, balsamic vinegar, and honey and bring to a boil. Reduce the heat to medium and cook at a brisk simmer until the liquid evaporates into a glaze, about 5 minutes. Stir in the thyme. Season to taste with the salt and pepper. Transfer to a small bowl and let cool. (The shallot marmalade can be cooled, covered, and refrigerated for 3 days. Reheat gently before using.)

5. Position a broiler rack about 6 inches from the source of heat and preheat the broiler on high. Using a serrated knife, trim the sides of the pizza bianca into a 9-by-6-inch rectangle, reserving the trimmings for another use (such as breadcrumbs or croutons). Brush the pizza bianca with olive oil. Broil until the pizza bianca is golden brown, 1 to 2 minutes. Spread the mousse over the pizza bianca. Using a sharp knife, cut the pizza into 12 strips, each 3 inches long and 1½ inches wide. Top each strip with an equal amount of the shallot marmalade. Serve immediately.

Note: *Duck fat is sold in the butcher department of many supermarkets. Shelf-stable brands can be purchased online. It freezes very well and is an excellent fat for sautéing. Duck fat–fried potatoes are a guilty pleasure of mine.*

AVOCADO, LEMON,
and ESPELETTE FOCACCIA

MAKES
16
TOASTS

6 TO 8 SERVINGS

Avocado toast is now ubiquitous on menus, and I have to weigh in with my version, which I have been serving for years. It is a great way to party, day or night. Not only does the lemony vinaigrette keep the avocado looking fresh and vibrant; the bright citrus dressing awakens the palate as any starter should. It's best to buy your avocados a few days ahead so they can soften at room temperature. And, if you can, frying the basil really makes this simple dish pop.

AVOCADO TOPPING

Finely grated zest of ½ lemon

1½ tablespoons fresh lemon juice

¼ teaspoon Dijon mustard

Fine sea salt and freshly ground black pepper

2 tablespoons extra-virgin olive oil

2 ripe Hass avocados, peeled, pitted, and cut into ½-inch dice

TOASTS

Pizza Bianca (page 43) or store-bought focaccia

¼ cup extra-virgin olive oil

1 tablespoon unsalted butter

About ½ teaspoon Piment d'Espelette (see Chef Talk, this page), as needed, for serving

16 fresh basil leaves, fried if you like (see Note)

Flaky sea salt, preferably Maldon, for serving

CHEF TALK

Piment d'Espelette

Piment d'Espelette ("pepper of Espelette" in French), a relatively mild chile, is named for the small town in the French Pyrenees where it is grown. When dried and ground, it is great as a seasoning for many dishes, including eggs and simply prepared vegetables, when you want a not-too-hard kick.

1. To make the topping: Whisk the lemon zest and juice, mustard, ¼ teaspoon salt, and ⅛ teaspoon pepper together in a medium bowl. Gradually whisk in the oil. Add the avocado and mix gently. (The avocado topping can be covered, with the plastic wrap pressed directly on to the surface, and refrigerated for up to 8 hours.)

2. To assemble the toasts: Using a serrated knife, cut the pizza into 16 strips, each about 4 inches long and 1½ inches wide. Trim the tops of the strips so they are flat and about ¾ inch tall. (The trimmings can be saved and used for another purpose, such as making croutons or processing into bread crumbs.)

3. Heat a ridged grill pan over medium-high heat. Mix the olive oil and butter together in a small bowl. Brush the pizza bianca strips on both sides with the oil mixture. In batches, place the strips on the grill pan and cook, turning once, until seared with grill marks, about 2 minutes per side. Place the strips on a platter or plates.

4. Spread each strip with an equal amount of the avocado mixture. Sprinkle with the Piment d'Espelette, followed by the basil, and finished with the flaky salt. Serve immediately.

Note: *Fried basil leaves have a beautiful transparent look and make an especially attractive (but optional) garnish. Heat a small sauce-pan of vegetable or canola oil to 350°F on a deep-frying thermometer over high heat. Add the basil leaves, a few at a time, and fry just until they look transparent and slightly crisp, about 15 seconds. Using a wire spider or slotted spoon, transfer the basil to paper towels to drain. Use immediately.*

CRAB CORN DOGS

with OLD BAY AIOLI

OLD BAY AIOLI

¾ cup House Aioli (page 50)

2 teaspoons Old Bay seasoning

¼ teaspoon hot pepper sauce,
such as Tabasco

CRAB CAKES

½ cup House Aioli (page 50)

4 tablespoons (½ stick) unsalted
butter, at very soft room temperature

1 pound lump crabmeat, picked
over for cartilage

½ cup panko (Japanese bread
crumbs), processed in a food
processor until very fine

1 tablespoon finely chopped fresh
chives

¾ teaspoon Old Bay seasoning

¼ teaspoon hot pepper sauce,
such as Tabasco

¼ teaspoon kosher salt

¼ teaspoon freshly ground
black pepper

BATTER

½ cup (70 grams) unbleached
all-purpose flour

1 teaspoon sugar

¾ teaspoon baking powder

½ teaspoon kosher salt

1½ cups buttermilk

1 cup fine yellow cornmeal

1 large egg, beaten to blend

Vegetable oil, for deep-frying

Special Equipment: 24 bamboo
party skewers

One bite of a corn dog, and I am instantly transported back to the circuses and fairs of my childhood in Rhode Island. I really wanted to make an upscale version, so I brainstormed with my fellow New Englander, chef Ryan Angulo. We couldn't resist giving our local favorite, crab cakes, the corn dog treatment. The Old Bay aioli is an easy dip, but I also love to serve them with the Corn Vinaigrette on page 80.

1. To make the Old Bay aioli: Whisk all of the ingredients together in a small bowl. Cover and refrigerate for at least 1 hour or up to 4 hours. Remove from the refrigerator about 30 minutes before serving.

2. To make the crab cakes: Whisk the house aioli and butter together until smooth. Add the crabmeat, panko, chives, Old Bay, hot pepper sauce, salt, and pepper and fold together until combined. Cover and refrigerate until firm enough to shape, at least 1 hour or up to 4 hours.

3. Line a large baking sheet with parchment or waxed paper. Using wet hands, for each crab cake, shape about 2 tablespoons of the crab mixture into an oval about 1½ inches long. Transfer to the lined baking sheet and cover loosely with plastic wrap. Refrigerate to firm slightly, at least 1 hour or up to 4 hours.

4. To make the batter: About 20 minutes before deep-frying, whisk the flour, sugar, baking powder, and salt together in a small bowl; set aside. Whisk 1 cup of the buttermilk with the cornmeal in a large bowl. Let stand until thickened, about 15 minutes. Whisk in the remaining ½ cup buttermilk and the egg. Add the flour mixture and stir to combine.

5. Position a rack in the center of the oven and preheat the oven to 200°F. Line an 18-by-13-inch half-sheet pan with a wire rack. Pour enough oil to come 2 inches up the sides of a large deep saucepan and heat over high heat until it registers 350°F on a deep-frying thermometer. Set up the cornmeal batter and crab "dogs" near the oil. ➤➤

6. Working in batches of about 6 corn dogs, being sure not to crowd them in the oil, dip a crab dog in the batter and coat, smearing the batter in a thin layer with your fingers. Lift the crab dog out of the batter, and scrape it gently against the bowl edges to remove excess batter. Immediately transfer the crab dog to the oil and deep-fry until golden brown, 1½ to 2½ minutes. You will be able to tell which crab dogs are done first by their color. (A few notes here: The batter layer should not be thick, and your fingers will get coated with batter when coating the dogs. You might want to fry a test crab dog to estimate the proper amount of batter. If the batter is thick, the crab dog will be too puffy.) Using a wire spider or slotted spoon, transfer the crab dogs to the wire rack and keep warm in the oven while frying the remaining dogs.

7. Spear a cocktail skewer into one end of each crab dog. Serve the crab dogs immediately, with the aioli for dipping.

HOUSE AIOLI

Makes about 1¼ cups

In its most basic form, aioli is garlic mayonnaise. My aioli has a deeper flavor and thicker consistency than other versions, and it can be mixed with other ingredients to make many useful variations.

- 2 large egg yolks, at room temperature
- 1 tablespoon Dijon mustard
- Finely grated zest of 1 lime
- 1 small garlic clove, shredded on a Microplane zester
- Kosher salt
- ⅛ teaspoon pure ground ancho chile
- ½ cup vegetable or canola oil
- ½ cup olive oil (not extra-virgin)

Combine the yolks, mustard, lime zest, garlic, ¼ teaspoon salt, and ground ancho in a food processor. With the machine running, very gradually drizzle in the oil and process to make a thick mayonnaise-like consistency. Season to taste with additional salt. (The aioli can be covered and refrigerated for 5 days.)

NORI-SPICED
TUNA POKE CRISPS

MAKES

24

CRISPS
6 TO 8
SERVINGS

Tuna tartare is always a surefire way to begin any party. I like my tartare to have a driving ingredient that elevates it from your typical rendition. Here, that role is played by Japanese *furikake*, one of the world's all-time great condiments, generally used as a rice topping. *Poke* (pronounced po-kay) is a Hawaiian raw tuna dish, but the fish is chopped larger than tartare.

WONTON CRISPS

Vegetable oil, for deep-frying

12 wonton wrappers, cut on a diagonal to make 24 triangles

POKE

8 ounces sashimi-grade tuna, cut into ¼- to ½-inch dice

1 tablespoon Japanese soy sauce

2 teaspoons finely chopped fresh cilantro

1 teaspoon Asian sesame oil

1 tablespoon thinly sliced scallion (white and green parts)

1 teaspoon sambal oelek or other Asian chili paste

1 tablespoon nori fumi furikake (see Chef Talk, below)

AVOCADO MOUSSE

1 ripe Hass avocado, peeled, pitted, and coarsely chopped

2 tablespoons fresh lime juice

About 3 tablespoons water, as needed

Kosher salt and freshly ground black pepper

———

¼ cup wasabi-coated peas, pulsed in a food processor until coarsely crushed

2 radishes, cut into thin shreds, for garnish

Lime wedges, for serving

1. To fry the wontons: Line a large baking sheet with paper towels. Pour enough oil into a large deep skillet to come about ½ inch up the sides and heat over high heat until is very hot and shimmering but not smoking. In batches, add the wonton triangles and cook, turning once, until they are golden brown, about 30 seconds. Using a wire spider or slotted spoon, transfer them to the paper towels to drain and cool. (The crisps can be stored at room temperature for up to 8 hours.)

2. To make the poke: Mix the tuna, soy sauce, cilantro, sesame oil, scallion, sambal oelek, and furikake in a medium bowl. (The poke can be covered and refrigerated for up to 8 hours.)

3. To make the mousse: Process the avocado and lime juice in a blender, occasionally stopping to scrape down the jar, adding enough water to make a smooth puree. Season with salt and pepper. Transfer to a food-safe plastic squeeze bottle.

4. To assemble the crisps: Just before serving, arrange the wonton triangles on a serving platter. Top each crisp with a spoonful of the poke. Squeeze some of the avocado purée over each, and sprinkle with the crushed wasabi peas and radish shreds. Serve immediately with the lime wedges.

CHEF TALK

Furikake

Furikake is a Japanese dry seasoning for cooked rice that comes in many flavors and colors. For the poke crisps, I like the basic nori fumi furikake with sesame seeds and flaked nori seaweed. There are many other versions, including furikake with dehydrated pink salmon, yellow egg yolk, or green citrus.

SOUR CREAM DOUGH

4 cups (560 grams) unbleached
all-purpose flour

¼ teaspoon baking powder

1 teaspoon kosher salt

½ cup full-fat sour cream

½ cup warm water

2 large eggs

2 teaspoons canola oil

POTATO FILLING

2 large Yukon Gold potatoes,
about 9 ounces each, peeled

2 teaspoons extra-virgin olive oil

½ cup finely chopped red onion

¾ cup (6 ounces) goat cheese,
at room temperature

1 teaspoon minced fresh chives

2 tablespoons heavy cream

Kosher salt and freshly ground
black pepper

CARAMELIZED ONIONS

2 tablespoons unsalted butter

1 large yellow onion, cut into thin
half-moons

½ teaspoon finely chopped fresh thyme

Kosher salt and freshly ground
black pepper

TRUFFLE CRÈME FRAÎCHE

¾ cup crème fraîche or sour cream,
for serving

2 teaspoons white truffle oil

ASSEMBLY

Flour, for rolling out the dough

1 large egg, beaten until foamy

About 2 tablespoons vegetable oil,
as needed

Finely chopped fresh chives, for garnish
(optional)

Special Equipment: 3-inch round
cookie cutter

POTATO *and* GOAT CHEESE
Pierogi
with Caramelized Onions

After work, I used to hang out at the Polish coffee shop Veselka, which is known as much as an after-hours chef hangout as it is for its incredible pierogi. Some people eat pierogi as a main course, but I prefer them as a hearty appetizer. I add goat cheese to the potato filling for extra creaminess, and a dash of truffle oil to the crème fraîche for a luxe finish. My mom says this is her favorite dish of all my creations, and that's saying something.

1. To make the dough: Whisk the flour, baking powder, and salt together in the bowl of a heavy-duty standing electric mixer (or in a large bowl). Whisk the sour cream, water, eggs, and oil together in a small bowl, then pour into the flour mixture. Using the paddle attachment, mix on low speed (or stir with a wooden spoon), adding more water if the dough is too dry, to make a soft dough. Change to the dough hook and mix on medium-low speed until the dough is smooth and supple, 6 to 8 minutes. (Or turn out the dough onto a lightly floured surface and knead by hand for 8 to 10 minutes.) Wrap the dough in plastic wrap and let stand at room temperature for 1 to 2 hours.

2. Meanwhile, make the filling: Put the potatoes in a large saucepan and add enough cold salted water to cover by 1 inch. Bring to a boil over high heat. Reduce the heat to medium and cook until the potatoes are tender, about 20 minutes. Drain well. Press the potatoes through a potato ricer (or rub them through a coarse wire sieve) into a medium bowl and let them cool.

3. Heat the olive oil in a small skillet over medium heat. Add the red onion and cook, stirring occasionally, until tender but not browned, about 3 minutes. Stir the onion into the potatoes, along with the goat cheese and chives. Stir in the cream and season to taste with salt and pepper.

4. To assemble the pierogi: Line a large rimmed baking sheet with parchment paper. Working with one half of the dough at a time, roll it out on a lightly floured work surface until about ⅛ inch thick. Using a 3-inch round cookie cutter, cut out rounds of the dough, reserving the trimmings. ➤

Cooking with Friends

Spoon about 1 teaspoon filling on the bottom half of each round. Brush the edge of each round with beaten egg, fold in half to enclose the filling, and seal closed with a fork. Transfer to the baking sheet. Knead the dough scraps together until smooth and let rest for about 10 minutes. Then repeat with the remaining dough and filling. (The pierogi can be covered with plastic wrap and refrigerated for up to 8 hours.)

5. To caramelize the onion: Melt the butter in a large saucepan over medium heat. Add the yellow onion and cook, stirring occasionally, until very tender and caramelized, about 25 minutes. Stir in the thyme and season to taste with the salt and pepper. Let cool. Coarsely chop the onions and transfer to a small bowl. (The onions can be covered and refrigerated for up to 8 hours. Bring to room temperature before using.)

6. To make the truffle crème fraîche: Mix the crème fraîche and truffle oil in a small bowl. (The crème fraîche can be covered and refrigerated for up to 8 hours. Bring to room temperature before using.)

7. Position a rack in the center of the oven and preheat the oven to 200°F. Line another large rimmed baking sheet with paper towels.

8. To cook the pierogi: Heat the oil in a large skillet, preferably nonstick, over medium heat. In batches, without crowding, add the pierogi, flat sides down, and cook, turning once, until golden brown on both sides, 4 to 5 minutes. Using a slotted spoon, transfer the pierogi to the baking sheet and keep warm in the oven while cooking the remaining pierogi, adding more oil to the skillet as needed.

9. Arrange the pierogi on a platter. Top each with a dab of the caramelized onions and sprinkle with the chives, if using. Serve immediately, with the truffle crème fraîche.

TOMATO "TARTARE"
on BRIOCHE CROSTINI

This is simply one of those dishes that you have to taste to believe: I have taken the flavors of beef tartare and applied them to roasted tomatoes for a meatless "tartare" that will not have you asking, "Where's the beef?" It's a great dish for vegetarians who don't get to have tartare! (For vegans, be sure to omit the egg yolks and substitute soy sauce for the Worcestershire sauce.) This technique yields amazing results from even the most average tomatoes by concentrating the tomato flavor through slow roasting.

1. To make the tomato tartare: Position a rack in the center of the oven and preheat the oven to 250°F. Line a large rimmed baking sheet with parchment paper.

2. Place the tomatoes, cut side up, on the baking sheet and brush lightly with oil. Bake until they are beginning to shrink and brown lightly around the edges but are still juicy, about 3½ hours. Let cool.

3. Working over a wire sieve placed in a medium bowl, remove the skin and seeds from the tomatoes. Separately reserve the juice in the bowl and the flesh, and discard the skin and seeds. Working on a cutting board with a well (to catch the tomato juices), finely chop the tomato flesh. Transfer the tomatoes to the sieve and squeeze them to extract more juice into the bowl. Pour any juice from chopping into the bowl. You should have about ¾ cup juice. Transfer the chopped tomato flesh to a medium bowl.

4. Bring the tomato juice to a boil in a small saucepan over medium heat. Boil until the juice is reduced by half, about 5 minutes. Pour over the tomato flesh and let cool.

5. Whisk 2 teaspoons olive oil with the mustard, soy sauce, sugar, hot sauce, and Worcestershire sauce in a small bowl. Stir in the capers, shallot, parsley, and garlic. Pour over the tomato mixture and mix well. Season to taste with salt and pepper. (The tomato tartare can be covered and refrigerated for up to 3 days. Bring to room temperature before serving.)

➤

TOMATO TARTARE

12 Roma (plum) tomatoes (about 3½ pounds), cored and halved lengthwise

Extra-virgin olive oil

1 teaspoon Dijon mustard

1 teaspoon Japanese soy sauce

1 teaspoon sugar

½ teaspoon hot red pepper sauce, such as Tabasco

½ teaspoon Worcestershire sauce

2 teaspoons finely chopped nonpareil capers

2 teaspoons finely chopped shallot

1 teaspoon minced fresh flat-leaf parsley or basil

½ teaspoon minced garlic

Kosher salt and freshly ground black pepper

BRIOCHE CROSTINI

1 loaf brioche or challah bread, cut into ¼-inch-thick slices

Extra-virgin olive oil, for brushing

Kosher salt and freshly ground black pepper

¼ cup (1 ounce) freshly grated Parmigiano-Reggiano cheese

ASSEMBLY

2 large egg yolks (optional)

Parmigiano-Reggiano cheese in a chunk, for grating, as needed

1 tablespoon very finely chopped fresh basil

Flaky sea salt, preferably Maldon

Extra-virgin olive oil, for drizzling

Special Equipment: 1½-inch round cookie cutter

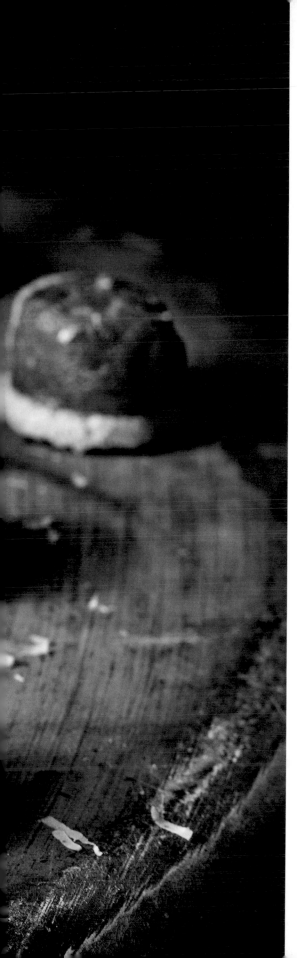

6. To make the crostini: Position a rack in the center of the oven and preheat the oven to 350°F. Line an 18-by-13-inch half-sheet pan with a silicone baking mat or parchment paper. Using a 1½-inch round cookie cutter, cut 24 rounds from the bread. Arrange the rounds on the half-sheet pan and brush with olive oil. Season with salt and pepper and sprinkle with the Parmigiano. Bake until the crostini are golden brown, about 10 minutes. Let cool. (The crostini can be covered and stored at room temperature for up to 8 hours.)

7. To assemble, place the crostini on a platter, and top each with an equal amount of the tomato tartare. For a finished look, use the cookie cutter as a mold. Place the round in the cutter, then spread 2 or 3 teaspoons of the tartare over the round in the cutter. Lift the cutter, leaving a neat layer of tartare on the round. (If desired, top each tartare with egg yolk. Beat the yolks in a small bowl to combine. Using an espresso spoon or a ¼-teaspoon measuring spoon, make a small indentation in each tartare. Fill the indentation with egg yolk.) Using a Microplane zester, grate a little Parmigiano over each. Sprinkle with the basil and salt, drizzle with olive oil, and serve immediately.

SPICY WOK-SEARED
EDAMAME

When you've eaten edamame in the past, they were probably served at a Japanese restaurant with some salt sprinkled on top. My edamame feature a spicy, sticky coating that transforms this basic bean into a powerhouse of flavor. With the finger licking required to eat them, a platter of sticky edamame is a surefire icebreaker, no matter who is sitting at the table. Don't be afraid to really char your pods, as the blackened spots are essential to the overall flavor.

MAKES
4 *to* 6
SERVINGS

2 tablespoons white (aka) miso

2 tablespoons futsu-shu (standard) sake, such as Gekkeikan

2 teaspoons Japanese soy sauce

2 teaspoons fresh ginger juice (see Note)

1 teaspoon sriracha

½ teaspoon Vietnamese or Thai fish sauce

½ teaspoon hoisin sauce

Pinch of Chinese five-spice powder

1 tablespoon canola oil

1 pound thawed frozen edamame in pods, patted completely dry

1. Whisk the miso, sake, soy sauce, ginger juice, sriracha, fish sauce, hoisin sauce, and five-spice powder together in a small bowl.

2. Heat a large wok or cast iron skillet over high heat until the wok is very hot. Pour the oil down the sides of the wok. Swirl the wok by its handle(s) to lightly coat the inside. Add the edamame, allowing the flat sides of as many edamame as possible to directly touch the wok sides. Cook, without stirring, until the pods are lightly charred, about 2 minutes. Stir and cook to create more charred spots, about 2 minutes more. Add ¼ cup water and cover the wok. Cook until the water is evaporated and the edamame is hot, about 2 minutes.

3. Stir in the miso mixture. Cook, stirring often, until the mixture has reduced to a glaze, about 1 minute. Transfer to a serving bowl. Serve hot, and eat the edamame with your fingers—with a lot of licking.

Note: *While you can buy bottled ginger juice in the baking aisle of some specialty markets, homemade juice is easy to make. To make it, purchase very fresh, plump ginger with tight, smooth skin. For each tablespoon of juice, shred about 1 inch of the ginger (no need to peel it) on the large holes of a box shredder. Working over a bowl, squeeze the shredded ginger in your fist to extract the juice. That's it.*

SAKE

When speaking of sake, which is quite a complex subject, there is really only one word that a cook needs to know: futsu-shu. In spite of all of the nuanced versions of the Japanese brewed spirit available (specified by the amount of outer grain removed before brewing), futsu-shu is a basic sake with a good balance of sweet to dry. It is not the sake to serve to friends to sip with fine sushi, but it is perfect for cooking and reasonably priced. If your liquor store carries only one brand, it is probably the commercial giant Gekkeikan, sold in a tall green screw-top bottle and actually made in California. Some people substitute dry sherry for sake, but now that sake is more available, it is really unnecessary to make the swap. Store leftover sake in the refrigerator, where it will keep for a few weeks, and even if the color darkens, it will be fine for cooking.

CITRUS-PICKLED
Vegetables

MAKES

2

QUARTS

These pickled vegetables are so easy to prepare that you just may make it a habit to always have a jar in the fridge. The touch of orange flavor gives them a tangy twist without overwhelming their pure briny flavor. Put them out with drinks, or serve as a side dish, as a snack, or with sandwiches. And because they are refrigerated and not stored at room temperature, you don't have to go through the hassle of hot-packing the jars.

VEGETABLES

1 large red bell pepper, seeded and cut into strips about ½ inch wide

1 large yellow bell pepper, seeded and cut into strips about ½ inch wide

2 large carrots, cut into ¼-inch rounds

1 standard cucumber, halved lengthwise, seeded, and cut into ½-inch half-moons

1 jalapeño, cut into ⅛-inch rounds, seeds shaken out

Ice water, to cover

CITRUS BRINE

1 quart water

1 cup distilled white vinegar

⅓ cup kosher salt

1½ tablespoons sugar

1 garlic clove, crushed under a knife and peeled

2 teaspoons yellow mustard seeds

2 teaspoons coriander seeds

2 teaspoons black peppercorns

½ teaspoon hot red pepper flakes

Zest strips from 1 navel orange, removed from the fruit with a vegetable peeler

2 tablespoons coarsely chopped fresh cilantro

1 bay leaf, broken in half

Special Equipment: Two 1-quart glass canning jars with lids

1. To prepare the vegetables: Mix the red and yellow bell peppers, carrots, cucumber, and jalapeño in a large bowl. Add enough ice water to cover the vegetables. Let stand for 15 to 30 minutes.

2. To make the brine, combine all the ingredients except the zest, cilantro, and bay leaf in a medium nonreactive saucepan. Bring to a full boil over high heat, stirring often to dissolve the salt and sugar.

3. Drain the vegetables well and discard any leftover ice cubes. Return the vegetables to the bowl and mix in the orange zest and cilantro. Divide the vegetable mixture equally among the jars. Pour the hot brine into the jars to cover the vegetables, discarding any leftover brine. Be sure to get most of the seasonings into the jars. Submerge a bay leaf half in each jar. Let the pickles cool, uncovered, until tepid, about 1 hour.

4. Cover the jars with their lids. Refrigerate at least 1 day before serving. (The pickles can be refrigerated for up to 2 months.)

Grilled *and* Chilled
HARICOTS VERTS

MAKES

6 *to* 8

SERVINGS

I love the idea of grilling green beans to add a layer of smokiness to this crisp, chilled starter. When I was growing up, there was always Italian dressing in our fridge and I would often find myself dipping various leftovers, such as crusty bread or raw vegetables, in the tangy mixture for impromptu snacks. The beans are best when made with thin haricots verts, but thicker regular green beans work well, too.

ITALIAN VINAIGRETTE

2 tablespoons champagne vinegar or white wine vinegar

1 small garlic clove, chopped

¼ teaspoon kosher salt

⅛ teaspoon freshly ground black pepper

Pinch of hot red pepper flakes

½ cup extra-virgin olive oil

2 tablespoons finely chopped red bell pepper

1 teaspoon minced fresh flat-leaf parsley

CROUTONS

3 slices slightly stale challah or brioche bread, cut into ½-inch cubes

2 tablespoons unsalted butter, melted

Kosher salt and freshly ground black pepper

GREEN BEANS

12 ounces haricots verts, stem ends trimmed

1 tablespoon extra-virgin olive oil

Kosher salt and freshly ground black pepper

---

1. To make the vinaigrette: Combine the vinegar, garlic, salt, black pepper, and red pepper flakes in a blender. With the machine running, gradually add the oil through the hole in the lid to emulsify. Pour into a bowl and stir in the red bell pepper and parsley. (The vinaigrette can be covered and refrigerated for up to 3 days.)

2. To make the croutons: Position a rack in the center of the oven and preheat the oven to 350°F. Toss the bread cubes and melted butter together in a medium bowl to coat the cubes, then season to taste with salt and pepper. Spread on a large rimmed baking sheet and bake, stirring occasionally, until they are lightly browned, about 10 minutes. Let cool completely. (The croutons can be stored, uncovered, at room temperature for up to 1 day.)

3. Toss the green beans with the oil in a large bowl and season lightly with salt and pepper. If you have an outdoor grill, cook the green beans over direct, medium heat (400°F) until seared and tender, about 5 minutes. (Using a perforated grilling pan over your grill rack can avoid the issue of the green beans falling through the cracks.) If you do not have an outdoor grill, heat a large rimmed grill pan over medium-high heat. In batches, spread the haricots verts in a single layer in the pan and cook until they are seared with grill marks and crisp-tender, about 3 minutes. Transfer to a plate and let cool. Cover and refrigerate the green beans until they are chilled, at least 1 hour or up to 1 day.

4. Toss the haricots verts and 2 to 3 tablespoons of the vinaigrette in a large bowl until the haricots are lightly coated. (Reserve the remaining vinaigrette for another use.) Season the beans to taste with salt and pepper. Heap onto a small serving platter and top with the croutons. Serve immediately.

SALADS AND A SOUP

The saying, "The whole is greater than the sum of its parts" applies to my salads. These recipes feature ingredients that run the gamut from crunchy to creamy, from savory to sweet-ish, and even sometimes spicy. If I am going to eat a plate of raw vegetables, I want them to pop with interesting flavor combinations and, above all, an incredible dressing. One of my favorite techniques is using reduced juice or vegetable puree as the main ingredient in a dressing—avocado, corn, apple, and carrot juice are essential components in some of my most delicious creations. Ultimately, all of these vibrant flavors and textures come together to create a truly memorable salad. While I typically steer clear of serving soups because they are difficult to share, my favorite tomato soup recipe is worth dirtying a few extra bowls!

ASPARAGUS RIBBON
and
SPRING PEA SALAD
with Lemon Ricotta

—

Cobb Salad Bites
with AVOCADO VINAIGRETTE

—

MY HOUSE SALAD
with Carrot Harissa Vinaigrette

—

KALE, APPLE, and PANCETTA
Salad

—

Panzanella
with
Tomato Vinaigrette
and
BLUE CHEESE

THAI MARINATED
Papaya Salad

—

Soba Noodle AND Beet Salad

—

SPINACH SALAD
with
Goat Cheese, Spicy Cashews, *and*
CORN VINAIGRETTE

—

Cream of Tomato Soup

ASPARAGUS RIBBON *and*
SPRING PEA SALAD
with LEMON RICOTTA

MAKES

6

SERVINGS

This beautiful salad, with many shades of green and accented with red radishes, has a surprise. The colorful presentation hides a lemony ricotta beneath the bounty of grilled asparagus ribbons and juicy green peas, giving each bite a tangy richness you wouldn't first expect. Inspired by a love of white pizza topped with green vegetables, this unique salad marries the greens and ricotta in a fresh and lighter way. If you can find some white asparagus, mix it up with the green spears.

LEMON RICOTTA

½ cup whole-milk ricotta, preferably fresh

Finely grated zest of 1 lemon

1 tablespoon fresh lemon juice

DIJON VINAIGRETTE

1 tablespoon fresh lemon juice

½ teaspoon Dijon mustard

¼ teaspoon kosher salt

Pinch of cayenne pepper

¼ cup extra-virgin olive oil

———

1 pound green asparagus, woody stems snapped off

1 pound peas in the pod, shelled (1 cup shelled peas)

1 (5-ounce) bag mixed baby greens

3 large radishes, cut into thin rounds

Kosher salt and freshly ground black pepper

1. To make the ricotta: Whisk all of the ingredients together in a small bowl. Cover and refrigerate until ready to serve. (The ricotta can be refrigerated for 8 hours.)

2. To make the vinaigrette: Whisk the lemon juice, mustard, salt, and cayenne together in a small bowl. Gradually whisk in the oil. (The vinaigrette can be covered and refrigerated for up to 8 hours. Whisk well before serving.)

3. Using a swivel vegetable peeler (preferably Y-shaped) and pressing firmly, shave the asparagus lengthwise into ribbons. Heat a ridged griddle or grill pan over high heat. In batches, spread the asparagus on the griddle in a single layer and cook just until seared with char marks, about 2 minutes. Transfer to a shallow bowl and let cool.

4. Bring a medium saucepan of salted water to a boil over high heat. Add the peas and cook until they are just tender, about 5 minutes. Drain the peas, rinse under cold running water, and rinse again. Pat the peas dry with paper towels. (The asparagus and peas can be covered and refrigerated for up to 4 hours.)

5. To serve, toss the mixed greens with the vinaigrette, asparagus, peas, and radishes in a large bowl. Season to taste with salt and pepper. Spread the bottom of your serving platter with the lemon ricotta. Top with the salad and serve immediately.

Cobb Salad Bites

with *AVOCADO VINAIGRETTE*

MAKES

24

PIECES

6 TO 8
SERVINGS

Cobb salad, invented at Hollywood's Brown Derby restaurant, is now served everywhere. I have taken the essential ingredients (bacon, eggs, avocado, blue cheese) and created bite-sized salads that emphasize my favorite ingredient of all, bacon. Shredded Brussels sprouts replace the typical iceberg lettuce to make the salad extra crisp and robust.

BACON CUPS

Vegetable oil cooking spray,
for the pans

6 slices thick-cut bacon, each cut
crosswise into quarters to make
24 pieces

AVOCADO VINAIGRETTE

½ ripe Hass avocado, pitted, peeled,
and coarsely chopped

2 tablespoons fresh lemon juice

½ teaspoon Dijon mustard

2 tablespoons vegetable oil

2 tablespoons olive oil

About 2 tablespoons water,
as needed

Fine sea salt and freshly ground
black pepper

COBB SALAD

½ ripe Hass avocado, peeled, pitted,
and finely diced (¼-inch)

1 teaspoon fresh lemon juice

10 ounces Brussels sprouts, trimmed

2 Roma (plum) tomatoes, seeded
and cut into ¼-inch dice

3 tablespoons finely chopped red onion

3 tablespoons finely crumbled blue
cheese, preferably Maytag

2 hard-boiled eggs, finely chopped

Special Equipment: Two 12-cup
mini-muffin pans

1. To make the bacon cups: Position racks in the top third and the center of the oven and preheat the oven to 375°F. Turn two 12-cup mini-muffin pans upside down and lightly spray the upturned cups with oil.

2. Center a piece over each cup. Place each muffin pan on an 18-by-13-inch half-sheet pan to catch the rendered fat. Bake until the bacon cups are crisp and browned, about 20 minutes. Let the cups cool briefly on the pans. Using kitchen tongs or a small sharp knife, carefully lift the bacon cups from the pans and transfer to paper towels to cool. (The bacon cups can be stored in an airtight container and refrigerated for up to 1 day. Bring them to room temperature before serving.)

3. To make the vinaigrette: Puree the avocado, lemon juice, and mustard in a blender (or food processor). Mix the vegetable oil and olive oil together. With the machine running, gradually pour the mixed oils through the hole in the blender lid (or processor feed tube). Add enough water to thin the vinaigrette to the consistency of heavy cream. Season to taste with salt and pepper. (Makes about 1 cup. The vinaigrette can be tightly covered and refrigerated for up to 1 day.)

4. To make the salad: Toss the diced avocado with the lemon juice in a large bowl. Shred the Brussels sprouts in a food processor (or with a large knife). Add them to the avocado, along with the tomato, onion, blue cheese, and eggs. Add about ½ cup of the vinaigrette (or more to taste) and toss gently. (Reserve the remaining vinaigrette for another use.)

5. Arrange the bacon cups on a large platter. Divide the salad, heaping it in tall mounds into the bacon cups. Serve immediately.

PICKLED CARROTS

½ cup white wine vinegar or champagne vinegar

2 teaspoons sugar

1 teaspoon kosher salt

1 teaspoon yellow mustard seeds

1 teaspoon coriander seeds

½ teaspoon pink peppercorns

½ teaspoon hot red pepper flakes

½ dried bay leaf

2 large carrots, shaved into 3-inch-long ribbons on a mandoline or V-slicer

CARROT HARISSA VINAIGRETTE

1½ cups carrot juice, freshly extracted or store-bought

2 teaspoons minced shallot

Grated zest of ½ lime

2 teaspoons fresh lime juice

1½ teaspoons harissa paste

1 teaspoon Dijon mustard

1 teaspoon honey

1 teaspoon kosher salt

¼ teaspoon freshly ground black pepper

⅓ cup extra-virgin olive oil

⅓ cup canola oil

1 tablespoon coarsely chopped fresh cilantro

CRISPY CHICKPEAS

Vegetable oil, for deep-frying

½ cup canned chickpeas (garbanzo beans), drained and patted dry with paper towels

¼ teaspoon sweet Spanish or Hungarian paprika

¼ teaspoon kosher salt

---

10 ounces mixed baby salad greens, preferably a combination of baby arugula and frisée

2 radishes, sliced into thin rounds on a mandoline or V-slicer

3 ounces Manchego cheese, in one piece, for shaving

MY HOUSE SALAD *with* CARROT HARISSA VINAIGRETTE

MAKES 4 to 6 SERVINGS

Chef Sarah Nelson created this extraordinary, very satisfying, and unique salad. If I'm going to make a salad, I want it to be something special and satisfying. The ingredients list may look long, but each step is easy and the reward is a multi-dimensional salad that is full of flavor—tart pickled ribbons of carrot, crispy garbanzo beans, and a bright carrot dressing. Try to include frisée as one of the greens, as its lacy texture will give the salad a nice height. If you like, use plain carrot ribbons and un-fried chickpeas; the salad will still be a winner.

1. To make the pickled carrots: Bring 1 cup water and the vinegar, sugar, salt, mustard seeds, coriander seeds, pink peppercorns, hot pepper flakes, and bay leaf to a boil in a medium saucepan. Reduce the heat to low and gently simmer, without reducing the liquid, for 10 minutes. Strain into a medium bowl. Add the carrot ribbons and let stand at room temperature for at least 1 hour. (The ribbons can be covered and refrigerated for up to 5 days.)

2. To make the vinaigrette: Boil the carrot juice in a small saucepan over high heat, stirring occasionally, until reduced to ½ cup. Let cool completely.

3. Process the cooled carrot juice, shallot, lime zest and juice, harissa, mustard, honey, salt, and pepper together in a blender (preferably a heavy-duty model) until very smooth, about 1 minute. With the machine running, gradually pour in the olive and canola oils through the feed tube. Add the cilantro and pulse until it is minced. (Makes about 1 cup. The vinaigrette can be covered and refrigerated for 3 days. If the dressing separates, process it again in the blender.)

4. To fry the chickpeas: Line a rimmed baking sheet with paper towels. Pour enough oil to come 1 inch up the sides of a medium saucepan and heat over high heat until the oil registers 350°F on a deep-frying thermometer. Carefully add the chickpeas, taking care that the oil does not bubble over, and cook until they are lightly browned, about 2 minutes. Using a wire spider or slotted spoon, transfer the chickpeas to the paper towels to drain. Let cool completely. Transfer the chickpeas to a small bowl and toss with the paprika and salt. (The chickpeas can be stored at room temperature for up to 8 hours.)

5. Toss the greens, radishes, and ¼ cup of the vinaigrette in a large deep platter. (Reserve the remaining vinaigrette for another use.) Drain the carrots and add to the salad, along with the chickpeas. Using a swivel vegetable peeler, shave 1 or 2 ounces' worth of Manchego curls over the salad and toss again. Transfer to a serving platter, fluffing the greens to give the salad height. Serve immediately.

CHEF TALK

Mandolines

Don't look at a mandoline or a plastic V-slicer as a chef's tool, but as something that will make your cooking more interesting and easier. Metal mandolines are pricey and an investment. However, plastic V-slicers are quite cheap and do the same job at a fraction of the mandoline's price. No matter which cutter you get, use extreme caution: Always cut with the guard and never with an unprotected hand — no matter what you might see the contestants on cooking shows do!

CHEF TALK

Shredding Soft Cheese

Shredding or grating soft cheese (like the goat cheese in this recipe) can be messy, with the end result looking much more smeared than shredded. To solve the problem, freeze the cheese until it is firm but not rock hard, about 30 minutes, depending on the size of the chunk and its consistency. The cheese can now be cleanly shredded on the large holes of a box grater, or even grated with a fine Microplane zester.

Kale, Apple,
and PANCETTA SALAD

MAKES

8

SERVINGS

There is kale salad... and then there is *this* kale salad developed by chef Kyle Kingrey, with its balanced trio of greens. The distinct apple vinaigrette, which gets it richness from reduced apple cider, could make even the simplest of salads a showstopper. Add some crispy pancetta, creamy goat cheese, and sweet candied pecans, and the salad will convert any kale skeptic into a superfan.

APPLE CIDER VINAIGRETTE

2 cups apple cider

½ cinnamon stick

Zest strips from ½ navel orange, removed with a vegetable peeler

1 sprig fresh thyme

3 tablespoons finely chopped shallots

3 tablespoons cider vinegar

1 large egg yolk

1 teaspoon Dijon mustard

Kosher salt and freshly ground black pepper

1 cup olive oil (not extra-virgin)

SALAD

5 ounces pancetta, cut into ⅓-inch dice

6 ounces lacinato or standard kale, thick stems discarded

1 medium head radicchio (12 ounces), cored

6 ounces leaf spinach, thick stems discarded

1 Granny Smith apple, cored and cut into thin strips on a mandoline or with a large knife

½ cup store-bought glazed pecans

Kosher salt and freshly ground black pepper

1 tablespoon finely chopped fresh chives

2 teaspoons finely chopped fresh tarragon

4 ounces goat cheese, frozen until firm

1. To make the vinaigrette: Bring the cider, cinnamon, orange zest, and thyme to a boil in a large saucepan over high heat. Cook until the liquid is syrupy and reduced to about ¼ cup, 10 to 15 minutes. Strain and discard the solids. Let the syrup cool completely.

2. Puree the apple syrup, shallots, vinegar, yolk, mustard, ½ teaspoon salt, and ¼ teaspoon pepper in a blender. With the machine running, pour the oil through the hole in the blender lid to make a thick vinaigrette. Season to taste with additional salt and pepper. (Makes about 1¾ cups. The vinaigrette can be covered and refrigerated for up to 2 days. Whisk well before using.)

3. To make the salad: Cook the pancetta in a medium skillet over medium heat, stirring occasionally, until crisp and brown, about 5 minutes. Using a slotted spoon, transfer the pancetta to paper towels to drain and cool. (The pancetta can be stored at room temperature for up to 2 hours.)

4. Using a large, sharp knife, cut the kale, radicchio, and spinach into long, thin shreds. You should have about 12 loosely packed cups.

5. Toss the kale, radicchio, and spinach with the pancetta, apple, and pecans in a large bowl. Add 1 cup of the apple cider vinaigrette and toss again. (Reserve the remaining vinaigrette for another use.) Season to taste with salt and pepper.

6. Heap the salad on a large platter. Sprinkle with the chives and tarragon. Using a Microplane zester, shred a generous amount of the goat cheese over the salad and serve immediately.

PANZANELLA

with *Tomato Vinaigrette* and **BLUE CHEESE**

MAKES 6 SERVINGS

Panzanella thinks it's a sandwich, which is why it is easily my favorite type of salad. While it's traditionally made with leftover chunks of bread, I recommend freshly toasted baguette cubes and some sharp blue cheese for a tasty detour from the original. Perfect as a stand-alone meal, I also love to serve this panzanella alongside a simply grilled steak for an ideal summer supper.

BREAD CUBES

10 ounces baguette (about ½ loaf), crust trimmed and bread cut into ¾-inch cubes, about 6 cups

1 tablespoon extra-virgin olive oil

Kosher salt and freshly ground black pepper

TOMATO VINAIGRETTE

2 tablespoons red wine vinegar

1 tablespoon tomato paste

⅓ cup extra-virgin olive oil

Kosher salt and freshly ground black pepper

---

1 head frisée or curly endive, torn into bite-sized pieces; or 6 ounces mixed baby greens

1 cup halved red cherry tomatoes

1 cup halved yellow cherry tomatoes

½ small red onion, cut into paper-thin slices

2 tablespoons chopped fresh chives

Kosher salt and freshly ground black pepper

1 cup (4 ounces) crumbled blue cheese, preferably Cabrales

1. To toast the bread: Position a rack in the center of the oven and preheat the oven to 350°F. Drizzle the bread cubes in a large bowl with the oil, season with salt and pepper, and toss well. Spread the coated bread on a rimmed baking sheet. Bake, stirring occasionally, until the bread is golden brown, 10 to 15 minutes. Let cool completely.

2. To make the vinaigrette: Whisk the vinegar and tomato paste together in a small bowl to dissolve the paste. Gradually whisk in the oil. Season the tomato vinaigrette to taste with salt and pepper.

3. Combine the bread cubes, frisée, red and yellow cherry tomatoes, red onion, and chives together in a large bowl. Drizzle with the vinaigrette and mix well. Season to taste with salt and pepper. Sprinkle with the blue cheese and serve immediately.

THAI MARINATED
PAPAYA SALAD

MAKES
8 *to* 12
SERVINGS

LEMONGRASS OIL

3 lemongrass stalks, tender bottom bulbs only, coarsely chopped

1¼ cups vegetable oil

MARINATED PAPAYA

1 green papaya (about 2¼ pounds), peeled, seeded, and cut on a mandoline or V-slicer into julienned strips about 3 inches long

1 (14-ounce) can unsweetened coconut milk (not cream of coconut)

¼ cup soy sauce

LEMONGRASS PEANUTS

¾ cup unsalted raw shelled peanuts

Kosher salt

MIDORI VINAIGRETTE

¼ cup fresh lime juice

3 tablespoons melon liqueur, preferably Midori

2 tablespoons mirin

2 tablespoons Thai sweet chili sauce

1 tablespoon rice vinegar

2 teaspoons Microplaned garlic

2 teaspoons peeled and Microplaned fresh ginger

½ teaspoon sriracha

½ teaspoon kosher salt

---

1 small red bell pepper, seeded

1 large ripe red papaya or 2 ripe yellow papayas, peeled and seeded

6 scallions, white and green parts, thinly sliced on a sharp diagonal

¼ cup hand-torn fresh Thai basil

¼ cup hand-torn fresh cilantro

¼ cup hand-torn fresh mint

Kosher salt

Sriracha

Green papaya is a staple of Thai and Vietnamese cooking. It is not sweet, as the more familiar variety that is sold ripened, and has a firm, crisp texture that makes one of the most refreshing salads on earth. There are some very simple green papaya salads, but I love this one with its overlapping flavors and textures.

1. To make the lemongrass oil: Smash the lemongrass with a meat mallet on a carving board. Warm and steep the oil and lemongrass together in a small saucepan over very low heat for 1 hour (don't worry if it bubbles lightly). Strain into a bowl, pressing hard on the solids, and let it cool completely. (Makes about 1 cup. The oil can be stored in a covered container and refrigerated for up to 1 month.)

2. To marinate the papaya: Combine the green papaya, coconut milk, and soy sauce together in a medium bowl. Cover and refrigerate for at least 1 hour or up to 4 hours.

3. To make the peanuts: Heat 2 teaspoons of the lemongrass oil in a small skillet over medium heat. Add the peanuts and cook, stirring occasionally, until they begin to darken, about 2 minutes. Remove from the heat and season with salt to taste. Transfer to a plate and let cool. Coarsely chop the peanuts. (The peanuts can be cooled, covered, and stored at room temperature for up to 1 day.)

4. To make the vinaigrette: Whisk all of the ingredients together in a medium bowl. Gradually whisk in ⅓ cup plus 2 tablespoons of the lemongrass oil. (Reserve the remaining lemongrass oil for another use. Makes about 1 cup dressing. The dressing can be stored in a covered container and refrigerated for up to 1 week.)

5. Cut the bell pepper and ripe papaya into 3-inch julienne (they do not require a mandoline). Briefly drain the marinated green papaya and transfer it to a large bowl. Add the bell pepper, ripe papaya, scallions, Thai basil, cilantro, and mint to the bowl and mix well. Add the vinaigrette and mix again. Season to taste with salt and sriracha. Transfer to a platter or serving bowl, sprinkle the peanuts, and serve.

Soba Noodle
and BEET SALAD

MAKES

4 *to* 6

SERVINGS

I serve this salad most often with the Wasabi Pea–Crusted Salmon on page 109. But it is so useful as a salad with other main courses (try it with grilled shrimp), that I am offering it here as a stand-alone recipe so it is sure to catch your attention. Ginger juice is a great ingredient as it adds spicy flavor without the tough texture of the chopped root. You'll be glad to have the leftover pesto to add zest to plain rice or noodles.

ASIAN DRESSING
2 tablespoons Asian Pesto (page 79)

1 tablespoon fresh ginger juice
(see page 58)

1 tablespoon fresh lime juice

1 teaspoon Asian sesame oil

1 teaspoon Japanese soy sauce

SOBA
½ cup Japanese soy sauce

1 (8-ounce) package soba

---

1 medium carrot, julienned with
a mandoline, V-slicer, or large knife

½ red bell pepper, cored and
cut into thin strips

½ yellow bell pepper, cored and
cut into thin strips

1 small beet, roasted
(see page 79), peeled, and
cut into ¼-inch dice

1 tablespoon finely chopped
roasted unsalted cashews

Kosher salt and freshly ground
black pepper

1. To make the dressing: Whisk the Asian pesto, ginger juice, lime juice, sesame oil, and soy sauce together in a large bowl; set aside. (Save the remaining pesto for another use.)

2. To cook the soba: Bring 4 quarts water to a boil in a large saucepan over high heat. Add the soy sauce and return to a boil. Add the soba and cook according to the package directions until barely tender. Drain in a colander and rinse quickly under cold running water just to stop the cooking.

Add the warm noodles to the dressing and let cool. Stir in the carrot, red and yellow pepper, beet, and cashews. Season to taste with salt and pepper. (The salad can be covered and refrigerated for up to 8 hours. Season again before using.)

➡

ASIAN PESTO

Makes about 1¼ cups

If you have lemons, make lemonade. If you have basil, make pesto! This version has Asian influences and, like the Italian original, can add an enormous amount of flavor and character to a dish with just a couple of tablespoons. Try it stirred into plain steamed rice or noodles, as a sandwich condiment (it is amazing on Vietnamese *bahn mi*), or slathered on grilled chicken toward the end of cooking.

¼ cup vegetable oil

¼ cup olive oil (not extra-virgin)

1 garlic clove, crushed under a knife and peeled

½ cup coarsely chopped roasted unsalted cashews

2 tablespoons fresh lime juice

1 tablespoon peeled and minced fresh ginger

1 teaspoon Vietnamese or Thai fish sauce

½ cup packed Thai basil leaves

½ cup packed Italian basil leaves

¼ cup packed mint leaves

1 tablespoon sambal oelek or Chinese chili paste

Fine sea salt

1. Combine the vegetable and olive oil in a liquid measuring cup; set aside. With the machine running, drop the garlic through the feed tube of a food processor to mince the garlic. Stop the machine and add the cashews, lime juice, ginger, fish sauce, Thai and Italian basil, mint, sambal oelek, and ¼ teaspoon salt. Pulse a few times to finely chop the ingredients.

2. With the machine running, pour the combined oils through the feed tube to make a paste. Season to taste with salt and pepper. (The pesto can be refrigerated in a covered container, with a very thin layer of vegetable oil poured on top to seal the surface, for up to 2 weeks, or frozen for up to 3 months. Bring to room temperature and stir well before using.)

ROASTING BEETS

Until recently, beets were mainly unloved. Their fortunes changed when cooks learned about roasted beets, which were vastly better than boiled beets. Roasted beets are sold at many supermarkets, but it is easy to roast your own.

Choose small to medium beets, no larger than 5 ounces each. (Large beets take forever to cook.) Scrub the beets well under cold running water and remove the top greens, saving them for another use. Rub the beets with olive oil and wrap tightly in a packet of aluminum foil. Roast in a 400°F oven until the beets are tender when pierced with the tip of a small sharp knife, about 1¼ hours. Be flexible with the roasting time, as the size and age of the beets are factors in the timing. Let stand until warm. Slip off the peels and let cool completely. Cover and refrigerate until chilled, at least 2 hours or up to 3 days.

SPINACH SALAD
with GOAT CHEESE, SPICY CASHEWS, AND CORN VINAIGRETTE

MAKES

6

SERVINGS

As you can see here (and with the Carrot Harissa Vinaigrette on page 70), I like to use vegetable purees and juices in my salads to create an intense depth of flavor. In this recipe, roasted corn is pureed into a beautiful pale yellow dressing that richly coats bright green spinach leaves. For a warm salad, toss the spinach very briefly in a large nonstick skillet with a dash of olive oil to warm the leaves before dressing, taking care not to wilt them.

SPICED CASHEWS

2 teaspoons unsalted butter

2 teaspoons dark brown sugar

1 teaspoon pure ground ancho chile

⅛ teaspoon cayenne pepper

⅛ teaspoon five-spice powder

½ teaspoon fine sea salt

¾ cup (3 ounces) roasted cashews

CORN VINAIGRETTE

½ cup roasted corn kernels (see Roasting Corn, page 81)

¼ cup Vegetable Stock (page 190) or water

1 tablespoon mayonnaise

2 teaspoons cider vinegar

1 teaspoon Dijon mustard

¼ cup canola oil

¼ teaspoon kosher salt

⅛ teaspoon freshly ground black pepper

———

12 ounces baby spinach

1 cup roasted corn kernels (see page 81)

4 ounces goat cheese, frozen until firm

Kosher salt and freshly ground black pepper

1. To make the cashews: Line a large rimmed baking sheet with a silicone baking mat, or butter the baking sheet well with softened butter. Melt the 2 teaspoons butter in a large skillet over medium heat. Add the brown sugar, ground ancho, cayenne pepper, five-spice powder, and salt and stir to melt the sugar. Add the cashews and mix to coat them well. Turn the cashew mixture onto the mat and let cool completely. In batches, break up the cashews into clusters and pulse them in a food processor until coarsely chopped. (The spiced cashews can be stored in an airtight container at room temperature for up to 1 day.)

2. Meanwhile, make the vinaigrette: Puree the roasted corn kernels with the stock in a blender. Add the mayonnaise, vinegar, and mustard. With the machine running, gradually add the canola oil through the hole in the blender lid and process until the vinaigrette is emulsified. Season with the salt and pepper. (Makes about 1 cup. The vinaigrette can be covered and refrigerated for up to 1 day.)

3. Toss the cashews, spinach, and corn with the vinaigrette in a large bowl. Using a Microplane zester, grate a generous amount of cheese over the salad. Toss again and season with salt and pepper. Serve immediately.

ROASTING CORN

Corn is naturally sweet, and roasting the kernels to a toasty brown color helps balance the sugary notes. You will get about ¾ cup kernels from an average-sized ear. Note that the corn should be husked so the kernels are directly exposed to the heat.

To roast the corn under a broiler, position the broiler pan about 8 inches from the source of heat and preheat the broiler on high. Place the husked corn on the rack and broil, turning occasionally, until the corn is lightly scorched with brown spots, about 8 minutes. (If you have an outdoor grill, cook the corn over medium-hot coals, with the grill lid closed, for about the same time.) Remove from the broiler and let cool completely.

Cut the wide end of the corn off to give it a solid base. Stand the ear on its cut end. Using a large knife, cut from top to bottom to remove the kernels where they meet the cob. Transfer the kernels to a bowl. Use the knife blade to scrape the corn "milk" from the cobs into the bowl.

Cream of
Tomato Soup

MAKES

6 *to* 8

SERVINGS

2 tablespoons extra-virgin olive oil

1 medium yellow onion, chopped

2 garlic cloves, thinly sliced

2 tablespoons tomato paste

2 pounds ripe Roma (plum) tomatoes, seeded and chopped

1 (28-ounce) can plum tomatoes, with their juice, chopped

1¼ cups tomato juice

1 tablespoon sugar

1½ teaspoons sriracha

½ cup heavy cream

1 tablespoon red wine vinegar

1 tablespoon finely chopped fresh basil

Kosher salt and freshly ground black pepper

Most of us have fond childhood memories of canned tomato soup. I set out to re-create that classic flavor and ended up with the best tomato soup I've ever tasted. With four different kinds, this soup is about tomatoes, tomatoes, tomatoes, and more tomatoes, with the cream playing a supporting role. This is the soup to serve with the "Grilled Cheese" Dumplings on page 36, one of my most popular restaurant recipes.

1. Heat the oil in a large saucepan over medium heat. Add the onion and garlic and cook, stirring occasionally, until the onion is translucent, about 4 minutes. Stir in the tomato paste and cook, stirring occasionally, until it begins to form a dark sticky film in the saucepan, about 2 minutes. Add the fresh tomatoes and cook, stirring up the paste on the bottom of the pan, until they give off juices and soften, about 10 minutes.

2. Stir in the canned tomatoes (with their juice), the 1¼ cups tomato juice, the sugar, and the sriracha and bring to a boil over high heat. Reduce the heat to medium-low and simmer until the soup is slightly reduced, about 45 minutes. During the last few minutes, stir in the cream, vinegar, and basil. Season to taste with salt and pepper.

3. Using a hand blender, puree the soup in the pot. Or let the soup cool until tepid, and puree in batches in a blender with the lid ajar. Strain and then return the soup to the pot. (The soup can be cooled, covered, and refrigerated. Reheat in the saucepan, adding water as needed if it is too thick.)

CHICKEN

Chicken—everyone loves it. But when I am cooking chicken, I consider it my goal to make a dish that is worth the time and effort and not just another familiar standard. In this chapter you'll find chicken dishes from all over the globe, although I seem to have a special affinity for Latin ingredients like chiles and cilantro. When you crave comfort food of the highest order, I recommend the spice-rubbed chicken wings or my quick-roasted chicken served with mascarpone polenta on pages 94 and 87. But no matter which recipe you choose, always buy the best poultry (preferably locally sourced and organically raised) that you can afford. You will be able to taste the difference.

SPATCHCOCKED
Roast Chicken
with Citrus Rub

—

Orange-Marinated
CHICKEN SATAY
with
PEANUT SAUCE

—

Arroz con Pollo
with Achiote Oil

—

CHICKEN MEATBALLS
in Creamy
Mushroom Sauce *with*
Whipped Ricotta

—

SMOKY
RUBBED
Chicken Wings
with Honey, Bourbon,
and Molasses Sauce

Open-Faced
CHICKEN AREPAS
with SALSA VERDE

—

Chilaquiles Verdes
with
CHIPOTLE
CHICKEN

—

Chicken Taquitos
with
Guacamole Puree

ROAST CHICKEN
with CITRUS RUB

MAKES

4

SERVINGS

A great roast chicken has juicy and flavorful meat with lots of crispy skin. Spatchcocking (also called *butterflying*) exposes all of the chicken skin to the hot temperature of the oven for an even golden brown on every surface. To ensure that your chicken has equal parts flavor and moisture, I pair a quick brine with an easy rub that's nuanced with citrus, garlic, and spice.

CHICKEN AND BRINE

1 chicken, giblets removed,
about 4 pounds

2 cups hot water

¼ cup plus 1 tablespoon sugar

¼ cup kosher salt

1½ quarts ice water

CITRUS RUB

2 tablespoons extra-virgin olive oil

Finely grated zest of 1 orange

Finely grated zest of 1 lemon

3 garlic cloves, shredded
on a Microplane zester

1 tablespoon finely chopped
fresh flat-leaf parsley

1½ teaspoons finely chopped
fresh thyme or ¾ teaspoon dried thyme

½ teaspoon hot red pepper flakes

Creamy Mascarpone Polenta
(page 206)

---

1. To prepare the chicken: Using kitchen shears or a large knife, cut down both sides of the chicken backbone and remove it. (Save the backbone for another use, like making stock.) Open the chicken, skin side up, on a work surface. Press hard on the breastbone to crack it and help the chicken lie flat.

2. To brine the chicken: Whisk the hot water, sugar, and salt well in a medium bowl to dissolve the sugar and salt. Let cool until tepid. Stir in the ice water.

3. Put the chicken in a 1- to 2-gallon self-sealing plastic bag, and place the bag in a bowl to hold it. Pour as much of the brine as needed into the bag to cover the chicken and seal the bag. Refrigerate for 1 to 4 hours.

4. To make the rub: Combine all the ingredients in a small bowl. Drain the chicken (do not rinse) and pat it dry with paper towels. Spread the rub all over the chicken. Lightly oil a half-sheet pan. Transfer the chicken, skin side up, onto the pan and let stand at room temperature for about 15 minutes.

5. Position a rack in the top third of the oven and preheat the oven to 400°F. Roast the chicken until an instant-read thermometer inserted in the thickest part of a thigh reads at least 165°F, 50 minutes to 1 hour. Remove from the oven and let the chicken stand for about 5 minutes.

6. Using the shears or a large knife, cut the chicken into quarters. Divide the polenta among 4 soup bowls. Top each bowl of polenta with a chicken quarter. Drizzle with the pan juices and serve.

Orange-Marinated
Chicken Satay
with PEANUT SAUCE

MAKES

4 *to* 6

SERVINGS

After a recent trip to Southeast Asia, I came back bursting with inspiration and ideas. This super-easy chicken satay incorporates some of the tricks I learned abroad, including a peanut sauce that requires only a handful of ingredients but is nonetheless chock-full of flavor. You can use any cut of boneless chicken you prefer—strips of boneless skinless breasts or thighs work as well as the tenders.

MARINADE AND CHICKEN

Finely grated zest of 1 large navel orange

½ cup fresh orange juice

¼ cup extra-virgin olive oil

2 tablespoons Japanese soy sauce

2 garlic cloves, shredded on a Microplane zester

2 pounds chicken tenders, trimmed of tendons and cut in half crosswise to make 24 pieces

PEANUT SAUCE

½ cup reduced-sodium chicken broth

¼ cup hoisin sauce

¼ cup smooth peanut butter

½ teaspoon sambal oelek or other Asian chili paste

1 garlic clove, shredded on a Microplane zester

Special Equipment: 24 (4- to 6-inch) bamboo skewers, soaked in water for at least 30 minutes and drained

1. To marinate the chicken: Whisk all of the marinade ingredients together in a medium bowl. Put the chicken in a 1-gallon self-sealing plastic bag. Pour in the marinade, seal the bag, and refrigerate for at least 1 hour or up to 8 hours.

2. To make the peanut sauce: Combine all the ingredients in a small saucepan. Cook over medium heat, whisking almost constantly, until simmering, smooth, and thickened. Remove from the heat and cover to keep warm.

3. Prepare an outdoor grill for direct cooking over medium heat (350°F to 450°F).

4. Remove the chicken from the marinade. Thread each chicken strip on a skewer. Place the meaty parts of the skewers over direct medium heat with the skewer handles facing the cooler part of the grill; slip a folded strip of aluminum foil under the handles (see Chef Talk, at right). Grill, with the lid closed, turning once, until browned and the chicken shows no sign of pink when pierced with the tip of a small knife, about 6 minutes. Transfer the satays to a platter.

5. Pour the peanut sauce into a serving bowl. Serve the satays with the peanut sauce for dipping.

CHEF TALK

Bamboo Skewers on the Grill

No matter how long you soak wooden skewers for grilling, they still tend to burn. Use this trick I learned from street vendors in Bangkok: First, prepare the fire so there is a cool area next to the hot cooking area. (This is easy to do on a gas grill, with one burner turned on and the adjacent burner turned off. With a charcoal grill, heap the coals in a mound in the center of the coal grate, leaving a cooler empty ring around the mound.) Arrange the meaty ends of the satays over the hot area, with the handles over the cool area. (With a charcoal grill, the satays will be in a circle.) Now, just slip double-thickness strips of aluminum foil under the handles to protect them from the heat. That's all there is to it.

MARINADE AND CHICKEN

6 garlic cloves, crushed under
a knife and peeled

1 medium green bell pepper, cored
and coarsely chopped

½ medium red bell pepper, cored
and coarsely chopped

½ large white onion, coarsely chopped

¼ cup packed fresh cilantro leaves

1 teaspoon kosher salt

½ teaspoon freshly ground
black pepper

¼ cup canola or vegetable oil

4 bone-in chicken thighs

4 chicken drumsticks

ACHIOTE OIL

⅓ cup canola or vegetable oil

1 teaspoon annatto seeds
(see Chef Talk, page 90)

────────

1½ tablespoons tomato paste

2 teaspoons cumin seeds, coarsely
ground in a mortar or spice grinder

1 teaspoon dried oregano

½ teaspoon granulated onion

½ teaspoon granulated garlic

Kosher salt and freshly ground
black pepper

1 bay leaf

⅓ cup dry white wine

½ cup water

1½ cups medium-grain rice, such
as arborio or Valencia

2 cups reduced-sodium chicken broth

1 cup dark beer, such as Negra Modelo
(not stout)

Pinch of crumbled saffron threads

1 cup thawed frozen green peas

1 large red pepper, roasted (see page 42),
seeded, and cut into ½-inch dice

Lemon wedges, for serving

ARROZ CON POLLO
with ACHIOTE OIL

Hanging out in the Lower East Side's many Latin restaurants has taught me a few things about delicious arroz con pollo, one of the all-time great comfort foods. I turned to Juan Borjas, who is one of my longtime chefs and from Puerto Rico, to help me create the ultimate version of this dish. Be sure to use medium-grain rice, which is slightly sticky after cooking, making serving much easier and neater than the fluffy long-grain variety.

1. To marinate the chicken: With the machine running, drop the garlic through the feed tube of a food processor to mince the garlic. Add the green and red bell peppers, onion, cilantro, salt, and pepper and pulse until the vegetables are finely chopped. With the machine running, pour the oil through the feed tube to make a puree.

2. Put the chicken thighs and legs in a 1-gallon self-sealing plastic bag and pour in the puree. Seal the bag and refrigerate, turning occasionally, for at least 8 hours or up to 24 hours.

3. To make the achiote oil: In a small saucepan, warm the oil and annato seeds together over low heat just until oil bubbles around the seeds, about 5 minutes. Do not overheat the oil or it will be bitter. Remove from the heat and let stand for 10 minutes. Strain the achiote oil into a small bowl and discard the seeds.

4. Remove the chicken from the marinade, shake off the excess marinade, and pat the chicken dry with paper towels. Pour 2 tablespoons of the achiote oil into a Dutch oven and heat over medium-high heat. Set the remaining oil aside for serving. In batches, add the chicken to the pot, skin side down, and cook, turning occasionally, until browned, about 5 minutes. Transfer the chicken to a plate.

5. Add the tomato paste to the pot and let it cook until it turns a darker shade of red, about 1 minute. Stir in the cumin, oregano, granulated onion, granulated garlic, ½ teaspoon salt, ½ teaspoon pepper, and bay leaf. Add the wine and bring to a boil, scraping up the browned bits in the pan with a wooden spoon and ➤➤

dissolving the tomato paste. Return the chicken, skin side down, to the skillet. Add the water and bring to a simmer. Reduce the heat to medium-low, cover the pot, and simmer for 20 minutes, until the chicken is about half-cooked.

6. Return the chicken to a plate. Increase the heat under the pot to high and cook until the cooking liquid is reduced to a glaze, about 1 minute. Add the rice to the pot and mix well. Stir in the broth, beer, saffron, and ½ teaspoon salt. Nestle the chicken in the rice and bring to a boil over high heat. Reduce the heat to medium-low and simmer until the rice is tender and absorbs the liquid and the chicken shows no sign of pink at the bone, about 20 minutes. During the last 5 minutes, scatter the peas and roasted red pepper into the pot.

7. Remove the pot from the heat and let stand, covered, for 5 minutes. Discard the bay leaf. Serve hot, with the lemon wedges and remaining achiote oil passed at the table for drizzling.

CHEF TALK

Annatto Seeds

Annatto seeds are triangular, rust-red seeds with a distinctive nutty-musky flavor. While they are considered a spice, the hard seeds are not used by themselves, but always processed with other ingredients into a seasoning oil or paste (*achiote*) that gives food a yellow-orange color. Look for annatto seeds at Latino markets in the spice aisle. If you can't find them, use plain olive oil, but you will sacrifice a bit of authentic barrio-style flavor and color.

CHICKEN MEATBALLS

in **Creamy Mushroom Sauce** *with* **Whipped Ricotta**

MAKES

4

SERVINGS

I began my restaurant career at an Italian restaurant in Rhode Island, so I know all about beef meatballs in red sauce. And I love them (my version is on page 142). But, for a fantastic and delicious change of pace, try these beauties made with ground chicken and served in rich mushroom gravy. The secret is to handle the meat very gently during mixing and shaping; the reward will be super-light meatballs that almost float off the plate.

MUSHROOM SAUCE

4 ounces white button mushrooms, coarsely chopped

½ medium celery rib, chopped

½ small yellow onion, chopped

1 tablespoon unsalted butter

2 cups reduced-sodium chicken broth, plus more if needed

½ cup heavy cream

Kosher salt and freshly ground black pepper

CHICKEN MEATBALLS

1 pound ground chicken

½ cup whole milk

2 tablespoons olive oil (not extra-virgin)

1 medium yellow onion, minced

2 garlic cloves, minced

¾ cup freshly grated Asiago or Parmigiano-Reggiano cheese

¾ cup panko (Japanese bread crumbs)

1 large egg, beaten

1 teaspoon minced fresh marjoram

½ teaspoon salt

½ teaspoon freshly ground black pepper

WHIPPED RICOTTA

1 cup whole-milk ricotta cheese

¼ teaspoon hot red pepper flakes

Vegetable oil, for deep-frying

White truffle oil, for serving (optional)

Finely sliced fresh chives, for garnish (optional)

1. To make the sauce: Pulse the mushrooms, celery, and chopped onion together in a food processor until they are finely chopped. Melt the butter in a medium saucepan over medium heat. Add the vegetable mixture and cook, stirring occasionally, until the mushroom liquid evaporates, about 10 minutes. Add the broth and bring to a boil over high heat. Cook, stirring occasionally, until the mixture reduces by half, about 15 minutes. Add the cream and boil until the sauce has thickened, about 10 minutes more. Puree the sauce with an immersion blender. If the sauce seems too thick, thin it with additional broth. Season to taste with salt and pepper. (The sauce can be cooled, covered, and refrigerated for up to 2 days. Reheat in a saucepan before serving.)

2. To make the meatballs: Put the ground chicken and milk in a bowl, mix gently, and let stand for 30 minutes.

3. Meanwhile, heat the oil in a medium skillet over medium heat. Add the minced onion and garlic and cook, stirring occasionally, until the onion is translucent, about 4 minutes. Remove from the heat and let the mixture cool slightly. Add the onion mixture, Asiago, panko, egg, marjoram, salt, and pepper to the chicken mixture and mix just until combined. Do not overmix or the meatballs will be heavy. Cover the bowl and refrigerate for at least 1 hour or up to 4 hours. ➤➤

SANTOS SIGNATURE

4. To whip the ricotta: Process the ricotta and hot pepper flakes together in a food processor until the mixture is very smooth, about 30 seconds. Transfer to a bowl and let stand at room temperature to lose its chill, about 30 minutes.

5. Position a rack in the center of the oven and preheat the oven to 350°F.

6. Using about ¼ cup for each, shape the chicken mixture into 12 balls and transfer to a plate.

7. To fry the meatballs: Line a baking sheet with paper towels and place near the stove. Pour enough oil into a large saucepan to come halfway up the sides and heat over high heat to 325°F on a deep-frying thermometer. In batches without crowding, add the meatballs and cook, turning them occasionally, until golden brown, 2½ to 3 minutes. The meatballs do not have to be entirely cooked through at this point. Using a wire spider or slotted spoon, transfer the browned meatballs to paper towels to drain.

8. Transfer the browned meatballs to a shallow baking dish and bake until they show no sign of pink when pierced to the center with a small sharp knife, about 15 minutes.

9. For each serving, spoon about ⅓ cup of the sauce into a shallow bowl and add 3 meatballs. Drizzle with truffle oil, if using, top with a dollop of the ricotta, and sprinkle with the chives, if using. Serve hot.

SMOKY RUBBED
CHICKEN WINGS
with **Honey, Bourbon,** *and* **Molasses Sauce**

MAKES

6

SERVINGS

BARBECUE SAUCE

1 cup store-bought spicy barbecue sauce, such as Rattler BBQ Sauce

1 cup tomato ketchup

¼ cup molasses (not blackstrap)

½ cup bourbon, preferably Maker's Mark

½ cup honey

2 tablespoons cider vinegar

SMOKY RUB

⅓ cup packed light brown sugar

1 tablespoon kosher salt

1 tablespoon ground coriander seeds

1 tablespoon sweet smoked paprika

1½ teaspoons ground cumin

1½ teaspoons dried thyme

½ teaspoon ground allspice

½ teaspoon ground ginger

½ teaspoon hot red pepper flakes

¾ teaspoon celery salt

¾ teaspoon freshly ground black pepper

¾ teaspoon cayenne pepper

¼ teaspoon dry mustard

¼ teaspoon garlic powder

5½ pounds chicken wingettes (see Note)

I order chicken wings anytime I see them on a menu, and this recipe will make you realize just how incredible they can be. After a lot of trial and error, when I finally got the rub right I felt like I had unlocked a magic puzzle. There are a lot of ingredients in the rub, but they provide a perfect mix of sugar and spice, and the bourbon-spiked sauce coats the wings in yet another layer of bold flavor. If you prefer the grill to the oven, grill the wings over medium indirect heat (about 400°F) for about 40 minutes, until they are almost done, before adding the sauce.

1. To make the sauce: Bring all of the ingredients to a boil in a medium sauce-pan over medium-high heat, whisking often. Reduce the heat to medium-low and simmer, whisking occasionally to discourage scorching, until lightly thickened and reduced by about one-quarter, about 30 minutes. Remove from the heat and let cool. (The sauce can be covered and refrigerated for up to 2 weeks.)

2. To make the rub: Whisk all of the ingredients together in a small bowl.

3. Put the wingettes in a very large bowl and toss with the rub. Divide the wingettes among two 1-gallon self-sealing plastic bags, seal, and refrigerate for at least 4 hours or overnight.

4. Position racks in the top third and center of the oven and preheat the oven to 400°F. Line two 18-by-13-inch half-sheet pans with aluminum foil for easy cleanup.

5. Spread the wingettes out on the baking sheets, spacing them well apart. Roast the wingettes, turning the wings over and switching the positions of the baking sheets from top to bottom and front to back halfway through cooking, until the wings are crisp and cooked through, about 40 minutes. During the last 5 minutes, brush the wings with some of the sauce. Remove the wings from the oven.

6. Position a broiler about 8 inches from the source of heat and preheat the broiler on high. In batches, broil the wings to caramelize the sauce in spots, about 3 minutes. Serve hot, with any leftover sauce passed on the side.

Note: Chicken wingettes are chicken wings that have been chopped between the joints, with the wing tips discarded. Many of the large poultry producers sell chicken wing-ettes. Fresh wingettes are better than the frozen ones, as the latter tend to be dry when baked. Or do it yourself: Chop whole chicken wings between the joints with a cleaver or heavy knife and discard the tips (or save them for another use, such as stock).

Open-Faced
Chicken Arepas
with SALSA VERDE

MAKES
18
AREPAS
6 SERVINGS

I have always loved chiles since picking them with my grandfather as a child. Now that I am an adult, chipotle chiles in adobo have become my go-to when I'm looking to add smoky heat to any dish. An arepa is a Colombian corn cake that is usually split and filled with roasted meats and cheese. My open-faced arepas not only are easier to share, but are remarkably beautiful with the Manchego and pickled jalapeño garnish.

CHICKEN TOPPING

3 skinless, boneless chicken thighs, about 12 ounces total

1 tablespoon extra-virgin olive oil

Kosher salt and freshly ground black pepper

½ cup mayonnaise

1 chipotle chile in adobo, minced to a puree

1 tablespoon finely chopped fresh cilantro

AREPAS

1½ cups yellow arepa flour (see Note)

½ teaspoon kosher salt

About 1½ cups warm water

Vegetable oil, for frying

---

1 very ripe Hass avocado, peeled, pitted, and mashed

½ cup Salsa Verde (page 97), or as needed

9 slices Manchego cheese, cut to make 18 squares, or ½ cup (2 ounces) shredded Manchego

18 slices Pickled Jalapeños (page 157) or sliced jalapeños for nachos

---

Special Equipment: 1½-inch round cookie cutter

1. To make the topping: Position a rack in the center of the oven and preheat the oven to 400°F. Toss the chicken on a baking sheet with the oil, 1 teaspoon salt, and ¼ teaspoon pepper. Bake until the chicken shows no sign of pink when pierced with the tip of a knife, about 30 minutes. Remove from the oven and let cool just until warm. Using your fingers and a fork, pull the warm chicken into shreds. Let cool completely. Transfer to a medium bowl and stir in the mayonnaise, chipotle, and cilantro. Season to taste with salt and pepper. (The chicken topping can be covered and refrigerated for up to 1 day.)

2. To make the arepas: Whisk the arepa flour and salt together in a bowl. Gradually stir in enough of the water to make a soft dough. Cover with plastic wrap and let stand for 2 to 3 minutes. Transfer the dough to a large sheet of plastic wrap or waxed paper. Top with another sheet of plastic and pat or roll the dough to a ⅓-inch thickness. Remove the top sheet. Using a 1½-inch round cookie cutter, gathering up and patting out the scraps as needed, cut out 18 rounds of dough. (The dough rounds can be transferred to a parchment- or waxed paper–lined baking sheet, covered with plastic wrap, and refrigerated for up to 8 hours.)

3. Pour enough oil to come ½ inch up the sides of a large deep skillet and heat over high heat until the oil is hot and shimmering. Line an 18-by-13-inch half-sheet pan with paper towels.

4. In batches without crowding, add the arepa rounds to the oil and fry, turning once, until golden brown, about 2 minutes. Using a slotted spatula, transfer them to the paper towels and sprinkle lightly with salt.

5. Stir the avocado into the chicken mixture. With the arepa rounds still on the baking sheet, divide the chicken mixture evenly among the arepas, followed by about 1 teaspoon of the salsa. Top each arepa with a slice of Manchego and a jalapeño slice. Transfer to a serving platter and serve.

Note: Arepa flour (often sold as masarepa), is ground from precooked yellow or white corn and sold at Latino markets. It is different from Mexican-style masa or masa harina. If you can't find it, serve the chicken mixture on the "grits" rectangles for the Shrimp and Cheesy "Grits" on page 119.

SALSA VERDE

Makes about 1½ cups

This tangy, herbaceous salsa uses roasted tomatillos and chiles as its base. Beyond its role as topping for the arepas, it is a fantastic dip for tortilla chips and sauce for grilled fish.

3 tomatillos (8 ounces), husked and rinsed

1 poblano (fresh ancho) chile

1 jalapeño

1 tablespoon extra-virgin olive oil

½ cup chopped red onion

1 garlic clove, minced

2 tablespoons coarsely chopped fresh cilantro

Kosher salt and freshly ground black pepper

1. Position a broiler rack about 8 inches from the source of heat and preheat the broiler on high. On a broiler pan, place the tomatillos, poblano, and jalapeño. Broil the vegetables, turning occasionally, until the tomatillos are browned but not bursting, about 6 minutes. Carefully transfer the softened tomatillos to a small bowl. Continue broiling the chiles, turning them occasionally, until the skins are blackened and blistered, about 4 minutes more. Transfer the chiles to another small bowl, cover with plastic wrap, and let stand for 10 minutes. Peel and seed the chiles.

2. Heat the oil in a small skillet over medium heat. Add the red onion and garlic and cook, stirring occasionally, until the onion is translucent, about 4 minutes. Combine the onion mixture, tomatillos, chiles, and cilantro in a blender or food processor and process until pureed. Season to taste with salt and pepper. Transfer to a small bowl. (The salsa can be covered and refrigerated for up to 1 day.)

CHILAQUILES VERDES
with CHIPOTLE CHICKEN

MAKES

4

SERVINGS

Chilaquiles—tortilla chips simmered in a spicy sauce—is the best excuse that I know of for eating a pile of tortilla chips in one sitting. I learned how to make them one Sunday morning about 20 years ago, when one of my line cooks whipped them up as a hangover remedy. Hungover or not, I've been eating this Mexican specialty (and putting it on my menus) ever since! Don't let the fried egg trick you into thinking that chilaquiles is only for breakfast, as it is also great for dinner.

TOMATILLO SAUCE

1½ pounds tomatillos, husked and rinsed

1 cup chopped white onion

¼ cup coarsely chopped fresh cilantro

1 large jalapeño, seeded and coarsely chopped

2 garlic cloves, crushed under a knife and peeled

Kosher salt and freshly ground black pepper

CHIPOTLE CHICKEN

1 pound skinless, boneless chicken thighs

2 tablespoons canola or vegetable oil

Kosher salt and freshly ground black pepper

½ cup mayonnaise

2 tablespoons finely chopped fresh cilantro

1 tablespoon adobo sauce from canned chipotles

TORTILLAS

Vegetable oil, for deep-frying

10 corn tortillas, each cut into sixths, left to stand uncovered for a few hours to curl up and turn stale

⸻

⅓ cup crumbled feta cheese

1 tablespoon canola or vegetable oil

4 large eggs

Kosher salt and freshly ground black pepper

½ small red onion, thinly sliced, preferably pickled (see Chef Talk, page 100)

Finely chopped fresh cilantro, for garnish (optional)

1. To make the sauce: Put the whole tomatillos, onion, cilantro, jalapeño, and garlic in a medium saucepan and add just enough water to barely cover the tomatillos, about 1 quart. Bring to a simmer over high heat. Reduce the heat to low and simmer just until the tomatillos turn olive green and are very tender, 15 to 20 minutes. Using a handheld blender, puree the mixture in the saucepan. (Or let cool and puree in batches in a blender.) Return the sauce to the saucepan if necessary and boil over medium-high heat, stirring often, until reduced to 4 cups. Season to taste with salt and pepper. (The sauce can be cooled, covered, and refrigerated for up to 3 days.)

2. To cook the chicken: Position a rack in the center of the oven and preheat the oven to 400°F. Toss the chicken, oil, ½ teaspoon salt, and ¼ teaspoon pepper in a large bowl to coat. Arrange the chicken on a large rimmed baking sheet and bake until golden brown and the juices show no sign of pink when pierced with a knife, about 30 minutes. Let cool until the chicken is easy to handle. Tear the warm chicken into strips. Let cool completely.

3. Whisk the mayonnaise, cilantro, and adobo sauce together in a medium bowl. Add the chicken and toss to coat with the mayonnaise mixture. Season to taste with salt and pepper. (The chicken can be covered and refrigerated for up to 1 day.)

4. To fry the tortillas: Line a large rimmed baking sheet with paper towels. Pour enough vegetable oil to come 2 inches up the sides of a large deep saucepan and heat over high heat until it registers 350°F on a deep-frying thermometer. In batches, without crowding, add the tortillas and deep-fry, turning as needed, until golden, about 1 minute. Using a wire spider or slotted spoon, transfer the tortillas to the paper towels to drain.

➤

5. Bring the tomatillo sauce to a simmer in a large, deep skillet over medium heat. In batches, mix in the tortillas and cook, stirring occasionally, just until they begin to soften, about 2 minutes. Do not overcook the tortillas. Stir in the chicken and its sauce and cook just until the tortilla chips are al dente, about 1 minute more. Remove from the heat and sprinkle with the feta.

6. Meanwhile, heat the canola oil in a very large nonstick skillet over medium heat. Crack each egg into the skillet and cover. (If all of the eggs don't fit in the skillet, cook them in batches as needed.) Cook the eggs just until the egg whites have set, about 1½ minutes. Season the eggs with salt and pepper. Place the eggs on top of the chilaquiles. Garnish with the red onion rings and a sprinkle of cilantro, if using. Serve hot, spooning up one egg for each guest.

CHEF TALK

Pickled Red Onions

If you have the time, give the red onions a quick pickling: Bring ½ cup cider vinegar, 1½ teaspoons sugar, and 1½ teaspoons kosher salt to a boil in a small saucepan over high heat, stirring to dissolve the salt. Put the red onion slices in a small bowl and pour in the vinegar mixture. Let cool. Cover and refrigerate at least 2 hours before serving. The pickles can be refrigerated for up to 1 month. Drain before using.

Chicken Taquitos
with GUACAMOLE PUREE

GUACAMOLE SAUCE

1 ripe Hass avocado, pitted, peeled, and chopped

1 Roma (plum) tomato, seeded and chopped

1 tablespoon coarsely chopped fresh cilantro

1 tablespoon finely chopped red onion

1 tablespoon fresh lime juice

2 teaspoons minced seeded jalapeño

Kosher salt and freshly ground black pepper

CHICKEN FILLING

1 tablespoon extra-virgin olive oil

8 ounces ground chicken

½ cup finely chopped red bell pepper

½ cup finely chopped red onion

1 teaspoon sugar

1 teaspoon dried oregano

¼ teaspoon ground cinnamon

⅛ teaspoon cayenne pepper

¾ cup (3 ounces) shredded white Cheddar cheese

Kosher salt and freshly ground black pepper

---

6 (6-inch) taco-sized flour tortillas (see Note on page 103)

Vegetable or canola oil, for shallow-frying

½ cup Mexican crema or full-fat sour cream, for serving

Guajillo Sauce (page 103), for serving

Finely chopped fresh cilantro, for garnish (optional)

Taquitos are another street food that I cannot get enough of. While they are similar to the stuffed fried tortillas called *flautas*, **taquitos' ends are folded in like a burrito. Serving the taquitos with a trio of sauce options allows your guests to customize each bite per their unique preferences, but you can certainly just make the guac alone.**

1. To make the guacamole sauce: Puree all of the ingredients (except salt and pepper) in a food processor to make a smooth sauce. (This smooth guacamole is easier to use as a dip than the chunky style.) Season to taste with salt and pepper. Transfer to a small bowl, cover with plastic wrap with the wrap pressing directly on the guacamole, and refrigerate. (The guacamole can be refrigerated for up to 1 day.)

2. To make the filling: Heat the olive oil in a large skillet over medium-high heat. Add the ground chicken and cook, stirring often and breaking up the meat with the side of the spoon, until the chicken loses its raw look, about 5 minutes. Add the bell pepper and red onion and cook, stirring occasionally, until the onion is translucent, about 4 minutes. Stir in the sugar, oregano, cinnamon, and cayenne pepper. Transfer to a medium bowl and stir the cheese into the warm mixture. Season to taste with salt and pepper. Let cool completely. (The filling can be covered and refrigerated for up to 1 day.)

3. For each taquito, spoon about 3 tablespoons of the filling in a strip at the bottom third of a tortilla, leaving about a ½-inch border at the right and left sides. Fold in the sides, then roll up the tortilla from the bottom to enclose the filling, closing the open end with a toothpick. Be sure that the ends are tucked in and the filling is not exposed. Transfer the taquitos, seam side down, to a rimmed baking sheet and loosely cover with plastic wrap. (The taquitos can be refrigerated up to 4 hours ahead.)

4. Position a rack in the center of the oven and preheat the oven to 200°F. Line a large rimmed baking sheet with a wire cake rack. ➤➤

5. Pour enough oil to come ½ inch up the sides of a large deep skillet and heat over high heat to 350°F on a deep-frying thermometer. In batches, add the taquitos and cook, turning occasionally, until golden brown, about 3 minutes. Transfer to the wire rack and keep warm in the oven while frying the remaining taquitos.

6. Place the guacamole sauce, crema, and guajillo sauce in three small serving bowls. Cut each taquito in thirds crosswise. Arrange the taquitos on a platter, sprinkle with the cilantro if using, and serve immediately, allowing guests to add the sauces to their plates as desired for dipping.

Note: Standard flour tortillas (not the puffy, soft taco variety) work best for this recipe.

GUAJILLO SAUCE

Makes about 3 cups

Smooth, dark red, and not too spicy, this is a fantastic all-purpose Mexican sauce for dousing tacos, burritos, and the like.

- 2 cups reduced-sodium chicken broth
- 5 dried guajillo chiles, stemmed, seeded, and roughly torn into large pieces
- 2 dried chiles de arbol, stemmed
- ¾ cup coarsely chopped red onion
- 4 garlic cloves, crushed under a knife and peeled
- 3 whole cloves
- ½ teaspoon ground cumin
- Kosher salt and freshly ground black pepper

1. Combine all of the ingredients (except salt and pepper) in a medium saucepan and bring to a boil over high heat. Reduce the heat to low and simmer until the chiles are very tender and the liquid has reduced by about one-quarter, about 25 minutes. Remove from the heat and let cool.

2. In batches, puree the mixture in a blender. Return to the saucepan and bring to a boil over high heat. Reduce the heat to medium and cook at a brisk simmer, stirring often to avoid scorching, until the sauce has reduced and thickened to the consistency of heavy cream, about 10 minutes. Season to taste with the salt and pepper. Transfer the sauce to a bowl. (The sauce can be cooled, covered, and refrigerated up to 3 days or frozen for up to 3 months.)

SEAFOOD

Fresh, delicately flavored fish and shellfish are naturally beautiful ingredients that can easily be accentuated to create something spectacular for your guests. Since seafood cooks quickly, it is a great choice when you are looking for a recipe that requires a minimum of last-minute attention. I offer a wide range of possibilities here, from super-elegant olive oil–poached cod (page 106) to down-home shrimp on cheesy "grits" (page 119). As with all of the recipes in this book, the various components are made ahead, and then the finished dish can be assembled right before serving. One important caveat when cooking seafood is to avoid overcooking in order to ensure that each bite is moist and delicious.

OLIVE OIL–POACHED COD
with Beet, Orange, and Tangerine Salad

—

WASABI PEA–Crusted Salmon
with Soba Noodle and Beet Salad

—

RED SNAPPER Mini-Tacos
with MANGO SALSA and GUACAMOLE

—

Seared **TUNA**
with Fried Black Rice and Spicy Miso Sauce

GRILLED CHIPOTLE *Shrimp*
with Tomatillo, Roasted Corn, and Feta Salsa

—

SHRIMP and **CHEESY "GRITS"**
with SMOKY RED PEPPER SAUCE

—

SALT-AND-PEPPER Shrimp with
Thai Papaya Salad

—

APPLE-CIDER **Mussels**
with Roasted Fall Vegetables and Mustard Butter

OLIVE OIL-POACHED COD
with Beet, Orange, and Tangerine Salad

MAKES

4

SERVINGS

For a sophisticated yet light entrée, you really can't do much better than this colorful salad with tender, pale cod contrasting with warm magenta beets and bright orange tangerines. The oil-poaching technique gives the fish a lush texture that you just cannot get with any other cooking method. Because you won't be able to reuse the oil, choose one that is good quality, but not artisanal.

TANGERINES AND SHERRY VINAIGRETTE

3 tangerines

1 tablespoon sherry vinegar

1 teaspoon minced shallot

½ teaspoon kosher salt

¼ teaspoon freshly ground black pepper

2 tablespoons extra-virgin olive oil

OLIVE OIL AND COD

4 cups olive oil, preferably extra-virgin, or more as needed

Zest strips of ½ lemon, removed with a vegetable peeler

8 sprigs fresh flat-leaf parsley

4 sprigs fresh rosemary

4 cod fillets, about 6 ounces each

SALAD

2 cups baby arugula, about 2½ ounces

2 small beets, about 6 ounces, roasted (see page 79), peeled, and cut into ½-inch dice

¼ cup fresh whole flat-leaf parsley leaves

Flaky sea salt, such as Maldon or fleur de sel, for serving

Freshly ground black pepper

⅓ cup (about 2 ounces) roasted, peeled, and chopped hazelnuts (see Note) for garnish

Special Equipment: Kitchen torch (optional)

1. To prepare the tangerines: Using a vegetable peeler, remove strips of zest from 1 tangerine and set aside for the poaching oil. Peel all of the tangerines, and separate them into segments. Arrange the tangerine segments on a baking sheet. Using a kitchen torch, lightly brown the tangerines. (You can skip this step, but it does add color and flavor to the tangerines. Or you can broil them about 4 inches from the heat source until they brown.) Set the tangerines aside.

2. To make the vinaigrette: Whisk the sherry vinegar, shallot, salt, and pepper together in a small bowl. Gradually whisk in the oil. Set the vinaigrette aside.

3. To poach the cod: Combine the oil, reserved tangerine zest strips, the lemon zest strips, parsley sprigs, and rosemary sprigs in a large skillet. Heat over medium-low heat just until the oil mixture reaches 180°F on an instant-read thermometer. Add the cod to the oil—the oil should barely cover the fish, so add more if needed. Let the cod poach slowly in the oil just until it turns snowy white throughout, 12 to 15 minutes.

4. To assemble the salad: Toss the tangerines, arugula, beets, parsley leaves, and sherry vinaigrette together in a medium bowl. Arrange the salad on a large platter. Using a slotted spatula, top the salad with the cod fillets. Sprinkle with the sea salt and pepper. Sprinkle with the hazelnuts and serve immediately.

Note: *To toast unskinned hazelnuts, spread them on a rimmed baking sheet. Bake in a preheated 350°F oven until the skins crack and the flesh under the skin is light brown, about 10 minutes. Transfer the hazelnuts to a kitchen towel and cool for 10 minutes. Using the towel, rub off the skins (you don't have to remove every last bit). Cool completely and use as needed.*

Wasabi Pea–
Crusted Salmon
with SOBA NOODLE and BEET SALAD

MAKES

6

SERVINGS

Salmon is a very popular fish for cooking but can be challenging to make interesting. A few years ago, I came up with a spicy, crunchy coating made from crushed wasabi peas. Using wasabi paste to help adhere the pea crumbs adds an extra layer of intensity to the spicy salmon.

---

4 skinless salmon fillets, each about 4 ounces and 1½ inches wide

Fine sea salt and freshly ground black pepper

2 tablespoons wasabi powder

About 1 tablespoon water, as needed

⅔ cup wasabi-coated peas

2 teaspoons canola oil

Soba Noodle and Beet Salad (page 77)

---

1. Position a rack in the center of the oven and preheat the oven to 450°F.

2. Season the salmon lightly with salt and pepper. Stir the wasabi powder with enough water to make a spreadable paste. Spread the paste on the skinned side of each fillet. Pulse the wasabi peas in a food processor until they are coarsely crushed and spread on a plate. Dip the coated side of each fillet in the peas to coat, then press them to adhere.

3. Heat the oil in a very large ovenproof skillet over medium heat. Add the salmon, crusted side down, and cook until the peas are just beginning to brown, about 3 minutes. Carefully flip the fillets over and transfer the skillet with the salmon to the oven. Roast until the salmon is barely opaque with a rosy center when pierced with the tip of a small knife, about 5 minutes.

4. Serve immediately with the noodle salad on the side.

RED SNAPPER
MINI-TACOS
with Mango Salsa and Guacamole

Most fish tacos are made with fish that is either grilled, or battered and fried. My favorite version follows, where the snapper filling is escabeche-style—sautéed and marinated in a chile-lime vinaigrette. The mini-taco shells definitely provide a *wow* factor, but you can also just fry the whole tortillas, and layer the taco fillings on top, tostada-style.

SNAPPER FILLING

¼ cup extra-virgin olive oil

2 skinless red snapper, perch, or tilapia fillets, about 6 ounces each

1 tablespoon sambal oelek or other Asian chili paste

1½ teaspoons pure ground ancho chile

½ teaspoon kosher salt

½ cup fresh lime juice

¼ cup coarsely chopped fresh cilantro

CHIPOTLE CREAM

½ cup sour cream or Mexican crema

1 canned chipotle in adobo, minced

Pinch of pure ground ancho chile

¼ teaspoon kosher salt

MANGO SALSA

1 ripe mango, peeled, pitted, and cut into ⅛-inch dice

1 small red bell pepper, seeded and cut into ⅛-inch dice

⅓ cup chopped red onion

2 tablespoons fresh lime juice

2 tablespoons finely chopped fresh cilantro

½ teaspoon pure ground ancho chile

Pinch of cayenne pepper

Kosher salt

GUACAMOLE

1 ripe Hass avocado, peeled, pitted, and cut into ½-inch dice

1 Roma (plum) tomato, seeded and cut into ¼-inch dice

2 tablespoons minced fresh cilantro

2 tablespoons minced red onion

2 teaspoons seeded and minced jalapeño

1 tablespoon fresh lime juice

Kosher salt

TACOS

18 corn tortillas

Vegetable oil, for the tortillas

Lime wedges, for serving

2 tablespoons finely chopped fresh cilantro

Special Equipment: 3-inch round cookie cutter; 6 small (½-inch-wide) cannoli forms

1. To make the filling: Heat the olive oil in a large nonstick skillet over medium-high heat until it is very hot but not smoking. Add the fish and cook, carefully turning once to avoid breaking the fillets, until lightly browned on both sides, about 3 minutes.

2. Mix the sambal oelek, ground ancho, and salt together. Spread generously over the fish (don't worry if some of it spills into the skillet) and continue cooking until the fish is barely opaque when flaked with the tip of a small knife, about 2 minutes more. Remove from the heat and add the lime juice and cilantro. Let the fish cool completely in the liquid. (The snapper and its liquid can be transferred to a shallow dish, covered, and refrigerated for 1 day.)

3. To make the chipotle cream: Whisk all of the ingredients together in a small bowl. (The cream can be covered and refrigerated for up to 8 hours.)

4. To make the mango salsa: Combine all of the ingredients together in a medium bowl, seasoning to taste with salt. (The salsa can be covered and refrigerated for up to 4 hours. Bring to room temperature before serving.)

5. To make the guacamole: Combine all of the ingredients together in a medium bowl, seasoning to taste with the salt. (The guacamole can be covered, with plastic wrap pressed directly on the guacamole surface, for up to 4 hours.)

6. To make the tacos: Using a 3-inch round biscuit cutter, cut out 18 rounds from the tortillas (see Note). Pour enough vegetable oil to come about ¾ inch up the sides of a heavy, deep skillet and heat over medium-high heat until the oil is shimmering. Line a baking sheet with paper towels and place near the skillet. Have ready 6 small (½-inch-wide) cannoli forms. (If you have more forms, use them, but if you only have 6, they can be reused after they cool.)

7. Working with one tortilla round at a time, use kitchen tongs to dip a round in the oil just until it softens, about 3 seconds. Transfer to the paper towels. Place a cannoli form across the center of the round. Let the round cool slightly, and fold up the sides to make a taco-shell shape. Holding the round and mold together with the tongs, transfer the shell to the hot oil and fry until the shell holds its shape around the form, about 15 seconds. Let go of the shell, and continue deep-frying until the shell is golden brown, about 30 seconds more. Return to the paper towels. (With practice, this operation will take less than a minute per shell, and you can do more than one at the same time.) Let cool. Slide the warm form out of the shell. (The shells can be covered loosely with plastic wrap and stored at room temperature for up to 6 hours.)

8. Drain the fish and discard the marinade. Heat a large nonstick skillet over medium heat. Add the fish and cook, turning once, until warmed through, about 2 minutes. Do not overcook. Remove from the heat. Smear about ½ cup of the guacamole over the fish and set aside to warm the guacamole, about 2 minutes. Transfer to a bowl and use two forks to break the fish mixture into bite-sized pieces.

9. Divide the fish filling among the taco shells. To each taco, add about 1 tablespoon of the salsa and a drizzle of the cream. Transfer to a platter, add the lime wedges, and sprinkle with the cilantro. Serve immediately, with any remaining salsa, guacamole, and cream on the side.

Note: You will have tortilla scraps from cutting out the mini-taco shells. Just cut them into irregular chip-sized pieces, fry them up, and salt lightly. Serve the chips along with the tacos and any leftover guacamole and salsa.

Seared Tuna
with FRIED BLACK RICE and
SPICY MISO SAUCE

MAKES

4

SERVINGS

Here's a way to dress up your basic tuna dish with exciting Asian flavors and unexpected color. Black rice, which has a distinctly nutty flavor, is such an easy and underutilized ingredient; it is a beautiful contrast against the crimson center of the sliced tuna. The dramatic presentation will surely impress your guests. Remember that all fried rice must be made with cold rice, or it will clump.

FRIED BLACK RICE

2 tablespoons canola or vegetable oil

2 tablespoons minced fresh ginger

1 cup forbidden rice (also called Chinese black rice)

¼ cup dry white wine, such as Pinot Grigio

2 teaspoons unseasoned rice vinegar (see Note)

2 cups plus 2 tablespoons water

Kosher salt

4 large shiitake mushrooms, stemmed and thinly sliced

1 small Shanghai (baby) bok choy, cored and thinly sliced crosswise

SPICY MISO SAUCE

¼ cup (2 ounces) silky (soft) tofu

2 tablespoons fresh lime juice

2 tablespoons unseasoned rice vinegar (see Note)

1 tablespoon white (shiro) miso

2½ teaspoons sambal oelek or other Asian chili paste

¼ cup canola or vegetable oil

TOGARASHI-SEARED TUNA

2 teaspoons shichimi togarashi (see Chef Talk, page 113)

½ teaspoon kosher salt

4 sashimi-grade tuna steaks, each about 5 ounces and 1 inch thick

---

1 red radish, sliced paper thin on a mandoline or plastic V-slicer (optional)

1. To make the fried rice: A few hours before frying the rice, heat 1 tablespoon of the oil in a medium saucepan over medium heat. Add the ginger and cook, stirring often, until it softens, about 3 minutes. Add the rice and cook, stirring often, until it feels heavier in the spoon, about 2 minutes. Add the wine and vinegar, increase the heat to high, and cook until the liquids evaporate to 1 tablespoon, about 1 minute. Stir in 2 cups of the water and 1 teaspoon salt and bring to a boil. Reduce the heat to low and cover the saucepan. Simmer until the rice is tender and has absorbed the liquid, 45 minutes to 1 hour. (If the liquid has evaporated before the rice is tender, add about ¼ cup boiling water and keep cooking.) Remove from the heat and let stand for 5 minutes. Drain the rice, if necessary. Transfer to a medium bowl and let cool completely. Cover and refrigerate for at least 1 hour or up to 1 day. Set the mushrooms and bok choy aside while you make the sauce.

2. Meanwhile, to make the miso sauce: Process the tofu, lime juice, vinegar, miso, and sambal oelek in a blender until smooth. With the blender running, gradually add the oil through the hole in the lid to make a smooth dressing. Do not add salt—the miso is salty enough. Pour into a small bowl. (The sauce can be covered and refrigerated for up to 1 day.)

3. To finish the rice, heat a large wok or skillet over medium-high heat until it is very hot. Drizzle in the remaining 1 tablespoon oil. Add the mushrooms and bok choy and stir-fry until the mushrooms are tender, about 1 minute. Add the rice and remaining 2 tablespoons water. Cook, stirring often, until the rice mixture is hot, about 2 minutes. Season to taste with salt. Spread the rice on a platter and cover with aluminum foil to keep warm.

4. To sear the tuna: Heat a large nonstick skillet over medium-high heat. Mix the togarashi spice and salt together in a small bowl. Season the tuna all over with the spice mixture. Add the tuna to the skillet and cook until the underside is seared, about 2 minutes. Turn and sear the other side of the tuna, about 2 minute more. Transfer the tuna to a cutting board and let stand for 2 minutes.

5. Cut the tuna across the grain into ½-inch slices. Fan the slices over the rice, sprinkle with the radish, if using, and serve with the miso sauce on the side.

Note: *Unseasoned rice vinegar is the most common kind at both supermarkets and Asian grocers. Watch out and don't buy seasoned rice vinegar, which includes sugar and salt for flavoring warm rice to make sushi.*

CHEF TALK

Togarashi

Togarashi is a Japanese spice blend with a base of chile peppers used for seasoning. Like furikake (see pages 5 and 51), there are many different flavors, but shichimi togarashi has seven ingredients, including orange peel, black and white sesame seeds, and ginger. Togarashi is sold in small bottles so diners can carry it easily to season their food with their favorite variety as the mood strikes. (It's like being a Tabasco fan and having a bottle in hand when you find out that the restaurant you are dining at only serves Frank's RedHot.) It is sold at Asian markets and online. If you want to try your hand at making your own, there are plenty of recipes on the Web. I prefer to buy my togarashi.

There really isn't a Western substitute for togarashi, but for this recipe, you could use 2 teaspoons sesame seeds (preferably a mix of black and white) combined with ¼ teaspoon cayenne pepper.

Tuna Sushi Satays
with JICAMA-PEANUT SLAW

MAKES

4

SERVINGS

Tuna is such a versatile fish, yet it's prepared over and over with many of the same ingredients. Now for something entirely different: The insides of these crunchy satays retain a raw, sushi-like center, but their tortilla-chip-and-barbecue-sauce coating is completely nontraditional. The crunchy and refreshing slaw is the perfect counterpart to the savory skewers.

JICAMA-PEANUT SLAW

⅓ cup fresh orange juice

3 tablespoons mayonnaise

1 teaspoon sriracha

1 medium jicama, about 1 pound, peeled and cut into thin matchsticks with a mandoline or large knife

½ medium poblano (fresh ancho) chile, seeds and ribs removed, cut into ¼-inch strips

½ medium red bell pepper, seeds and ribs removed, cut into ¼-inch strips

3 scallions, white and green parts, thinly sliced

2 tablespoons fresh cilantro leaves

2 tablespoons coarsely chopped fresh Thai basil (optional)

Kosher salt and freshly ground black pepper

⅓ cup coarsely crushed roasted peanuts

TORTILLA-CHIP RUB

½ teaspoon ground coriander

½ teaspoon chili powder

½ teaspoon pure ground ancho chile

½ teaspoon Old Bay seasoning

¼ teaspoon hot red pepper flakes

⅛ teaspoon kosher salt

½ cup finely crushed tortilla chips

1½ pounds sashimi-grade tuna loin, cut into 16 chunks, each about 1¼ inches square

⅓ cup spicy store-bought barbecue sauce, such as Rattler BBQ Sauce

---

Special Equipment: 4 (6-inch) wooden skewers (no need to soak them)

1. To make the slaw: Whisk the orange juice, mayonnaise, and sriracha together in a large bowl. Add the jicama, poblano, bell pepper, half of the scallions, the cilantro, and the basil, if using, and mix well. Season to taste with salt and pepper. Set the remaining scallions and peanuts aside until just before serving. (The slaw can be covered and refrigerated for up to 8 hours.)

2. To make the rub: Whisk the coriander, chili powder, ground ancho, Old Bay, hot pepper flakes, and salt together in a small bowl. Add the tortilla chips and mix again.

3. Toss the tuna chunks in a large bowl with the barbecue sauce to coat the tuna. Sprinkle with the tortilla chip mixture to coat again. For each satay, thread 4 tuna chunks onto a 6-inch bamboo skewer.

4. Heat a griddle over medium-high heat. Add the tuna satays and cook, turning occasionally, until the crust is browned on all four sides but still raw in the center, about 4 minutes.

5. Add half of the peanuts to the slaw and mix well. Spread the slaw on a deep platter. Top with the satays and sprinkle with the remaining scallions and peanuts. Serve immediately.

MAKES
4
SERVINGS

Grilled CHIPOTLE SHRIMP
with Tomatillo, Roasted Corn, and Feta Salsa

MARINADE AND SHRIMP

3 canned chipotles in adobo with 1 tablespoon of their adobo sauce

3 tablespoons coarsely chopped fresh cilantro

3 garlic cloves, crushed under a knife and peeled

1 tablespoon fresh lime juice

1 teaspoon pure ground ancho chile

½ cup extra-virgin olive oil

32 jumbo (21 to 25 count) shrimp, peeled and deveined, with tail segment attached

THREE-PEPPER SAUCE

1 medium red bell pepper

1 medium yellow bell pepper, or another red bell pepper

1 jalapeño

⅓ cup extra-virgin olive oil

Kosher salt and freshly ground black pepper

TOMATILLO SALSA

1 ear fresh corn, husked

3 tomatillos, about 8 ounces, husked, rinsed, and cut into ¼-inch dice

⅓ cup finely chopped red onion

3 tablespoons minced fresh cilantro

½ teaspoon pure ground ancho chile

½ teaspoon ground cumin

¼ cup crumbled feta cheese

Kosher salt and freshly ground black pepper

Lime wedges, for serving (optional)

Special Equipment: 8 large wooden skewers, soaked in cold water to cover for at least 30 minutes

Chipotle-marinated shrimp was one of my first signature dishes. It's an especially good recipe to have in your repertoire during the summer grilling season. The bright salsa has the unique addition of feta, which offers a unique salty/creamy counterpart to roasted corn and tomatillos.

1. To marinate the shrimp: Process the chipotles, cilantro, garlic, lime juice, and ground ancho in a blender. With the machine running, gradually pour the oil into the mixture through the hole in the blender lid. Pour into a 1-gallon self-sealing plastic bag. Add the shrimp, toss to coat, and seal the bag. Refrigerate, turning the bag occasionally, for at least 1 hour or up to 12 hours.

2. Prepare an outdoor grill for direct cooking over medium heat (400°F to 450°F).

3. To make the sauce: Grill the bell peppers and jalapeño with the lid closed, turning them occasionally, until the skins are blackened and blistered, about 8 minutes for the jalapeño and 12 minutes for the bell peppers. Transfer to a bowl, cover with plastic wrap, and let stand for 15 minutes. Discard the skins and seeds. Puree the peppers and jalapeño with the oil in the blender. Season to taste with salt and pepper. (The sauce can be cooled, covered, and refrigerated for up to 6 hours. Reheat in a saucepan over low heat before serving.)

4. Meanwhile, to make the salsa: Add the corn to the grill and cook, turning occasionally, until the kernels are browned in spots, 12 to 15 minutes. Transfer to a cutting board and let it cool. Cut the kernels from the cob and transfer to a bowl. Add the tomatillo, red onion, cilantro, ground ancho, and cumin and mix gently. Add the feta and mix again. Season to taste with salt and pepper. (The salsa can be covered and refrigerated for up to 4 hours. Bring to room temperature before using.) ➡

5. To grill the shrimp: If necessary, reheat the grill. Drain the skewers. Wearing rubber gloves to protect your skin from the marinade, if desired, thread 4 shrimp onto each skewer. Discard the marinade in the bag. Place the skewers on the grill, perpendicular to the grid. Slide a strip of aluminum foil under the exposed skewer ends to protect them from the heat. Cook with the lid closed, turning halfway through cooking, until the shrimp are opaque, about 4 minutes.

6. Transfer the shrimp skewers to a platter. Serve hot with lime wedges, if using, and the pepper sauce and salsa passed on the side.

SHRIMP AND CHEESY "GRITS"
with SMOKY RED PEPPER SAUCE

CHEESY "GRITS" JOHNNYCAKES

¾ cup reduced-sodium chicken broth

¾ cup whole milk

¾ cup heavy cream

2 tablespoons unsalted butter

Kosher salt

½ cup yellow cornmeal, preferably stone-ground

1 cup (4 ounces) shredded mild Cheddar cheese

¼ cup (1 ounce) freshly grated Parmigiano-Reggiano cheese

¼ teaspoon freshly grated nutmeg

¼ teaspoon freshly ground black pepper

Vegetable oil, for the griddle

SMOKY RED PEPPER SAUCE

1 large red bell pepper, roasted (see page 42), peeled, seeded, and coarsely chopped

2 tablespoons finely chopped red onion

1 tablespoon red wine vinegar

1 canned chipotle in adobo

1 small garlic clove, minced

1 teaspoon honey

1 teaspoon Dijon mustard

¼ cup canola or vegetable oil

Kosher salt and freshly ground black pepper

MARINADE AND SHRIMP

½ cup canola or vegetable oil

1 tablespoon red wine vinegar

1 tablespoon Worcestershire sauce

2 tablespoons coarsely chopped fresh cilantro

1 tablespoon Cajun seasoning

5 garlic cloves, crushed under a knife and peeled

18 extra-jumbo (16 to 20 count) shrimp, peeled and deveined, with tail segment attached

———

2 tablespoons canola or vegetable oil, for the shrimp

2 scallions, white and green parts, finely chopped

Lime wedges, for garnish

As a native of Rhode Island, it's fair to say that I've eaten more than my share of johnnycakes, the local corn griddlecakes. I first had shrimp and grits the classic way, over cornmeal mush. But there are many ways to make this Southern dish, and I knew I would like it even more on top of my hometown favorite. This rendition, with Cajun shrimp, cheesy johnnycakes, and a smoky sauce, is always a hit at my dinner parties.

1. To start the johnnycakes: Bring the broth, milk, cream, butter, and ¾ teaspoon salt to a boil in a medium heavy-bottomed saucepan over medium heat, being sure that the mixture does not boil over. Gradually whisk in the cornmeal. Reduce the heat to medium-low and simmer, whisking often, until the mixture has thickened, 12 to 15 minutes. Whisk in the Cheddar and Parmigiano cheeses, nutmeg, and pepper and return to the simmer. Carefully taste (it's very hot) and season with additional salt if necessary. Pour the mixture into an oiled 11-by-8-inch baking dish and smooth the top. Let cool. Cover loosely with plastic wrap and refrigerate until the mixture is chilled and firm, at least 1 hour or up to 1 day.

2. To make the sauce: Puree the roasted pepper, onion, vinegar, chipotle, garlic, honey, and mustard together in a food processor. With the machine running, pour in the oil through the feed tube to make a smooth sauce. Transfer to a bowl and season to taste with salt and pepper. (The sauce can be covered and refrigerated for up to 1 day. Bring to room temperature before using.)

3. To marinate the shrimp: Process the oil, vinegar, Worcestershire sauce, cilantro, Cajun seasoning, and garlic together in a food processor to make a thick marinade. Combine the shrimp and marinade in a 1-gallon self-sealing plastic bag. Seal and refrigerate, turning the bag occasionally, for 30 minutes to 2 hours.

➞

4. To cook the johnnycakes: Run a dinner knife around the cornmeal slab in the baking dish, lifting the slab slightly at one end to break the air seal. Place a baking sheet on top of the dish and invert to turn out the slab in one piece. Cut the slab into 18 equal rectangular cakes. (Or use a 2½-inch round cookie cutter to cut out about 12 rounds, although this alternative creates scraps.)

5. Heat a large griddle, preferably nonstick, over medium heat. Lightly oil the griddle. Cook the cakes on the griddle, turning once, until golden brown, 4 to 5 minutes. The cheese will make the cakes brown fairly quickly, so adjust the heat as needed so they heat through without burning. Transfer to a large platter and tent with aluminum foil to keep warm.

6. To cook the shrimp: Drain the shrimp well. Heat a very large skillet over medium-high heat. Add the oil and swirl to coat the bottom of the skillet. Add the shrimp and cook, turning once, just until the shrimp turn opaque, about 3 minutes. Transfer to a plate.

7. Spoon about 1 tablespoon of the red pepper sauce over each cake and top each with a shrimp. Sprinkle with the scallions. Serve warm, with the lime wedges.

Salt-and-Pepper
SHRIMP
with Thai Papaya Salad

MAKES

4

SERVINGS

Also perfect as a party starter, this intensely peppered dish is incredibly easy to make and will take your palate on an international journey with just a few steps. The shrimp rub has a complex flavor from its handful of ingredients: The five-spice powder and furikake combined contain about a dozen ingredients! I like to wash this down with a cool, crisp white wine.

MISO-SAMBAL MAYONNAISE

¾ teaspoon white (aka) miso

½ teaspoon sambal oelek or other Asian chili sauce

½ cup mayonnaise, preferably Kewpie (see Chef Talk, page 197)

SALT-AND-PEPPER SHRIMP

½ teaspoon Sichuan peppercorns

½ teaspoon black peppercorns, preferably smoked

½ teaspoon katsuo fumi furikake (see Chef Talk, this page) or minced nori seaweed (optional)

¼ teaspoon Chinese five-spice powder

¼ teaspoon kosher salt

1½ pounds extra-jumbo (16 to 20 count) shrimp, peeled and deveined

2 teaspoons canola or vegetable oil

1 tablespoon extra-virgin olive oil

2 scallions, white and green parts, thinly sliced

1 tablespoon finely chopped peeled fresh ginger

2 garlic cloves, minced

½ recipe Thai Marinated Papaya Salad (page 76)

Lime slices, for garnish

1. To make the mayonnaise: Whisk the miso and sambal oelek together in a small bowl with a few drops of water to dissolve the miso. Add the mayonnaise and stir well.

2. To make the shrimp: Coarsely grind the Sichuan peppercorns and black peppercorns in a spice grinder. Add the furikake, if using, five-spice powder, and salt and pulse just to combine.

3. Toss the shrimp with the salt and pepper mixture. Heat a wok or large skillet over high heat until it is very hot. Drizzle in the canola oil and swirl to coat the inside of the skillet. Add the shrimp and cook until the underside is seared, about 30 seconds. Flip the shrimp and sear the other side for about 30 seconds more. Add the olive oil, scallions, ginger, and garlic and stir-fry just until the shrimp turn opaque, about 1 minute more. Transfer to one side of a platter.

4. Using a slotted spoon, transfer the papaya salad to the opposite side of the shrimp on the platter. Add the lime slices and serve with the miso-sambal mayonnaise passed on the side.

CHEF TALK

Furikake #2

In addition to nori fumi furikake (see Chef Talk, page 51), katsuo fumi furikake (made of sesame, nori, and bonito) is sold at Asian markets and many supermarkets. Be sure to use it as a topping on plain rice, too!

APPLE-CIDER
MUSSELS

with **Roasted Fall Vegetables**
and **Mustard Butter**

MAKES

4

SERVINGS

One of my oldest friends, and most trusted kitchen advisors, Timothy Peterson, introduced me to this mussel recipe and it's been my go-to ever since. It includes the usual suspects—wine, garlic, and butter— but is elevated with mustard and apple cider. My favorite part is the addition of roasted cauliflower and fennel, which transforms a pot of mussels into a meal on its own.

MUSTARD BUTTER

½ cup (1 stick) unsalted butter,
at room temperature

2 tablespoons finely chopped
yellow onion

2 tablespoons mashed Roasted Garlic
(page 134); or 2 garlic cloves, minced

1 tablespoon Dijon mustard

1½ teaspoons sriracha

1 teaspoon cider vinegar

¼ teaspoon freshly ground black
peppercorns, preferably smoked

ROASTED VEGETABLES

2 tablespoons fresh lemon juice

2 tablespoons extra-virgin olive oil

4 garlic cloves, minced

½ head cauliflower, broken into florets

1 small bulb fennel, fronds removed,
cored, and cut on a diagonal into
¼-inch slices

APPLE-CIDER MUSSELS

1½ cups apple cider

½ cup dry white wine, such
as Pinot Grigio

3 pounds mussels, preferably Prince
Edward Island (see Note), scrubbed

Kosher salt and freshly ground
black pepper

1. To make the mustard butter: Melt 1 tablespoon of the butter in a small skillet over medium heat. Add the onion and cook, stirring occasionally, until softened, about 3 minutes. Reduce the heat to medium-low and cook, stirring occasionally, until the onion is golden brown, about 10 minutes. Let cool completely.

2. Process the onion, roasted (or minced) garlic, mustard, sriracha, vinegar, and pepper with the remaining 7 tablespoons butter in a mini–food processor until the mixture is well combined. Transfer to a small bowl. (The butter can be covered and refrigerated for 1 day. Bring to room temperature before using.)

3. To roast the vegetables: Position racks in the top third and center of the oven and preheat the oven to 400°F.

4. Whisk the lemon juice, oil, and minced garlic together in a small bowl. Toss 2 tablespoons of the oil mixture with the cauliflower in a large bowl and spread on one side of an 18-by-13-inch half-sheet pan. Repeat with the fennel and remaining oil mixture, and spread on the opposite side of the sheet. Bake, occasionally stirring each vegetable without mixing them, until they are lightly browned but al dente, about 20 minutes.

5. To cook the mussels: Bring the apple cider and wine to a boil in a large stockpot over high heat. Add the mussels and cover tightly. Cook over high heat, shaking the pot occasionally, until all of the mussels have opened, about 5 minutes. During the last minute of cooking, add the roasted vegetables. Season to taste with salt and pepper.

6. Divide the mussels, vegetables, and cooking liquid among 4 large deep bowls. Top each with one-quarter of the mustard butter. Toss and serve immediately.

Note: *Prince Edward Island mussels, harvested in Nova Scotia, are "beardless," so do not have the thick cord-like protrusion that would otherwise need to be removed before cooking. Standard mussels use the beards to attach themselves to rocks and pilings. If you use standard mussels, use a pair of pliers to tug the beard from each mussel.*

SEARED-SQUID
LETTUCE WRAPS
with SPICY CARROT SLAW

MAKES

4 *to* **6**

SERVINGS

When many people think of squid, their brain instantly goes to Italian fried calamari, but squid is a very versatile and easy-to-cook seafood that cooks should get to know in other guises. This recipe is essentially a quick stir-fry with Southeast Asian seasonings that is used as a stuffing for crisp lettuce leaves. Be sure that the oil in your wok is searing hot before adding the calamari to ensure the perfect char without overcooking.

JALAPEÑO SOY SAUCE

⅓ cup water

¼ cup Japanese soy sauce

1 tablespoon balsamic vinegar

1 jalapeño, thinly sliced, with seeds

2 teaspoons minced shallot

2 teaspoons sugar

SPICY CARROT SLAW

2 tablespoons Asian sesame oil

1 tablespoon white wine vinegar

2 teaspoons Japanese soy sauce

2 teaspoons sugar

½ teaspoon sambal oelek or other Asian chili paste

½ teaspoon kosher salt

1 small garlic clove, minced

1 pound carrots (see Note), peeled and cut into julienne with a mandoline, V-slicer, or large knife

2 scallions, white and green parts, thinly sliced

MISO MAYONNAISE

½ cup mayonnaise

1½ tablespoons white (shiro) miso

1 teaspoon Dijon mustard

1 teaspoon honey

1½ pounds cleaned calamari

1 head green leaf lettuce, separated into leaves

1 tablespoon canola or vegetable oil

1 tablespoon chopped fresh mint

1. To make the jalapeño soy sauce: Whisk all of the ingredients in a medium bowl until the sugar dissolves. (The soy sauce can be stored at room temperature for up to 8 hours.)

2. To make the slaw: Whisk the sesame oil, vinegar, soy sauce, sugar, sambal oelek, salt, and garlic together in a medium bowl until the sugar dissolves. Add the carrots and scallions and mix well. (The slaw can be covered and refrigerated for up to 8 hours.)

3. To make the miso mayonnaise: Whisk all of the ingredients together in a small bowl. (The mayonnaise can be covered and refrigerated for up to 6 hours.)

4. Using the tip of a large knife, score the calamari bodies in a crosshatch pattern. Cut the bodies into ¼-inch rings. Coarsely chop the tentacles. Pat the calamari completely dry with paper towels.

5. Reserve 2 tablespoons of the jalapeño soy sauce. Transfer the remaining jalapeño soy sauce, the slaw, and the miso mayonnaise into separate serving bowls. Heap the lettuce leaves on a plate.

6. Heat a large wok or skillet over high heat until the wok is very hot, at least 3 minutes. Drizzle the oil down the sides of the wok (it will smoke). Add the calamari and cook, without turning, until it is seared, about 1 minute. Sprinkle in the mint. Add the reserved 2 tablespoons jalapeño soy sauce and stir-fry until the calamari just turns opaque, about 1 minute more, making sure not to overcook. Transfer to a serving bowl.

7. Serve the calamari, jalapeño soy sauce, carrot slaw, miso mayonnaise, and lettuce so diners can make their own wraps at the table.

Note: *If you have green papaya, substitute it for all or part of the carrots.*

MEAT

For many people, meat and potatoes is a classic combination, but my feeling is that when it comes to entertaining, there are so many more things to do with beef, pork, and lamb than to pair them with root vegetables. With my pull-apart baby back ribs (page 151), you'll never need another sparerib recipe. For a quick dinner, the pork tenderloin (page 147) has the most incredible caramel glaze; and for a true steakhouse experience at home, cook the Ribeye with the garlic-butter baste (page 133). And my mother would never forgive me unless I brought special attention to her chouriço and peppers (page 158), a simple, one-pot dish that has been my absolute favorite since childhood.

HANGER STEAK
with Red Pepper and Olive Chimichurri

—

INDIVIDUAL
Beef Wellingtons

—

Ribeye Steak
with Garlic-Butter Baste and Mustard-Bourbon Sauce

—

"Beef and Broccoli"
(*Asian Braised Short Ribs with Broccoli Puree*)

—

SEXY SLIDERS
with Fancy Sauce and Cola Onions

—

OLD-SCHOOL
Meatballs
with **Marinara Sauce**

—

KOREAN
Short Rib Tacos
with Kimchi

—

PORK TENDERLOIN
with **Ancho-Caramel Glaze** and **BBQ Beans**

Brined Pork Milanese
with Tomato-Balsamic Sauce

—

BABY BACK RIBS
WITH *Jägermeister–Black Cherry Cola Glaze*

—

PORK BELLY
BLT TACOS
with **Charred-Lime Vinaigrette**

—

Cajun Bacon
RISOTTO

—

Grilled Cheddar
AND Jalapeño
Bacon Sandwiches

—

Chouriço *and* Pepper
SLOPPY JOES

—

LAMB SOUVLAKI
with Tzatziki and Lime-Harissa Aioli

Hanger Steak

with Red Pepper and Olive Chimichurri

MAKES

4

SERVINGS

I have always loved a good chimichurri, the classic Argentine steak sauce/pesto. After I traveled to Argentina with chef Jonathan Kavourakis, we both became hooked. Following our travels, we began toying with our own variations, and Jonathan's rendition, heavy on red bell pepper and olives, has become our clear favorite.

CHIMICHURRI

1 medium red bell pepper, seeded and coarsely chopped

3 tablespoons coarsely chopped pitted black kalamata olives

3 tablespoons coarsely chopped pitted green olives

1 small garlic clove, shredded on a Microplane zester

2 tablespoons red wine vinegar

¾ teaspoon smoked paprika

¾ teaspoon dried oregano

Pinch of cayenne pepper

¼ cup extra-virgin olive oil

Kosher salt and freshly ground black pepper

HANGER STEAK

1 teaspoon black peppercorns, preferably 1 teaspoon each black and smoked peppercorns

1 teaspoon kosher salt

2 pounds hanger steaks, cut into 4 portions

Canola or vegetable oil, for brushing

1. To make the chimichurri: Pulse the bell pepper, black olives, green olives, and garlic in a food processor until combined. Add the vinegar, paprika, oregano, and cayenne pepper and pulse until finely chopped. Transfer to a medium bowl. Whisk in the oil and season to taste with salt and pepper. Cover and let stand at room temperature for at least 1 hour or up to 4 hours to marry the flavors. (The chimichurri can be refrigerated for up to 1 week. Bring to room temperature before using.)

2. To cook the hanger steak: Coarsely grind the peppercorns in a mortar or spice grinder. Transfer to a small bowl and mix in the salt. Brush the steaks lightly with the oil and season all over with the pepper mixture. Let the steaks stand at room temperature for 30 minutes.

3. Heat a very large heavy skillet, preferably cast iron, over medium-high heat. Turn on the kitchen exhaust fan. Add the steaks to the hot pan and cook, turning halfway through cooking, until they are well browned and an instant-read thermometer inserted in the center registers 125°F for medium-rare, about 6 minutes. Transfer to a carving board and let stand for 3 to 5 minutes. Slice across the grain and serve with the chimichurri.

INDIVIDUAL
BEEF WELLINGTONS

MAKES
6
SERVINGS

Beef Wellington is a dish that has "class" written all over it. When I am trying to impress my friends with a more upscale dinner, this is the first dish that I turn to—a seared filet of beef layered with cooked minced mushrooms (duxelles) and pâté, then wrapped in puff pastry and baked. While some people use an entire beef tenderloin, I opt for individual beef Wellingtons so that each guest gets an ample amount of buttery pastry. I like to serve this by itself, after My House Salad (page 70).

DUXELLES

1 tablespoon canola or vegetable oil

10 ounces white button mushrooms, sliced

2 tablespoons finely chopped shallot

1 teaspoon minced fresh thyme

3 tablespoons dry white wine

Kosher salt and freshly ground black pepper

BORDELAISE SAUCE

2 teaspoons canola or vegetable oil

¼ cup coarsely chopped white or yellow onion

2 sprigs fresh thyme

¼ teaspoon black peppercorns

1 small bay leaf

½ cup hearty red wine, such as Shiraz

1 cup store-bought demi-glace (see Chef Talk, page 132)

2 tablespoons cold unsalted butter, cut into ½-inch cubes

Kosher salt and freshly ground black pepper

FILETS AND PASTRY

6 filet mignon steaks, each about 3 ounces and 1 inch thick

Kosher salt and freshly ground black pepper

1¼ pounds thawed frozen puff pastry (about 1½ boxes, see Note, page 132)

All-purpose flour, for rolling the dough

6 ounces liver mousse pâté, preferably foie gras, as needed

1 large egg, beaten well

———

Truffle oil, for serving

Fresh thyme sprigs, for garnish

Flaky sea salt, preferably Maldon, for serving

1. To make the duxelles: Heat a large skillet over medium-high heat until very hot. Add the oil, followed by the mushrooms, shallot, and thyme. Cook, stirring occasionally, until the juices are evaporated and the mushrooms are deeply browned around the edges, about 8 minutes. Add the wine and cook until it evaporates, about 1 minute. Remove from the heat and season to taste with salt and pepper. Let cool completely. Transfer the mushroom mixture to a food processor and pulse until finely chopped, but not a paste. (The duxelles can be covered and refrigerated for up to 1 day.)

2. To start the sauce: Heat the oil in a small saucepan over medium heat. Add the onion, thyme, peppercorns, and bay leaf and cook, stirring occasionally, until the onion is lightly browned, about 5 minutes. Pour in the wine and cook until reduced to a glaze, about 5 minutes. Add the demi-glace and bring to a boil. Reduce the heat to medium and cook at a brisk simmer until reduced by about one-fourth, about 10 minutes. Strain through a wire sieve into a small bowl and discard the solids. Keep the cubed butter cold while you prepare the beef and pastry. (The sauce base can be cooled, covered, and refrigerated for up to 1 day.)

3. To prepare the beef filets and pastry wrap: Heat a large skillet, preferably a ridged grilling skillet, over medium-high heat. Season the filets with salt and pepper. In batches without crowding, add the filets to the skillet and cook, turning once, until browned on both sides but still very rare, about 2 minutes. Do not overcook. Transfer to a wire cake rack and let cool completely. ➤

4. Line a half-sheet pan with parchment paper. On a lightly floured work surface, roll out the puff pastry to remove its creases. Using a pizza wheel or large knife, cut the pastry into six 6-inch squares. Spoon equal amounts of the pâté onto the center of each pastry square, making the pâté about as wide as each seared filet. Top each with equal amounts of the cooled duxelles, followed by a filet. Brush the border of each square lightly with beaten egg. Bring the pastry corners up to meet in the center, and press the seams closed to enclose the filet. Place the packets seam side down on the baking sheet, and pat each into a rough round shape. Loosely cover the pastry packets with plastic wrap. Refrigerate for at least 1 hour or up to 6 hours.

5. Position a rack in the center of the oven and preheat the oven to 425°F.

6. Brush the tops and sides of the packets with some of the egg wash. Bake until the pastry is golden brown, 17 to 20 minutes for medium-rare. Transfer each beef Wellington to a plate.

7. To finish the sauce: Quickly bring the sauce base to a boil in the saucepan over high heat. Remove from the heat. One cube at a time, whisk the butter into the warm sauce base to enrich and lightly thicken it. Taste and season with salt and pepper. Spoon the sauce around each beef Wellington and drizzle with the truffle oil. Add a thyme sprig and a sprinkle of salt to each, and serve immediately.

Note: All-butter frozen puff pastry, sold at specialty markets, is preferable to the shortening-based supermarket variety. You will need about 1½ (14-ounce) boxes for the Wellingtons, so plan another use for the remaining puff pastry.

CHEF TALK

Demi-Glace

Demi-glace is a brown veal stock that has been reduced to intensify its flavor. It is becoming increasingly available at supermarkets, specialty stores, and butchers. D'Artagnan is the most common brand. You can substitute a high-quality store-bought beef or veal stock, but the sauce base will need to be thickened slightly: After the sauce base has reduced by one-fourth, stir in a slurry (¼ teaspoon cornstarch whisked into 1 tablespoon water) and cook just until slightly thickened, about 30 seconds.

RIBEYE STEAK
with Garlic-Butter Baste
and Mustard-Bourbon Sauce

MAKES

4

SERVINGS

A big steak is one of life's huge pleasures, but like so many things, its preparation is important. Start with the best, well-marbled steak you can find (preferably aged prime), and don't skimp on the smoky peppercorn rub. Basting your steak with a rich garlic butter and finishing with a mustardy sauce amps up the *wow* factor. The Angry Potatoes on page 202 are a great accompaniment if you like the age-old combination of meat and potatoes.

GARLIC-BUTTER BASTE

2 tablespoons extra-virgin olive oil

1 tablespoon mashed Roasted Garlic (page 134)

4 tablespoons (½ stick) unsalted butter, at room temperature

2 teaspoons finely chopped chives

¼ teaspoon kosher salt

⅛ teaspoon freshly ground black pepper

MUSTARD-BOURBON SAUCE

1 tablespoon unsalted butter

3 tablespoons minced shallots

¼ cup bourbon

1 cup heavy cream

¼ cup store-bought demi-glace (see Chef Talk, page 132) or high-quality beef stock

3 tablespoons Worcestershire sauce

3 tablespoons whole-grain mustard

4 tablespoons (½ stick) cold unsalted butter, cut into ½-inch dice

Kosher salt and freshly ground black pepper

STEAK

1 (2-inch-thick) ribeye or porterhouse steak, about 2½ pounds

2 teaspoons black peppercorns, preferably 1 teaspoon each plain and smoked peppercorns

2 teaspoons kosher salt

Bunch of thyme sprigs, for serving

1. To make the baste: Puree the oil and roasted garlic in a mini–food processor or blender and transfer to a medium bowl. Add the butter, chives, salt, and pepper and mash the ingredients together with a rubber spatula. (The baste can be covered tightly and refrigerated for up to 2 days. Bring to room temperature before using.)

2. To start the sauce: Melt the 1 tablespoon butter in a medium saucepan over medium-low heat. Add the shallots and cook, stirring occasionally, until translucent, about 3 minutes. Add the bourbon and remove from the heat. Carefully ignite the bourbon with a long-handled match and let the flames burn down. (If they don't extinguish on their own after 30 seconds, tightly cover the saucepan with its lid.) Stir in the cream, demi-glace, Worcestershire sauce, and mustard. Bring to a boil over high heat, being sure the mixture doesn't boil over. Reduce the heat to medium-low and cook at a brisk simmer, stirring occasionally, until the sauce has reduced by half, 15 to 20 minutes. Remove from the heat. Refrigerate the 4 table-spoons cold butter while you prepare the steak. (The sauce can be stored at room temperature for up to 2 hours.)

3. To prepare the steak: Trim the excess fat from the perimeter of the steak, leaving a ¼-inch layer and reserving the trimmed fat. Coarsely grind the peppercorns in a mortar or spice grinder. Transfer to a small bowl and mix in the salt. Season the steak all over with the salt mixture and let stand for 15 to 20 minutes at room temperature. ➤

ROASTED GARLIC

Makes about ½ cup

Garlic, of course, is an essential seasoning, but there are times when I prefer the milder, nutty flavor of roasted garlic cloves, so I always keep a small container of roasted garlic, covered with olive oil, in the fridge. And the garlic-flavored oil can come in handy for salads and pastas, too.

   1 large, plump head of garlic

   Kosher salt and freshly ground black pepper

   ½ cup olive oil (either extra-virgin or standard), as needed

Position a rack in the center of the oven and preheat the oven to 350°F. Separate the garlic into individual cloves. Using a small sharp knife, peel the cloves, keeping them as intact as possible. Place the garlic cloves in the center of a piece of aluminum foil about 12 inches square. Season the garlic lightly with salt and pepper and drizzle with about 1 tablespoon of oil. Wrap the garlic into a packet with the seam on top to contain the oil. Place on a baking sheet and bake until the garlic is very tender and beige, 30 to 40 minutes. Let cool completely. Transfer to a small covered container and add enough oil to cover the garlic. (The garlic can be refrigerated for up to 2 weeks.)

4. Position a rack in the center of the oven and preheat the oven to 450°F. Turn on your kitchen fan.

5. Heat a very large, heavy ovenproof skillet (preferably cast iron) over high heat until very hot. Using tongs, quickly rub the inside of the skillet with the reserved fat to apply a thin layer of grease. Add the steak and let cook until the underside is well browned, about 5 minutes. Flip the steak and cook to brown well for 5 minutes more. Transfer the skillet with the steak to the oven. Roast, flipping the steak halfway through cooking, until an instant-read thermometer inserted horizontally in the center of the fillet section of the steak registers 125°F for medium-rare, 5 to 10 minutes more. Remove the skillet with the steak from the oven. Dollop the basting butter all over the steak and into the skillet and let it melt, spooning the butter over the steak. Transfer the steak to a platter and let it stand for 3 to 5 minutes, setting the skillet with the butter aside.

6. Meanwhile, finish the sauce: Reheat the mustard sauce to a simmer over medium heat, whisking constantly. Remove from the heat. A few pieces at a time, whisk in the cold butter, letting the sauce absorb the first addition before adding another. Season to taste with salt and pepper. Transfer the sauce to a small serving bowl.

7. Transfer the steak to a carving board. Carve the steak off the bone, and cut the meat across the grain into thick slices. Return the bone to the platter and arrange the sliced meat around the bone. Place the thyme sprigs over the steak, and pour the butter mixture from the pan and any carving juices on top. Serve immediately with the mustard sauce.

"BEEF AND BROCCOLI"

(Asian Braised Short Ribs *with* Broccoli Puree)

MAKES

4 *to* 6

SERVINGS

My friend and fellow chef Derrick Prince knows that no Chinese meal is ever complete without my order of beef and broccoli. This dish is a fresh take on the familiar takeout standby—long-braised short ribs are served on crisp rice cakes with a green broccoli sauce. The brilliant green color of the puree means a feast for the eyes as well as the palate.

1. To marinate the beef: Combine all the marinade ingredients in a jumbo 2½-gallon zip-tight plastic bag. Add the short ribs, seal the bag, and refrigerate, turning occasionally, for at least 2 hours or up to 18 hours.

2. To braise the beef: Position a rack in the center of the oven and preheat the oven to 325°F. Remove the beef ribs from the marinade, reserving the marinade and solids, and pat the ribs dry with paper towels. Season with the Sichuan peppercorns and ½ teaspoon salt.

3. Heat the oil in a large Dutch oven over medium-high heat. In batches, add the ribs and cook, turning occasionally, adjusting the heat to avoid scorching the pan juices, until browned, about 5 minutes.

4. Pour in the broth and the reserved marinade with its solids, adding water to cover the beef if needed. Bring to a boil over high heat. Cover tightly, transfer to the oven, and bake until the meat is very tender, about 2 hours.

5. Uncover and let stand for 5 minutes. Transfer the meat to a platter and let cool until easy to handle, about 15 minutes. Using your fingers, shred the beef, discarding the bones. (The beef can be cooled, covered, and refrigerated for up to 1 day.)

Skim off any fat from the surface of the liquid in the pot and let the liquid cool until tepid. In batches, puree the liquid with its solids in a blender with the lid ajar. Return the puree to the Dutch oven and bring to a boil over high heat. Cook, stirring occasionally,

➡

MARINADE

1 Granny Smith apple, cored and sliced

1 medium yellow onion, sliced

⅓ cup Japanese soy sauce

¼ cup packed fresh cilantro leaves

3 tablespoons unseasoned rice vinegar

2 tablespoons finely chopped fresh ginger

1 tablespoon Thai or Vietnamese fish sauce

1 tablespoon finely chopped jalapeño, with seeds

2 teaspoons sriracha

3 garlic cloves, crushed under a knife and peeled

1 whole star anise, broken into individual points

½ teaspoon whole coriander seeds

SHORT RIBS

2 pounds cross-cut (flanken or Korean-style) bone-in short ribs

2 teaspoons ground Sichuan peppercorns (ground in spice grinder or mortar)

Kosher salt

2 tablespoons canola oil

1 quart reduced-sodium chicken broth

BROCCOLI PUREE

8 ounces broccoli crowns, stems peeled, tops and stems coarsely chopped, about 2 cups

1 tablespoon canola oil

½ cup chopped seeded green bell pepper

3 tablespoons chopped white onion

2 teaspoons minced fresh ginger

1 garlic clove, minced

2 tablespoons finely chopped fresh cilantro

2 teaspoons Japanese soy sauce

1 teaspoon sriracha

About ½ cup reduced-sodium chicken broth, as needed

2 teaspoons Asian sesame oil

---

18 Sticky Rice Cakes (1 recipe, page 207)

1 raw broccoli floret, cut into very tiny florets, for garnish (optional)

until the puree has thickened and reduced to about 2 cups, about 30 minutes. (The sauce can be cooled, covered, and refrigerated for up to 1 day.)

6. To make the broccoli puree: In a collapsible steamer basket over boiling water, steam the broccoli florets and stems until bright green and barely tender, about 5 minutes. Transfer the broccoli to a large bowl of ice water and let cool completely. Drain well. Heat the oil in a medium skillet over medium heat. Add the green pepper and onion and cook, stirring occasionally, until the onion is translucent, about 4 minutes. Stir in the ginger and garlic and cook until fragrant, about 1 minute more. Transfer to a blender and add the broccoli, cilantro, soy sauce, and sriracha. Process, adding enough of the broth to make a smooth, thick puree. Adjust the seasoning with soy sauce and sriracha. Add the sesame oil and pulse the blender to combine. (The puree can be cooled, covered, and refrigerated for up to 1 day.)

7. Transfer the broccoli puree to a medium saucepan and heat over medium heat. Reduce the heat to low to keep the puree warm.

8. Reheat the beef with its sauce in a medium saucepan over medium heat, about 5 minutes. Spoon 9 tablespoons of the broccoli puree in individual pools on a platter. Top with 9 of the rice cakes, followed by 9 portions of the beef. Scatter the broccoli florets around the platter, if using. Repeat on a second platter with the remaining cakes, beef, sauce, and florets. Serve immediately.

SEXY SLIDERS
with **Fancy Sauce** and **Cola Onions**

SLIDER PATTIES

6 ounces boneless short ribs

7 ounces boneless ribeye steak
(preferably aged prime)

9 ounces boneless beef chuck

2 ounces beef fat trimmed from
ribeye steak

1½ ounces sliced double-smoked
bacon, preferably Neuske's

1½ teaspoons kosher salt

¾ teaspoon freshly ground black
pepper

FANCY SAUCE

¼ cup mayonnaise

3 tablespoons tomato ketchup

2 tablespoons Dijon mustard

1 tablespoon finely chopped shallots

1 tablespoon finely chopped cornichons

2 teaspoons fresh lemon juice

¾ teaspoon hot red pepper sauce, such
as Tabasco

COLA-BRAISED ONIONS

1 tablespoon unsalted butter

1 medium white onion, cut into half-
moons about ½ inch thick

1 tablespoon sugar

½ cup cola soda (not diet)

Kosher salt

———

Kosher salt and freshly ground
black pepper

3 slices American cheese, each cut into
quarters to make 12 pieces total

3 leaves Bibb lettuce, each torn into
quarters to make 12 pieces total

12 brioche or potato dinner rolls, split

———

Special Equipment: 12 cocktail
skewers, for serving

These are as voluptuous and sexy as burgers get. They
have a personalized ground meat mix with three kinds
of beef, plus bacon and extra beef fat. You don't need a
meat grinder, as the partially frozen meat is chopped in
a food processor. Searing the burgers in a smoking hot
pan gives them that flavorful crust that you just don't get
from grilling over coals. And a specially made, "fancy"
sauce like this one is never a bad idea.

1. To make the patties: Cut the short ribs, ribeye, chuck,
the fat from the ribeye, and bacon into 1-inch chunks. Toss
together on a baking sheet and freeze until partially frozen, 1 to
2 hours. In three or four batches, pulse all the meat and fat in a
food processor until the mixture is finely ground but not a paste.
Transfer the ground meats to a medium bowl, season with
the salt and pepper, and mix gently. Divide the mixture into
12 equal portions and shape into patties about 2 inches wide.
(The patties can be covered and refrigerated for up to 6 hours.
Remove from the refrigerator 30 minutes before cooking.)

2. To make the sauce: Mix all of the ingredients together in
a medium bowl until combined. (The sauce can be covered and
refrigerated for up to 3 days.)

3. To braise the onions: Melt the butter in a large skillet over
medium heat. Add the onion and sugar and cook, stirring
occasionally, until the onion is lightly browned, 8 to 10 minutes.
Add the cola, bring to a boil, and cook until the liquid has reduced
to a glaze, about 5 minutes. Season to taste with salt and cover
the skillet with its lid to keep the onions warm. (The onions can
be cooled, covered, and refrigerated for up to 1 day. Reheat the
onions in the skillet before using.)

To cook the burgers: Lightly season the patties all over with
salt and pepper. Heat a large griddle or two large skillets over
medium-high heat. Cook the patties on the griddle until the
undersides are well browned, about 2 minutes. ➤━━➤

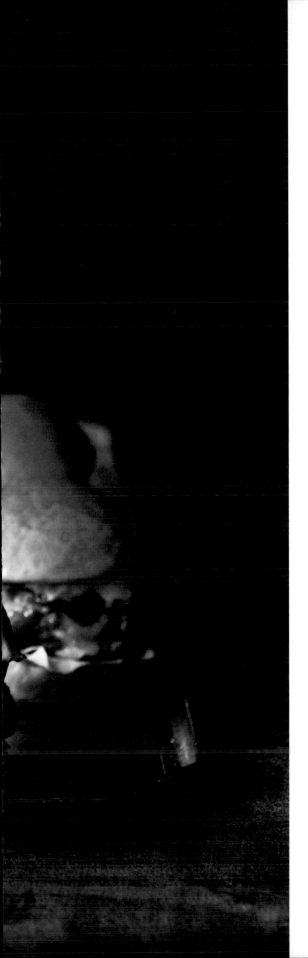

Turn and continue cooking until the other sides are browned, about 3 minutes for medium-rare (the patties will feel somewhat soft and barely beginning to firm when pressed on top with a fingertip). During the last 30 seconds of cooking, top each patty with a cheese quarter. Remove from the griddle.

4. To build each slider, place a lettuce quarter on a roll bottom, then add a patty, about 1 tablespoon each of the onions and sauce, and the roll top. Spear each slider with a skewer (if desired), transfer to a platter, and serve immediately.

OLD-SCHOOL
Meatballs
with MARINARA SAUCE

MAKES

4 *to* 6

SERVINGS

You've heard this before—"My grandmother made the *best* meatballs!"— but my grandmother actually *did*. Her secret was a combination of three meats and extra cheese in the mix. I love them simply served in a simple homemade marinara, but they also go great with pasta, of course. At Beauty & Essex, we serve the meatballs and sauce with the homemade manicotti on page 184. Some may call that combination overkill, but I call it outrageously good!

MARINARA SAUCE

¼ cup extra-virgin olive oil

⅓ cup finely chopped fresh basil

⅓ cup finely chopped fresh flat-leaf parsley

1 small white onion, finely chopped

2 garlic cloves, minced

1 (28-ounce) can plus 1 (14-ounce) can whole peeled tomatoes in juice, preferably San Marzano, coarsely chopped, juices reserved

2 tablespoons balsamic vinegar

1 tablespoon sugar

Kosher salt

MEATBALLS

2 tablespoons extra-virgin olive oil, plus more for frying

1 medium yellow onion, finely chopped

2 garlic cloves, minced

¼ cup whole milk

1 large egg plus 1 large egg yolk

½ cup finely ground panko (Japanese bread crumbs), processed in a blender

1½ teaspoons kosher salt

½ teaspoon freshly ground black pepper

8 ounces ground beef chuck

8 ounces ground pork

8 ounces ground veal

1 cup (4 ounces) freshly grated Parmigiano-Reggiano cheese, plus more for serving

1. To make the marinara: Heat the oil in a Dutch oven over medium heat. Add the basil and parsley and cook, stirring often, until the oil turns green, about 1 minute. Stir in the onion and cook, stirring occasionally, until it is translucent, about 4 minutes. Stir in the garlic and cook until it gives off its aroma, about 1 minute. Add both cans of tomatoes and their juices and bring to a boil over high heat. Reduce the heat to medium-low and simmer, uncovered and stirring occasionally, until reduced by about one-quarter, about 1 hour. Stir in the balsamic vinegar and sugar, and season to taste with salt. (The sauce can be cooled, covered, and refrigerated for up to 2 days. Reheat to simmering in the Dutch oven.)

2. Meanwhile, prepare the meatballs: Heat the oil in a medium skillet over medium heat. Add the onion and garlic and cook, stirring often, until the onion is translucent, about 4 minutes. Transfer the onion mixture to a large bowl and let cool.

3. Stir the milk, egg, yolk, panko, salt, and pepper into the onion mixture. Add the ground beef, ground pork, ground veal, and Parmigiano and mix with your hands until combined. Cover and refrigerate until chilled, about 30 minutes. Shape into 18 equally sized meatballs.

4. Pour enough olive oil to come about ⅛ inch up the sides of a large skillet, preferably nonstick, and heat over medium-high heat until very hot but not smoking. In batches without crowding, add the meatballs and cook, turning occasionally, until they are browned on all sides, about 5 minutes. Using a slotted spoon, transfer the meatballs to the marinara sauce. Reduce the heat to low and cover. Simmer, gently stirring occasionally, until the meatballs are very tender, about 1 hour.

5. Transfer the meatballs and sauce to a large serving bowl. Serve, passing Parmigiano on the side.

Korean Short Rib
TACOS *with* KIMCHI

MAKES

12

TACOS

4 TO 6

SERVINGS

One of the reasons Korean food is so incredible is the use of fermented condiments like *gochujang* and *chunjang* (see Chef Talk, page 146). These soft tacos are a happy marriage between Korean and Mexican cuisines. The marinade is packed with intense umami flavor, making the sweet and spicy beef the main event. If you wish, purchase kimchi instead of making your own.

CLASSIC KIMCHI

2 pounds napa cabbage, cored and cut crosswise into ⅛-inch ribbons

2 tablespoons kosher salt

2 tablespoons sugar

½ medium white onion, thinly sliced

1 small carrot, cut into 1½-inch julienne

2 scallions, white and green parts, cut into 1½-inch julienne

2 garlic cloves, minced

2 garlic cloves, shredded on a Microplane zester

1 teaspoon finely shredded fresh ginger (use a Microplane zester)

2 tablespoons Japanese soy sauce

1½ tablespoons gochugaru (red chili flakes for kimchi)

BEEF AND MARINADE

¼ cup Japanese soy sauce

¼ cup gochujang (Korean chili paste)

¼ cup chunjang (Korean black bean paste)

1 tablespoon Thai or Vietnamese fish sauce

2 teaspoons fresh lime juice

2½ pounds bone-in flanken (cross-cut short ribs)

GOCHUJANG AIOLI

½ cup House Aioli (page 50)

2 tablespoons gochujang (Korean chili paste)

---

12 corn tortillas

Fresh cilantro leaves, for garnish

1. To make the kimchi: At least 2 days before serving, toss the cabbage, salt, and sugar together in a colander. Let the mixture drain in the sink for 2 to 3 hours.

2. Rinse the cabbage mixture well under cold water. A handful at a time, squeeze out the excess moisture and transfer the cabbage to a large bowl. Add the onion, carrot, scallions, garlic, and ginger and mix well. Add the soy sauce and chili flakes and mix again. Cover tightly and refrigerate for at least 2 days. (The kimchi can be refrigerated for up to 1 week. The flavor will improve as it ages.)

3. To marinate the beef: Whisk the soy sauce, gochujang, chunjang, fish sauce, and lime juice together in a medium bowl. Place the short ribs in a 1-gallon self-sealing plastic bag and pour in the marinade. Seal and refrigerate, occasionally turning the bag, for at least 6 hours or up to 24 hours. Remove from the refrigerator and let stand at room temperature for 30 minutes before grilling.

4. To grill the short ribs: Prepare a grill for direct cooking over high heat (about 500°F). (Or position the broiler rack about 6 inches from the source of heat and preheat the broiler on high.) Brush the grill grates clean.

5. Remove the ribs from the marinade and shake off the excess marinade. Grill, with the lid closed as much as possible, turning once, until browned on both sides, about 6 minutes. (Or broil according to the same directions above.) Transfer the beef to a carving board and let stand for 3 to 5 minutes. ➤➤

6. Meanwhile, make the gochujang aioli: Combine the house aioli and gochugang in a small bowl.

7. Brush the grill grates clean again. Grill the tortillas, turning once, until hot, about 30 seconds. Transfer to a cloth napkin–lined bowl and wrap to keep warm.

8. Cut off and reserve the bones from the short ribs. Cut the meat into 1-inch pieces and transfer to a bowl.

9. For each taco, spread a tortilla with about ½ tablespoon of the aioli. Top with a few beef chunks, about 2 tablespoons of the kimchi, and a sprinkle of cilantro. Fold the taco in half and transfer to a platter. (Or offer bowls of the sliced beef, kimchi, aioli, and cilantro with the bowl of tortillas and let diners make their tacos at the table.) Serve immediately, with the bones for nibbling.

CHEF TALK

Korean Seasonings

Once you have gochujang and chunjang (Korean chili paste and black bean paste) in your kitchen, you will find all sorts of uses— try them in barbecue sauces. In addition, gochugaru can be used like cayenne pepper. The condiments are sold at Asian markets, especially ones that cater to Korean clientele (such as H Mart on both coasts), and online.

PORK TENDERLOIN *with*
Ancho-Caramel Glaze and **BBQ Beans**

At Al Forno in Providence, Rhode Island, the late, great chef George Germon made me a terrific "dirty" steak, cooked directly on charcoal and served with a caramel sauce. Inspired by that combination, I developed this dish using pork tenderloin instead of beef. Don't let the caramel-making process scare you off; a candy thermometer is not required and you can tell when the caramel is at the right stage by its sharp aroma.

MAKES
6 *to* 8
SERVINGS

ANCHO-CARAMEL GLAZE

½ cup sugar

3 tablespoons water

⅓ cup heavy cream

3 tablespoons pure ground ancho chile

BBQ BEANS

4 slices bacon, cut into ½-inch dice

2 tablespoons extra-virgin olive oil

½ cup (¼-inch) diced red bell pepper (or use half red and half yellow pepper)

¼ cup (¼-inch) diced red onion

¼ cup (¼-inch) diced celery

¼ cup (¼-inch) diced carrot

1 tablespoon seeded and minced fresh jalapeño

1 garlic clove, minced

1 teaspoon ground cumin

1 teaspoon ground coriander seeds

1 teaspoon pure ground ancho chile

3 (19.5-ounce) cans seasoned whole black beans, such as La Costena (see Note, page 148) drained and rinsed

1 cup reduced-sodium chicken broth

1 cup store-bought spicy barbecue sauce, preferably Rattler BBQ Sauce

Kosher salt and freshly ground black pepper

PORK

2 pork tenderloins, each about 1 pound, trimmed of excess fat and silver skin

1 tablespoon canola or vegetable oil

1 teaspoon kosher salt

———

Flaky sea salt, such as Maldon, for serving

Cilantro leaves, for garnish

---

1. To make the glaze: Pour the sugar into a heavy medium saucepan and stir in the water. Cook over high heat, stirring often, until the sugar is melted and boiling. Stop stirring and cook, occasionally swirling the saucepan by its handle and wiping down any crystals that form on the inside of the saucepan with a bristle pastry brush dipped in cold water, until the caramel has a sharp, distinct aroma, turns the color of an old penny, and is smoking, 3 to 5 minutes. Reduce the heat to low and carefully pour in the cream (be careful of splatters). Stir until the caramel is melted. Transfer to a small bowl. Stir in the ground ancho and let cool completely. (The glaze can be covered and refrigerated for 1 day. Reheat until fluid in a saucepan or microwave oven.)

2. To make the beans: Position a rack in the center of the oven and preheat the oven to 350°F. Meanwhile, cook the bacon and oil together in a medium flameproof casserole over medium heat, stirring often, until the bacon is beginning to brown, about 5 minutes. Add the bell pepper, onion, celery, carrot, jalapeño, and garlic. Cook, stirring occasionally, until the vegetables are tender, about 5 minutes. Stir in the cumin, coriander, and ground ancho.

3. Add the beans, broth, and barbecue sauce, mix well, and bring to a simmer. Season to taste with salt and pepper. Transfer to the oven and bake, uncovered and without

➡

stirring, until thickened and glazed, about 45 minutes. Remove from the oven and cover with aluminum foil to keep warm. (The beans can be cooled, covered, and refrigerated for 1 day. Reheat in a 350°F oven in the covered casserole for 30 minutes.)

4. To cook the pork: Increase the oven temperature to 400°F. Fold the thin ends of the tenderloins back and tie them in place with kitchen twine to give the tenderloins equal thickness throughout their length. Heat the oil in a large ovenproof skillet over medium-high heat. Season the pork with the kosher salt. Cook the pork, turning occasionally, until well browned on all sides, about 7 minutes. Brush the top of the pork, still in the skillet, with some of the ancho glaze. Transfer the skillet and pork to the oven and roast for 6 minutes. Turn the pork and brush with the remaining glaze. Roast until the pork reaches 145°F on an instant-read thermometer, 5 to 8 minutes longer. Transfer the pork to a carving board and let stand for 3 to 5 minutes. Set the skillet with the cooking juices aside.

5. Cut the pork into ½-inch slices, arrange on a serving platter, and drizzle with some of the juices (but not the fat) from the skillet. Season with the flaky salt and sprinkle with the cilantro. Serve immediately with the baked beans.

Note: Be sure to use whole black beans seasoned with onion and peppers. It may not clearly state "seasoned" on the label, so check the ingredients list. La Costena is my favorite brand.

MAKES

4

SERVINGS

BRINE AND PORK CHOPS

2 cups water

⅓ cup plus 1 tablespoon sugar

¼ cup kosher salt

Zest strips of ½ large orange, removed with a vegetable peeler

1½ quarts ice water

2 boneless pork chops, each 8 ounces

TOMATO-BALSAMIC SAUCE

2 tablespoons extra-virgin olive oil

2 garlic cloves, crushed under a knife and peeled

½ teaspoon hot red pepper flakes

1 (28-ounce) can plum tomatoes, coarsely crushed by hand

Finely grated zest of 1 lemon

⅓ cup coarsely chopped fresh basil

1 tablespoon finely chopped fresh oregano

1 tablespoon balsamic vinegar, preferably aged balsamic

1 teaspoon sugar

COATING

½ cup unbleached all-purpose flour

2 large eggs

½ teaspoon kosher salt

½ teaspoon freshly ground black pepper

½ cup Sicilian Bread Crumbs (page 181)

½ cup panko (Japanese bread crumbs)

2 tablespoons finely chopped fresh parsley

Grated zest of 1 lemon

¼ teaspoon crushed hot red pepper flakes

———

Vegetable oil, for frying

BRINED
Pork Milanese
with TOMATO-BALSAMIC SAUCE

Boneless pork chops get a bad rap for being tough after cooking, but this well-priced meat can be succulent and tender if you give your chops a little TLC. A quick brine adds moisture throughout the pork, and crisp panko adds a protective coating. The tomato sauce that goes with it is rustically chunky, with a mouthwatering sweet-and-sour flavor. For easier serving to a group, cut the fried chops into strips.

1. To brine the chops: Combine the water, sugar, salt, and orange zest in a medium saucepan. Bring to a boil over high heat, stirring often to dissolve the sugar and salt. Transfer to a medium heatproof bowl and let cool (see Chef Talk, this page). Stir in the ice water—the brine must be very cold.

2. Meanwhile, one at a time, place a pork chop between two sheets of plastic wrap. Pound the chop with the flat side of a meat pounder until it is about ⅓ inch thick. Put the pork in a 1-gallon zippered plastic bag and pour in the brine. Seal the bag tightly, place in a bowl, and refrigerate for at least 1 hour or up to 2 hours, no longer.

CHEF TALK

Brining

Brining is a popular technique for adding moisture to meat and poultry, but there is one detail that is often omitted: The brine must be ice-cold to work well. The problem is, this brine is boiled to infuse the liquid with orange flavor. You can let the base cool naturally by itself, but that takes at least 30 minutes. To speed the cooling, place the bowl with the salt mixture in a larger bowl of icy water, and let it stand until chilled, about 10 minutes.

---

3. Meanwhile, make the sauce: Heat the oil and garlic together in a medium saucepan over medium heat until the garlic is toasted to golden brown, about 2 minutes. Using a slotted spoon, remove and discard the garlic. Stir the hot pepper flakes into the oil. Stir in the tomatoes with their juices and the lemon zest. Bring to a boil. Reduce the heat to low and simmer, stirring occasionally, until slightly reduced, about 1 hour. During the last few minutes, stir in the basil, oregano, balsamic vinegar, and sugar. (The sauce can be cooled, covered, and refrigerated for up to 3 days. Reheat before serving.)

4. To coat the pork chops: Remove the pork from the marinade and pat it dry with paper towels. Spread the flour in a wide shallow bowl. Beat the eggs, salt, and pepper together in a second shallow bowl. Mix the Sicilian crumbs, panko, parsley, lemon zest, and hot pepper flakes in a third bowl. One at a time, coat the pork in the flour, shaking off the excess, then dip on both sides in the egg mixture and coat evenly with the panko mixture, patting it in gently to adhere. Transfer to a platter. Let the pork stand for about 10 minutes to set the coating.

5. Line a large baking sheet with paper towels. Pour enough oil into a very large skillet to come ¼ inch up the sides and heat over medium-high heat until shimmering. Add the pork to the oil and cook, adjusting the heat so the pork bubbles steadily in the oil without browning too quickly, until the underside is golden brown, about 3 minutes. Turn the pork over and brown the other side, about 3 minutes more. Transfer to the paper towels and drain briefly. Cut each pork chop crosswise into ½ inch strips. Transfer to a platter and serve immediately, with the tomato sauce on the side.

Baby Back Ribs

WITH
JÄGERMEISTER-BLACK CHERRY COLA GLAZE

MAKES
8
SERVINGS

To a city dweller without an outdoor grill, it can be a challenge to make succulent, fall-off-the-bone ribs in an oven. No problem here! In my recipe, the ribs are simmered in a deeply flavored brew that includes Jägermeister, the German liqueur that brings 56 herbs, spices, roots, and fruits to the braising liquid, then baked in the oven for 2 hours. Afterward, the liquid is boiled down into a decadent glaze for the baby backs.

RIBS

3 racks pork baby back ribs (about 9 pounds total), each rack cut in half vertically

2 tablespoons kosher salt

¼ cup sriracha

2 tablespoons freshly ground black pepper, preferably smoked black pepper

2 tablespoons pure ground ancho chile

2 tablespoons smoked paprika

2 tablespoons onion powder

JÄGERMEISTER BBQ SAUCE

3 (12-ounce) bottles (3 cups) store-bought spicy barbecue sauce, such as Rattler BBQ Sauce

½ cup fresh orange juice

½ cup Jägermeister (see Note, page 152)

1 navel orange, cut into thin rounds

1 medium red onion, cut into thin rounds

12 large sprigs fresh mint

2 (12-ounce) cans black cherry cola (not diet)

1. To prepare the ribs: Season the ribs all over with the salt. Place on an 18-by-13-inch half-sheet pan and let them stand at room temperature for 15 to 30 minutes.

2. Brush the ribs with sriracha on both sides. Stir the black pepper, ground ancho, paprika, and onion powder together in a small bowl. Spread the rub on top of the sriracha over both sides of the racks.

3. Position the broiler rack about 6 inches from the heat source and preheat the broiler on high. Arrange the ribs on a broiler pan. Broil, turning once or twice, until the ribs are browned, about 10 minutes. (Or prepare an outdoor grill for direct cooking over medium heat. Add the ribs to the cooking grate and cover the grill. Cook the ribs until lightly browned, about 5 minutes per side. If the dripping fat causes flare-ups, move the ribs to a part of the grill that isn't directly over the heat.)

4. Position a rack in the lower third of the oven and preheat the oven to 300°F. Transfer the ribs to a large, deep flameproof roasting pan, about 14 by 10 by 3 inches, arranging them in a single layer and overlapping as needed.

5. For the sauce: Whisk the barbecue sauce, orange juice, and Jägermeister together in a large bowl. Pour the mixture over the ribs. Scatter the orange rounds, red onion, and mint on top. Pour in the soda. Bring the mixture to a boil on the stove over medium heat. Tightly cover the pan with aluminum foil.

➤➤

6. Bake in the oven until the ribs are very tender and the meat is pulling away from the bone, about 2 hours. Transfer the ribs to a baking sheet. (The ribs can be cooled, covered with aluminum foil, and refrigerated for up to 1 day.)

7. Meanwhile, let the sauce in the roasting pan stand for about 5 minutes, then skim any fat from the surface. Bring the sauce in the pan to a boil over high heat. Reduce to medium heat and simmer, stirring occasionally, until the sauce thickens and reduces to about 4 cups of glaze, about 10 minutes. Strain the glaze through a wire sieve into a medium bowl. (The glaze can be cooled, covered, and refrigerated for up to 1 day.)

8. When ready to serve, position the broiler rack about 6 inches from the heat source and preheat the broiler on high. Arrange the ribs on the broiler pan and broil, turning once, until lightly browned and sizzling, about 3 minutes per side. Brush the tops with some of the glaze and broil until it is bubbling, about 3 minutes. Turn the ribs over, brush with more glaze, and broil until the other side is bubbling, about 3 minutes more. (Or brown and glaze on an outdoor grill over medium direct heat.) Transfer the ribs to a chopping board and let stand for 3 minutes. Chop between the bones to cut the slab into individual ribs. Serve hot.

Note: You can substitute bourbon for the Jägermeister, but I prefer the latter.

12

TACOS

4 SERVINGS

BRAISED PORK BELLY

1½ pounds pork belly, in one piece

3 tablespoons sriracha

1 teaspoon pure ground ancho chile

1 teaspoon smoked paprika

1 teaspoon celery salt

1 teaspoon garlic powder

1 teaspoon freshly ground black pepper

½ teaspoon mustard powder

½ teaspoon kosher salt

¼ cup packed fresh cilantro leaves

2 bay leaves

1 quart reduced-sodium chicken broth

1 cup lager beer

TOMATO-GUAJILLO SAUCE

1 cup Guajillo Sauce (page 103)

2 drained sun-dried tomato halves

1 tablespoon fresh lime juice

½ teaspoon sugar

Pinch of cayenne pepper

1 sprig fresh thyme, leaves only

CHARRED-LIME VINAIGRETTE

2 large limes

2 tablespoons extra-virgin olive oil

2 teaspoons honey

Kosher salt and freshly ground black pepper

AVOCADO CREMA

2 Hass avocados, peeled, pitted, and chopped

2 tablespoons fresh lime juice

———

12 (6-inch) soft taco flour tortillas

2 cups packed cilantro leaves

152 SHARE

PORK BELLY
BLT Tacos *with*
CHARRED-LIME VINAIGRETTE

Here is my spicy taco take on a BLT, without being super-literal about it. After all, when pork belly is smoked, it becomes bacon. You do have to start a day ahead with this recipe, as the pork is cured, simmered, and chilled before a final crisping, and each step builds up the flavor. The other components include a cilantro salad (tossed with a vinaigrette spiked with charred lime), tangy pureed avocado, and a spicy tomato sauce.

1. To braise the pork belly: Using a sharp knife, score the pork belly skin in a crosshatch pattern. Place the pork in a shallow glass or ceramic baking dish. Mix the sriracha, ground ancho, paprika, celery salt, garlic powder, pepper, mustard, and salt together in a small bowl. Smear a thick layer of the paste all over the pork. Sprinkle the cilantro and bay leaves on the pork. Cover with plastic wrap and refrigerate for at least 4 or up to 24 hours.

2. Position a rack in the center of the oven and preheat the oven to 300°F. Transfer the coated pork belly to a Dutch oven. Pour in the broth and beer; if needed, add enough water to barely cover the pork. Bring to a boil over high heat. Cover tightly and bake, adding more water to the pot to keep the pork covered if needed, until the pork is very tender, 2½ to 3 hours. Remove from the oven, uncover, and let the pork cool in the liquid. Discard the cooking liquid and wrap the pork tightly in plastic wrap. Refrigerate for at least 4 hours or up to 24 hours. (The pork is easiest to cut if it is chilled.)

3. To make the sauce: Puree all the ingredients together in a blender. Transfer to a serving bowl. (The sauce can be covered and refrigerated for up to 2 days.)

4. To make the vinaigrette: Position a broiler rack about 6 inches from the source of heat and preheat the broiler on high. Using a thin-bladed sharp knife, trim the top and bottom from the limes. One at a time, stand a lime on end and cut away the peel where it meets the flesh. Broil the peeled limes, turning occasionally, until the flesh is charred in spots, about 8 minutes. Let the limes cool. Chop and press the limes in a wire sieve over a bowl to extract the juice. Whisk 2 tablespoons charred lime juice with the olive oil and honey; discard the remaining juice. Season to taste with salt and pepper. (The vinaigrette can be stored at room temperature for up to 4 hours.)

5. To make the crema: Beat the avocados and lime juice together in a small bowl with a handheld electric mixer until smooth. Transfer to a small bowl and cover with plastic wrap pressed directly on the crema surface. (The crema can be refrigerated in the bowl for up to 4 hours.)

6. For the tortillas: Position a rack in the center of the oven and preheat the oven to 350°F. Have a napkin lined–basket near the stove to hold the tortillas.

7. Meanwhile, cut the chilled pork belly crosswise into ⅓-inch slices, keeping the skin, but discarding the bones. Heat two large skillets over high heat. Add the pork slices and cook, turning occasionally, until browned and crispy, about 5 minutes.

8. Bake the tortillas directly on the oven rungs until hot, about 5 minutes. Transfer to the basket and wrap in the napkin to keep warm. Toss the cilantro leaves and vinaigrette together in a medium bowl.

9. Serve the pork belly slices, avocado crema, tomato-guajillo sauce, and cilantro salad with the tortillas. Allow each guest to make their own tacos from the ingredients.

CAJUN BACON
RISOTTO

Risotto is the perfect dish for sharing because your guests can take part in the experience while you are cooking it. My kitchen is part of my living space, so guests hang out while I stir risotto to perfect doneness. (Stirring is important, as it coaxes the starch from the rice to achieve ideal creaminess.) The intensity of the bacon flavor in this risotto is off the charts. If you really want to go all out, top your risotto with poached lobster tails or sautéed shrimp.

MAKES

4 *to* **6**

SERVINGS

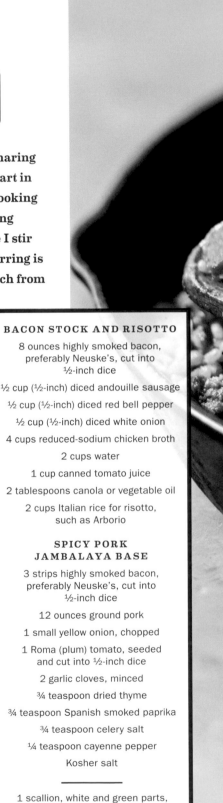

BACON STOCK AND RISOTTO

8 ounces highly smoked bacon, preferably Neuske's, cut into ½-inch dice

½ cup (½-inch) diced andouille sausage

½ cup (½-inch) diced red bell pepper

½ cup (½-inch) diced white onion

4 cups reduced-sodium chicken broth

2 cups water

1 cup canned tomato juice

2 tablespoons canola or vegetable oil

2 cups Italian rice for risotto, such as Arborio

SPICY PORK JAMBALAYA BASE

3 strips highly smoked bacon, preferably Neuske's, cut into ½-inch dice

12 ounces ground pork

1 small yellow onion, chopped

1 Roma (plum) tomato, seeded and cut into ½-inch dice

2 garlic cloves, minced

¾ teaspoon dried thyme

¾ teaspoon Spanish smoked paprika

¾ teaspoon celery salt

¼ teaspoon cayenne pepper

Kosher salt

———

1 scallion, white and green parts, thinly sliced, for garnish (optional)

1. To make the bacon stock: Cook the bacon in a large saucepan over medium-high heat, stirring occasionally, until it renders some of its fat and is beginning to brown, 6 to 8 minutes. Stir in the andouille, bell pepper, and onion and cook, stirring occasionally, until the onion is translucent, about 5 minutes. Add the broth, water, and tomato juice and bring to a boil over high heat. Reduce the heat to medium-low and simmer, uncovered, until the mixture is full flavored, about 1 hour. *Do not strain the stock.* Keep the stock warm over very low heat. (Or the stock can be cooled, covered, and refrigerated for 1 day. Do not remove the bacon fat on the surface of the stock. Reheat the stock in the saucepan over medium heat until simmering, and then keep warm over very low heat.)

2. To make the risotto: Heat the oil in a large, wide saucepan over medium heat. Add the rice and cook, stirring occasionally, until it feels heavier in the spoon, about 3 minutes. Do not brown the rice. About 1 cup at a time, stir in the hot bacon stock and let it come to a boil. Reduce the heat to medium-low and simmer, stirring almost constantly, until the rice has absorbed almost all of the liquid, about 2 minutes. Continue stirring in the remaining stock, 1 cup at a time, until the rice is al dente, about 20 minutes total. Do not overcook the rice. If you run out of stock, use hot water. (If you have any leftover stock, cool, cover, and refrigerate for up to 8 hours. Reheat to steaming before using.)

3. To make the base: Cook the bacon in a large, wide saucepan over medium heat, stirring occasionally, until it has rendered some of its fat and is beginning to brown, about 5 minutes. Add the ground pork. Cook, stirring occasionally and breaking up the pork with the spoon, until it begins to brown, about 5 minutes. Stir in the onion, tomato, and garlic and cook, stirring occasionally, until the onion is translucent, about 5 minutes. (The base can be cooled, covered, and refrigerated for up to 8 hours. Reheat in the saucepan over medium heat.)

4. Stir the thyme, paprika, celery salt, cayenne, and ½ teaspoon salt into the base. Add the risotto and hot stock (or 1 cup hot water). Cook, stirring often, adding more hot water as needed, until the risotto is hot and has a somewhat loose, spoonable consistency, about 3 minutes. Season to taste with salt. Transfer to individual serving bowls, sprinkle with the scallion if using, and serve immediately.

GRILLED CHEDDAR
AND JALAPEÑO BACON
SANDWICHES

MAKES

4 to 6

SERVINGS

When is a grilled cheese sandwich more than just a grilled cheese sandwich? When it is made with cilantro Cheddar, tempura-coated tomatillos, and chile-cured bacon. Keep the simple bacon-curing technique in mind whenever you want to amp up your breakfast bacon with some chile heat. It's especially good for brunch and lunch.

JALAPEÑO BACON

6 slices high-quality bacon, such as Hormel Black Label

1 tablespoon pure ground ancho chile

½ jalapeño, seeded and minced

LEMON AIOLI

⅓ cup mayonnaise

1 small garlic clove, crushed through a press

Finely grated zest of ½ lemon

1 teaspoon fresh lemon juice

CILANTRO CHEDDAR

2 cups (8 ounces) shredded sharp Cheddar cheese

¼ cup finely chopped fresh cilantro

TEMPURA TOMATILLOS

Vegetable oil, for deep-frying

½ cup unbleached all-purpose flour

½ cup cornstarch

Pinch of kosher salt

⅔ cup chilled club soda or seltzer

1 chilled large egg, beaten

3 medium tomatillos, husked, rinsed, and cut into 12 (¼-inch) slices

---

8 slices wide sourdough bread, cut from a batard

⅓ cup drained Pickled Jalapeños (see page 157) or store-bought sliced jalapeños for nachos

1. To cure and bake the jalapeño bacon: Sprinkle the bacon on both sides with the ground ancho and jalapeño. Transfer to a 1-gallon plastic bag, seal, and refrigerate for at least 1 hour or up to 24 hours.

2. Position a rack in the center of the oven and preheat the oven to 375°F. Arrange the bacon and any clinging seasoning on an 18-by-13-inch half-sheet pan. Bake until the bacon is crisp and browned, about 20 minutes. Transfer the bacon to paper towels to drain and cool. Cut the bacon slices in half crosswise.

3. To make the aioli: Whisk together all the ingredients in a small bowl to combine. (The aioli can be covered and refrigerated for up to 1 day.)

4. To prepare the cilantro Cheddar: Mix the cheese and cilantro together in a medium bowl.

5. To make the tempura tomatillos: Pour enough oil to come halfway up the sides of a large saucepan and heat to 350°F on a deep-frying thermometer over high heat. Line a baking sheet with a wire cake rack and place it near the stove.

6. Whisk the flour, cornstarch, and salt together in a medium bowl. Add the club soda and egg and whisk gently just until the batter is combined, but not entirely smooth. In batches without crowding, dip the tomatillo slices in the batter, letting the excess batter drip back into the bowl. Add to the oil and fry until golden brown, turning once, about 2 minutes. Using a wire spider or slotted spoon, transfer to the wire rack to drain.

7. Position the broiler rack about 8 inches from the source of heat and preheat the broiler on high. Line an 18-by-13-inch half-sheet pan with aluminum foil (this helps clean up any melted cheese). Arrange the bread slices on the baking sheet. Toast the bread slices on one side under the broiler, about 1 minute. Remove from the broiler.

8. Turn the bread over and spread the untoasted sides with the aioli. Divide the cilantro Cheddar evenly over the bread. Return to the broiler and cook until the cheese melts, about 1 minute. Remove from the broiler.

9. Divide the tomatillo slices, pickled jalapeños, and bacon equally over 4 of the bread slices. Top with the remaining 4 bread slices, cheese side down. Using a serrated knife, cut each sandwich diagonally into halves or quarters. Transfer to a platter and serve immediately.

PICKLED JALAPEÑOS

Makes about 1 cup

I like to have a jar of these pickled chiles in the fridge to spice up sandwiches, tacos, chilaquiles... just about anything that could use a spark of spice. The flavor is much better than the bottled nacho slices, which I suppose you could use in a pinch.

1 cup unseasoned rice vinegar

⅓ cup sugar

1 tablespoon minced peeled fresh ginger

1 teaspoon kosher salt

¼ teaspoon hot red pepper flakes

4 jalapeños, cut crosswise into ⅛-inch rounds, seeds included

1. Bring the vinegar, sugar, ginger, salt, and hot pepper flakes to a boil in a small nonreactive saucepan over high heat, stirring to dissolve the sugar.

2. Put the jalapeño rounds in a 1-pint canning jar or covered container. Pour in the vinegar solution to cover. Let cool. Cover the jar and refrigerate for at least 2 days before using. (The jalapeños can be refrigerated for up to 2 months.)

Chouriço and Pepper
SLOPPY JOES

MAKES

12

SLIDERS

4 TO 6
SERVINGS

These hearty sandwiches are my mom Mary Lou's specialty, and they are always waiting for me when I come home for a visit. They feature the spicy Portuguese sausage, chouriço, but Spanish chorizo will do. We like to serve a big bowl of the filling with rolls on the side so each person can make an overstuffed sandwich according to his or her own appetite. If you can find Portuguese rolls (which are famously soft with a thin, but crisp, crust), so much the better, although you'll have to cut them up if you plan to share.

3 tablespoons olive oil

8 ounces Portuguese chouriço or Spanish chorizo links, cut into ½-inch dice

1 large yellow onion, sliced into thin half-moons

1 large green bell pepper, seeded and cut into ½-inch strips

1 pound ground round beef
2½ cups Marinara Sauce (page 142 or see Note), made without fresh basil and parsley

1 cup water

1 teaspoon dried basil

3 tablespoons finely chopped fresh flat-leaf parsley

Kosher salt and freshly ground black pepper

12 potato slider rolls, split

1. Heat 2 tablespoons of the oil in a Dutch oven over medium heat. Add the chouriço and cook, stirring occasionally, until browned, about 5 minutes. Using a slotted spoon, transfer the sausage to paper towels, leaving the oil in the pot. Add the onion and bell pepper to the pot and cook, stirring occasionally, until softened, about 4 minutes.

2. Meanwhile, heat the remaining 1 tablespoon oil in a large skillet over medium-high heat. Add the beef and cook, stirring occasionally and breaking up the meat with the side of the spoon, until browned, about 8 minutes. Drain off the excess oil.

3. Add the chouriço and the beef to the Dutch oven, along with the marinara sauce, water and basil, and stir well. Bring to a simmer and reduce the heat to low. Simmer, uncovered, until the sauce has thickened and the vegetables are tender, about 45 minutes. During the last few minutes, stir in the parsley. Season to taste with salt and pepper.

4. Divide the meat mixture among the rolls and serve immediately with plenty of napkins.

Note: Mom makes this with one 24- to 26-ounce jar store-bought marinara sauce, and you can too.

LAMB

1 pound ground lamb (see Note)

½ cup soft bread crumbs, made from slightly stale crusty bread

1 large egg, beaten

⅓ cup minced red onion

1½ tablespoons finely chopped fresh cilantro

1½ tablespoons finely chopped fresh mint

1 garlic clove, shredded on a Microplane zester

1½ teaspoons turmeric powder

1½ teaspoons ground allspice

1½ teaspoons ground cumin

1 teaspoon kosher salt

½ teaspoon chili powder

½ teaspoon ground cinnamon

¼ teaspoon finely ground black pepper

TZATZIKI

1 large standard cucumber, peeled, sliced lengthwise, and seeds scooped out

Kosher salt

½ cup plain Greek yogurt

2 tablespoons finely chopped fresh mint

2 tablespoons fresh lime juice

1 garlic clove, shredded on a Microplane zester

Freshly ground black pepper

LIME-HARISSA AIOLI

½ cup mayonnaise

1 teaspoon harissa paste

½ teaspoon sriracha

1 garlic clove, shredded on a Microplane zester

—————

6 burrito-sized flour tortillas

Chopped fresh cilantro, for serving

4 lime wedges, for serving

—————

Special Equipment: 3½-inch round biscuit cutter; 4 to 6 long bamboo skewers, for serving

Lamb Souvlaki
with TZATZIKI AND LIME-HARISSA AIOLI

MAKES
12
SOUVLAKI
4 TO 6 SERVINGS

People associate souvlaki with street food, which is why it's so much fun to make them at home and really surprise your guests with beautiful mini kebabs. Souvlaki is often made with chunks of lamb, but you must try my ground lamb version with aromatic spices running through every bite. If you have an outdoor grill, cook the lamb over direct medium-high heat (450°F) for about 8 minutes for medium-rare.

1. To prepare the lamb: Combine all of the ingredients with your hands in a large bowl. Shape into 12 sausage shapes, each about 3 inches long and 1½ inches wide. Transfer to a platter, cover, and refrigerate for at least 30 minutes or up to 8 hours.

2. To make the tzatziki: Shred the cucumber on the large holes of a box grater. Toss the cucumber with ½ teaspoon salt in a wire sieve and let drain for 30 minutes to 1 hour. Press to remove as much liquid as possible from the mixture. Transfer to a medium bowl and mix in the yogurt, mint, lime juice, and garlic. Season to taste with salt and pepper. Cover and refrigerate for at least 1 hour or up to 1 day.

3. To make the aioli: Whisk all the ingredients together in a small bowl. Cover and refrigerate for at least 1 hour or up to 1 day.

4. Using a 3½-inch round cookie cutter, cut 12 rounds from the tortillas, discarding the trimmings. Cover the rounds with plastic wrap and set them aside.

5. Position a rack in the center of the oven and preheat the oven to 300°F.

6. Heat a large skillet over medium-high heat. Add the lamb oblongs and cook, turning occasionally, until well browned, about 5 minutes for medium. (These don't need to be served rare.) Transfer to paper towels and drain briefly.

7. Place the tortilla rounds directly on the oven racks and bake until heated but not crisp, about 1½ minutes. Remove from the oven.

8. Spread about 1 teaspoon of the harissa aioli onto each tortilla. Add 1 lamb oblong and fold the tortilla to enclose the lamb. Using a bamboo skewer, spear 2 to 3 souvlakis through their centers to hold them together and place on a platter. Top each with about 2 teaspoons of the tzatziki and sprinkle with the cilantro. Serve immediately with lime wedges.

Note: *If your butcher doesn't carry ground lamb as a matter of course, ask to have boned lamb shoulder freshly ground for you. Do not use leg of lamb, as it is too lean.*

PASTA

Every cuisine has some kind of noodle culture, and this chapter has international inspirations—but always with my unique twists. For example, my rich and creamy carbonara (page 164) replaces traditional guanciale, which can be hard to find, with crispy yet tender bits of braised pork belly. I'll bet that my Bolognese sauce (page 170), with its underlying warmth from Moroccan spices, is unlike any red sauce that you've had before. And I love my fully loaded mac 'n' cheese that's bursting with chorizo and roasted peppers (page 169). Pasta is another instance where sourcing the best pays off—buy imported Italian pasta over everyday domestic brands—or else go for the gold with my homemade manicotti (page 184).

Pork Belly
CARBONARA

—

ORECCHIETTE
with **Sausage,
Leeks, Mushrooms,
and Red Peppers**

—

Mac 'n' Cheese
with CHORIZO *and*
POBLANOS

—

PASTA WITH
Spicy Veal
and
Lamb Bolognese

—

RIGATONI
with *MERGUEZ,
RICOTTA SALATA,
and BROWN BUTTER*

—

Asian Noodles
with **Shrimp,
Miso Butter,** *and*
Spicy Peanuts

PASTA with
**Mushroom Ragout,
Walnuts,**
and **Pecorino**

—

CREAMY
ORZO
with Pancetta
and Vegetables

—

SPAGHETTI
CAPRESE
with **Tomatoes,
Mozzarella, and
Spinach**

—

Spaghettini
with **ZUCCHINI** and
PARSLEY PESTO

—

RICOTTA
and
BASIL MANICOTTI

PORK BELLY
Carbonara

MAKES

4 *to* **6**

SERVINGS

The typical carbonara is made with guanciale, Italian cured pork jowl. I developed my carbonara with braised pork belly instead, infusing the meat with wine and vegetables along the way. Start the pork early in the day (or even the day before) because it must be chilled to slice properly. Finding nuggets of the rich pork belly in the pasta really drives home the deep flavors in this standout dish.

BRAISED PORK BELLY

1 pound pork belly, in
a single slab

½ small yellow onion,
coarsely chopped

1 small carrot, coarsely
chopped

½ small celery rib, coarsely
chopped

2 garlic cloves, smashed under
a knife and peeled

1 teaspoon canola or vegetable oil

1¼ teaspoons very coarse sea salt
(not kosher salt, see Note, page 166)

1½ cups reduced-sodium
chicken broth

1 cup dry white wine,
such as Pinot Grigio

4 sprigs fresh thyme

---

1 pound dried fettuccine

1 cup heavy cream

3 large egg yolks

⅔ cup freshly grated
Pecorino Romano cheese,
plus more for serving

Kosher salt and freshly grated
black pepper

---

1. To braise the pork belly: Position a rack in the center of the oven and preheat the oven to 250°F.

2. Lightly score the pork skin in a wide crisscross pattern with a large knife. Stand the pork belly, skin side up, in a small Dutch oven and surround it with the onion, carrot, celery, and garlic. Rub the skin with the oil, and sprinkle with the sea salt. Pour the broth and wine around (not over) the pork and scatter the thyme into the liquid. Bring to a simmer over high heat.

3. Cover and transfer the Dutch oven to the oven. Bake for 1½ hours. Uncover and increase the heat to 350°F. Continue baking until the skin is crispy and browned and the pork is very tender when pierced with a meat fork, about 1½ hours longer. Increase the oven temperature to 450°F and roast until the skin crisps, 25 to 30 minutes. Transfer the pork belly to a plate and let cool. Discard the solids in the pot. Wrap in aluminum foil and refrigerate until chilled and firm, at least 3 hours or up to 1 day.

4. Bring a large pot of salted water to a boil over high heat.

While the water is coming to a boil, slice and crisp the pork belly: Cut four to six 1-inch-thick slices from the pork belly. Cut the remaining pork into strips about ½ inch wide and ½ inch thick. Each strip should have layers of skin, fat, and meat. Heat a very large skillet over medium-high heat. Add the pork belly strips and cook, flipping them occasionally, until sizzling and crispy, about 5 minutes. Using a slotted spoon, transfer the

➤

crispy pork to paper towels to drain; discard the fat in the skillet. Add the pork chunks to the skillet and cook, turning halfway through cooking, until the slices are sizzling and crispy, about 5 minutes. Transfer to the paper towels with the strips.

5. Add the fettuccine to the water and cook according to the package directions until it is al dente. Drain in a colander. Return to the cooking pot. Reduce the heat to very low.

6. Whisk the cream, yolks, and cheese together in a small bowl. Pour it over the pasta and cook, tossing with two large spoons, until the sauce is lightly thickened but is not simmering, about 1 minute. Remove from the heat. Add the pork strips and quickly toss again. Season with kosher salt and pepper to taste. Immediately transfer to a deep serving bowl. Sprinkle with more black pepper and serve with more Romano cheese on the side. Serve the pasta in individual bowls, adding a pork chunk to each portion.

Note: *The sea salt needed for the pork belly skin is the type used to fill salt grinders. A common supermarket brand is La Baleine* sel de mer gros. *Be sure to use the coarse, and not fine, crystals. You can also use other very coarse salt, such as pink Himalayan.*

ORECCHIETTE
with SAUSAGE, LEEKS, MUSHROOMS, AND RED PEPPERS

MAKES

4 *to* 6

SERVINGS

This comforting, Sunday-supper kind of dish is not your nonna's pasta. The surprising combination of ginger juice, basil, sambal oelek, and soy sauce creates an intense umami flavor that will have your guests trying to guess the ingredients at the dinner table. Ear-shaped orecchiette is especially good because its hollows catch the luscious sauce, but you could also use shell-shaped pasta.

---

2 large leeks, white and pale green parts, cut crosswise into thin rounds

4 tablespoons (½ stick) unsalted butter, at room temperature

Kosher salt and freshly ground black pepper

1 garlic clove, minced

2 tablespoons extra-virgin olive oil

1 medium red bell pepper, seeded and cut into ½-inch dice

10 ounces cremini mushrooms, thinly sliced

12 ounces sweet Italian chicken or turkey sausage, casings removed

2 tablespoons soy sauce

1 tablespoon fresh ginger juice (see page 58)

1½ cups reduced-sodium chicken broth

1 cup heavy cream

½ teaspoon sambal oelek or sriracha

¼ cup finely chopped fresh basil (or use 2 tablespoons each basil and finely chopped fresh cilantro), plus more for serving

1 pound orecchiette, or shell- or tube-shaped pasta

---

1. Wash the leeks well in a bowl of cold water, separating the rounds into rings. Lift the rings out of the water, leaving the grit in the bowl. You should have about 2 cups leeks.

2. Heat 1 tablespoon of the butter in a medium skillet over medium heat. Add the leeks, season with ¼ teaspoon salt and ⅛ teaspoon pepper, and cover tightly. Cook, stirring occasionally, until the leeks soften, about 5 minutes. Uncover and cook, stirring occasionally, until they are light brown and very tender, about 20 minutes. During the last few minutes, stir in the garlic. Transfer the leeks to a large serving bowl.

3. Meanwhile, in large skillet, heat the oil over medium-high heat. Add the red bell pepper and cook, stirring occasionally, until softened, about 3 minutes. Add the mushrooms and cook, stirring occasionally, until the mushrooms give off their juices and are beginning to brown, about 8 minutes. Transfer the vegetables to the bowl.

4. Add the sausage to the skillet and cook, stirring occasionally and breaking it up with the side of a spoon, until browned, about 7 minutes. Return the vegetable mixture and leeks to the skillet. Add the soy sauce and ginger juice and stir until the soy sauce evaporates, about 30 seconds. Add the broth and bring to a boil over high heat, stirring to scrape up the browned bits. Cook until the broth has reduced by half, about 10 minutes. Add the cream and sambal oelek, bring to a boil, and cook until the sauce has reduced by half and coats a wooden spoon, 7 to 10 minutes more. During the last few minutes, stir in the basil. Remove the sauce from the heat.

5. Meanwhile, bring a large pot of salted water to a boil over high heat. Add the orecchiette and cook according to the package directions until al dente. Drain well. Return the pasta to the cooking pot.

6. Add the sauce and remaining 3 tablespoons butter to the pasta and toss well, letting the butter melt into the sauce. Season to taste with salt and pepper. Transfer to a serving bowl and sprinkle with more basil. Serve immediately.

MAC 'N' CHEESE
with CHORIZO AND POBLANOS

MAKES
6
SERVINGS

HERBED BREAD CRUMBS

1 cup panko
(Japanese bread crumbs)

2 tablespoons unsalted
butter, melted

¼ cup (1 ounce) shredded
Gruyère cheese

2 tablespoons finely chopped
mixed fresh herbs, such as flat-leaf
parsley, or 1 tablespoon each parsley
and fresh chives

Kosher salt and freshly ground
black pepper

CHEESE SAUCE

1 (12-ounce) can evaporated milk
(see Chef Talk, below)

¼ cup whole milk

¼ cup heavy cream

2 cups (8 ounces) shredded
sharp Cheddar cheese

1 cup (4 ounces) shredded
Gruyère cheese

1 cup (4 ounces) crumbled
goat cheese

2 teaspoons sriracha

1 teaspoon dry mustard

Kosher salt and freshly ground
black pepper

———

1 tablespoon canola oil, plus
more for the baking dish

8 ounces smoked chorizo,
cut into ½-inch dice

1 pound radiatore or ziti pasta

2 poblano (fresh ancho) chiles,
roasted (see page 42), peeled,
seeded, and cut into ½-inch dice

2 large egg yolks

2 teaspoons finely chopped fresh
chives, for garnish (optional)

How do you make macaroni and cheese special? Try this one on for size. The spiciness of my Latin-inspired mac 'n' cheese may seem to make it an "adults only" version, but I have seen some adventurous kids eat it up, too. Mixing a few cheeses adds dimension to the sauce; if you have it, substitute 2 ounces of smoked goat cheese for 2 ounces of the unsmoked kind. Be sure to slightly undercook the pasta to al dente, as it will bake and soften further in the oven.

1. To make the herbed crumbs: Mix the panko and butter together in a small bowl, being sure that the panko is coated with the butter. Stir in the Gruyère and herbs. Season to taste with salt and pepper. Set the crumbs aside.

2. To make the cheese sauce: Bring the evaporated milk, whole milk, and cream to a boil in a large saucepan over medium heat, taking care that the mixture does not boil over. Remove from the heat. Gradually whisk in the Cheddar, Gruyère, and goat cheese and mix until the cheeses are melted. Whisk in the sriracha and mustard. Season to taste with the salt and pepper. Set the cheese sauce aside.

3. Heat the oil in a large skillet over medium heat. Add the chorizo and cook, stirring occasionally, until browned and crispy, about 5 minutes. Using a slotted spoon, transfer the chorizo to paper towels to drain.

4. Position a rack in the center of the oven and preheat the oven to 400°F. Lightly oil a large baking dish or cast iron skillet.

5. Bring a large pot of salted water to a boil over high heat. Add the radiatore and cook according to the package directions until almost al dente. Drain well. Return the pasta to the cooking pot and stir in the cheese sauce, chorizo, and poblanos. Stir in the yolks, mixing well.

6. Spread the mixture in the oiled dish and sprinkle the herbed crumbs on top. Bake until the crumbs are golden brown and the sauce is bubbling around the edges, about 20 minutes. Sprinkle with the chives, if using, and serve hot.

CHEF TALK

Evaporated Milk

Why do I use evaporated milk in this macaroni and cheese? Because much of the water has been removed, it gives a richer flavor than fresh milk, although you can use the latter if you don't happen to have canned on hand. In that case, I'd use 1½ cups fresh whole milk and ½ cup heavy cream.

PASTA *with*
Spicy Veal and Lamb Bolognese

MAKES

6

SERVINGS

PLUS ENOUGH
LEFTOVER SAUCE FOR
ANOTHER MEAL

Bolognese sauce is often made with veal and beef, but to shake things up a little I substitute lamb and Moroccan spices for the beef to make a particularly distinctive meat sauce. The Parmesan rind is a true secret ingredient, as it imparts an elusive flavor without being seen in the finished sauce. This recipe purposely makes a large batch, so you'll have enough sauce for another meal.

SPICY BOLOGNESE SAUCE

2 tablespoons unsalted butter

⅓ cup finely diced pancetta,
about 1½ ounces

2 slices bacon, finely diced,
or ⅓ cup additional pancetta

1 medium yellow onion, finely chopped

4 garlic cloves, minced

1½ pounds ground veal

1 pound ground lamb (see Note)

1 tablespoon harissa paste

½ cup hearty red wine, such as Shiraz

½ cup reduced-sodium chicken broth

1 (28-ounce) can whole plum tomatoes
in juice, coarsely chopped, with juices

3 tablespoons tomato paste

3 tablespoons coarsely
chopped seedless raisins

½ teaspoon hot red pepper flakes

Kosher salt and freshly ground
black pepper

1 (1½-ounce) chunk of
Parmigiano-Reggiano rind

2 teaspoons red wine vinegar

———

1 pound stubby pasta, such
as garganelli or ziti

1 cup whole-milk ricotta cheese,
preferably fresh, whisked well

Hot red pepper flakes, for serving

Aged balsamic vinegar or store-bought
balsamic glaze, for serving

Freshly grated Parmigiano-Reggiano
cheese, for serving

1. To make the Bolognese: Melt the butter in a Dutch oven over medium heat. Add the pancetta and bacon and cook, stirring occasionally, until the meats are lightly browned, about 5 minutes. Stir in the onion and garlic and cook, stirring occasionally, until the onion is translucent, about 4 minutes. Add the veal and lamb and increase the heat to high. Cook the mixture, uncovered, breaking up the meats with the side of a spoon, until they lose their raw look, 8 to 10 minutes. Tilt the pot to drain off all but about 2 tablespoons rendered fat.

2. Return to high heat and cook, without stirring, until the meat mixture forms a crust on the bottom of the pot, 3 to 5 minutes. Stir in the harissa and cook for 1 minute. Add the wine and broth and bring to a boil, scraping up the browned crust with a wooden spoon. Stir in the tomatoes and their juices, tomato paste, raisins, hot pepper flakes, 1½ teaspoons salt, and ½ teaspoon pepper. Bring to a boil. Reduce the heat to very low and submerge the Parmigiano rind in the sauce. Simmer, uncovered, stirring often, until the sauce is very thick and the liquids have reduced, about 1½ hours. Stir in the wine vinegar and season to taste with salt and pepper. Discard the rind. (The sauce can be cooled, covered, and refrigerated for up to 2 days. Reheat before serving.)

3. Bring a large pot of salted water to a boil over high heat. Add the pasta and cook according to the package directions until al dente. Drain well. Return the pasta to its cooking pot. Add half of the sauce (about 3½ cups) and mix well. (The remaining sauce can be frozen for up to 3 months.)

4. Transfer the pasta to a large serving bowl. Serve in individual bowls, topping each serving with a dollop of ricotta, a sprinkle of chili flakes, and a drizzle of balsamic vinegar, with the Parmigiano passed on the side.

Note: *If you wish, substitute the merguez sausage mixture on page 173 for the ground lamb and harissa.*

CHEF TALK

Parmigiano Rind

Italian cooks never throw away the rind from Parmigiano-Reggiano. It can be tossed into liquid dishes (such as spaghetti sauce, soup, and stew) to simmer and slowly release its flavor.

RIGATONI

with MERGUEZ, RICOTTA SALATA, AND BROWN BUTTER

MAKES

4 *to* 6

SERVINGS

Here it is—my favorite pasta dish. Ever. I learned to make it with *torchio*, an unusual funnel-shaped Venetian pasta, but any tube-shaped kind will do. The dish isn't saucy, so you can really taste the individual flavors, and the merguez, with its spicy harissa flavor, has an unexpected kick. Both parsley and mint provide fresh accents.

1 pound ziti or other
tube-shaped pasta

6 tablespoons (¾ stick)
unsalted butter

3 tablespoons extra-virgin olive oil,
plus more for serving

1 pound merguez sausage
(see Chef Talk, below),
casings removed

2 garlic cloves, minced

1 tablespoon tomato paste

1 tablespoon finely chopped
fresh flat-leaf parsley

Kosher salt and freshly ground
black pepper

¾ cup (3 ounces) shredded
ricotta salata cheese

½ cup Sicilian Bread Crumbs
(page 181) or pan-toasted
soft bread crumbs

3 tablespoons finely chopped
fresh mint

CHEF TALK

Merguez

Merguez is lamb sausage, boldly seasoned with harissa, the North African spice paste. Because it is pork-free, you'll often find merguez at halal and kosher butchers. As an easy substitute, mix 1 pound ground lamb, 1 to 2 tablespoons harissa (sold at specialty markets and online), 1 teaspoon kosher salt, and 2 garlic cloves, shredded on a Microplane zester.

1. Bring a large pot of salted water to a boil over high heat. Add the pasta and cook according to the package instructions until al dente. Drain well and rinse under cold running water.

2. Meanwhile, melt the butter in a small saucepan over medium heat. Continue cooking until the milk solids in the saucepan turn hazelnut brown, about 2 minutes. Immediately pour the melted butter into a small bowl.

3. Heat 1 tablespoon of the oil in a very large skillet over medium-high heat. Add the sausage and cook, occasionally stirring and breaking it up with the side of the spoon into bite-sized pieces, until lightly browned, about 8 minutes. Stir in the garlic and cook until it softens, about 1 minute. Stir in the tomato paste and parsley and mix well. Pour into a colander to drain the excess fat. Clean the skillet.

4. Heat the remaining 2 tablespoons oil in the skillet over medium-high heat. Add the pasta and cook, stirring occasionally, until it is lightly browned, about 2 minutes. Add the sausage mixture and stir well. Season to taste with salt and pepper.

5. Transfer the pasta mixture to a serving bowl. Add the browned butter and mix well. Top with the ricotta salata, bread crumbs, and mint. Drizzle with additional olive oil, toss, and serve immediately.

ASIAN NOODLES *with*
SHRIMP, MISO BUTTER, AND SPICY PEANUTS

MAKES

4

SERVINGS

These Chinese stir-fried noodles are dressed with butter and lemongrass paste, creating an unforgettable taste you'll never find in a takeout box. When buying the noodles, look for those with real eggs and not just yellow food coloring—you can substitute egg fettuccine, if necessary.

MISO BUTTER

6 tablespoons (¾ stick) unsalted butter, at room temperature

1½ tablespoons white (shiro) miso

1½ teaspoons Japanese soy sauce

LEMONGRASS PASTE

1 tablespoon chopped (pale bulb only) lemongrass

1 tablespoon chopped peeled fresh ginger

1 tablespoon chopped fresh cilantro stems (leaves reserved for serving)

2 garlic cloves, chopped

¼ teaspoon hot red pepper flakes

---

8 ounces dried Chinese egg noodles

2 tablespoons plus 2 teaspoons canola or vegetable oil

1 pound jumbo (21 to 25 count) shrimp, peeled and deveined

4 cups fresh bean sprouts

1 large red bell pepper, roasted (see page 42), seeded, and cut into ½-inch dice

2 scallions, white and green parts, thinly sliced

20 cilantro leaves, torn into small pieces

10 large Thai basil leaves, torn into small pieces

⅓ cup coarsely chopped sriracha-flavored peanuts

1. To make the miso butter: Mash the butter, miso, and soy sauce together in a small bowl.

2. To make the lemongrass paste: Pulse the lemongrass, ginger, cilantro stems, garlic, and hot pepper flakes together in a mini–food processor or electric spice grinder to make a coarse paste. Transfer to a ramekin or custard cup.

3. Bring a large pot of water to a boil over high heat. Add the noodles and cook according to the package directions until tender. Drain well and rinse under cold water. Drizzle the noodles with 2 teaspoons of the oil and toss well. (The noodles can be stored at room temperature for up to 2 hours.)

4. Heat a large wok or skillet over high heat until the wok is very hot. Drizzle the remaining 2 tablespoons oil down the sides of the wok (it will smoke). Add the shrimp, scattering them along the sides of the wok. Cook without stirring until the undersides turn opaque, about 1 minute. Add the lemongrass paste and stir, scraping the shrimp off the sides of the wok. Add the bean sprouts, roasted pepper, and scallions and stir-fry just until the shrimp turn almost completely opaque, about 1 minute. Add the noodles and stir-fry until they are hot, about 1 minute. Add the miso butter, cilantro, and Thai basil and toss until the butter melts and coats the noodle mixture, about 30 seconds.

5. Transfer the noodles to a large serving platter. Sprinkle with the peanuts and serve immediately.

Pasta
with Mushroom Ragout, Walnuts, and Pecorino

MAKES

4 *to* 6

SERVINGS

One of the best things about this pasta dish is its versatility. A mix of supermarket mushrooms (for example, cremini, oyster, and shiitake) can be just as good as foraged wild mushrooms like chanterelles and morels. To encourage the browning of the mushrooms, cook them in batches, because if they are crowded in the pan, they'll steam and give off too much liquid. For an entirely vegetarian dish, substitute Vegetable Stock (page 190) for the chicken broth. Don't forget to toast the walnuts!

6 tablespoons (¾ cup) unsalted butter

3 tablespoons finely chopped shallots

4 garlic cloves, minced

1½ pounds assorted mushrooms (such as shiitake caps, oyster, cremini, chanterelle, morels, and king, in any combination), sliced

Kosher salt and freshly ground black pepper

⅓ cup Madeira or dry Marsala

2 cups reduced-sodium chicken broth

1 cup heavy cream

2 tablespoons Japanese soy sauce

1½ teaspoons finely chopped fresh thyme

1 pound tube-shaped pasta, such as rigatoni or ziti

½ cup (2 ounces) freshly grated Pecorino Romano cheese, plus more for serving

½ cup coarsely chopped toasted walnuts (see Note)

2 tablespoons finely chopped fresh flat-leaf parsley, for serving

1. Melt 2 tablespoons of the butter in a very large, deep skillet over medium-high heat. Stir in half of the shallots and half of the garlic and cook just until they soften, about 1 minute. Stir in half of the mushrooms, season lightly with salt and pepper, and cook, stirring occasionally, until the mushrooms are browned and tender, about 8 minutes. Transfer the mushrooms to a bowl. Repeat with another 2 tablespoons butter and the remaining shallots, garlic, and mushrooms, seasoning with salt and pepper. Return the reserved mushrooms to the skillet.

2. Stir in the Madeira and cook until it reduces to a glaze, about 2 minutes. Stir in 1 cup of the broth and boil until it reduces to 2 tablespoons, about 5 minutes. Stir in the remaining 1 cup broth, the cream, soy sauce, and thyme and boil, stirring occasionally, until the liquid has thickened and reduced by half, about 10 minutes. Remove from the heat.

3. Meanwhile, bring a large pot of salted water to a boil over high heat. Add the pasta and cook according to the package directions until al dente. Drain in a colander. Return the pasta to its cooking pot.

4. Add the mushroom ragout, cheese, and remaining 2 tablespoons butter to the pasta and toss until the butter has melted. Season to taste with salt and pepper. Transfer to a serving bowl. Sprinkle with the walnuts and parsley and serve immediately, with more Pecorino passed on the side.

Note: To toast the walnuts, bake them on a rimmed baking sheet in a 350°F oven, stirring occasionally, until lightly browned and fragrant, 8 to 10 minutes. A toaster oven works, too.

CREAMY ORZO
with Pancetta and Vegetables

MAKES

4 *to* 6

SERVINGS

With nuggets of roasted butternut squash, this comforting dish is just the thing to make on a cool autumn evening. The creamy thyme sauce gives the rice-shaped pasta a rich, risotto-like consistency. I usually make this with guanciale (cured pork cheeks), but pancetta is an easy-to-find substitute.

ROASTED SQUASH

1 small butternut squash, about 1 pound, peeled, seeded, and cut into ¾-inch cubes

1 tablespoon extra-virgin olive oil

THYME CREAM

¾ cup heavy cream

6 sprigs fresh thyme

1 garlic clove, crushed under a knife and peeled

1 bay leaf, preferably fresh

---

8 ounces orzo pasta, about 1⅓ cups

1 tablespoon extra-virgin olive oil

2 bunches broccolini (see Note), stems trimmed, cut into 2-inch lengths

Kosher salt and freshly ground black pepper

3 ounces (¼-inch) diced pancetta

4 tablespoons (1 ounce) freshly grated Parmigiano-Reggiano cheese, plus more for serving

Grated zest of ½ lemon

½ teaspoon finely chopped fresh thyme

---

1. To roast the squash: Position a rack in the center of the oven and preheat the oven to 425°F. Toss the squash with the oil in a large bowl. Spread on an 18-by-13-inch half-sheet pan. Roast, stirring occasionally, until tender and lightly browned, about 30 minutes.

2. Meanwhile, to make the thyme cream: Bring the cream, thyme sprigs, garlic, and bay leaf to a simmer in a small saucepan over low heat. Remove from the heat and let steep for 10 minutes. Strain the mixture through a wire sieve into a small bowl, discarding the solids, and set the cream aside.

3. Bring a large saucepan of salted water to a boil over high heat. Add the orzo and cook according to the package directions until barely tender. Drain in a colander, rinse under cold running water, and drain again. Transfer to a bowl and toss with the oil.

4. Bring a medium saucepan of salted water to a boil over high heat. Add the broccolini and cook until barely tender, 4 to 5 minutes. Drain in the colander and rinse under cold running water. Pat dry and coarsely chop.

5. Cook the pancetta in a large saucepan over medium heat, stirring occasionally, until lightly browned, about 5 minutes. Add the thyme cream and bring to a simmer, stirring to scrape up any browned bits in the pan. Remove from the heat and stir in 2 tablespoons of the Parmigiano, the lemon zest, and the chopped thyme. Season to taste with salt and pepper. Reduce the heat to very low to keep warm.

6. Stir the butternut squash, orzo, and broccolini into the thyme cream and cook just until it is heated through, about 1 minute. Transfer the orzo mixture to a large, deep platter. Sprinkle with the remaining 2 tablespoons Parmigiano. Serve immediately, with extra Parmigiano passed at the table.

Note: Broccolini is really terrific in this dish, but if you wish, substitute 1 pound broccoli. Cut off the tops (save the stems for another use) and cut them into small florets, about the diameter of a dime. After cooking, coarsely chop the florets, cutting their stems into ½-inch dice.

SPAGHETTI CAPRESE

with TOMATOES, MOZZARELLA, AND SPINACH

MAKES

4 *to* 6

SERVINGS

The trattorias of Capri became known for their simple antipasto of sliced ripe tomatoes and fresh mozzarella with basil, and the combination became a classic. I especially like to use the concept with pasta, and perk it up with spinach and a bit of lemon and hot pepper. For the best flavor and appearance, use a combination of colorful heirloom tomatoes at their summertime peak. And be sure to use creamy fresh mozzarella, not the rubbery industrial kind.

¼ cup (½ stick) unsalted
butter, softened

4 tablespoons coarsely chopped
fresh basil

4 tablespoons freshly grated
Parmigiano-Reggiano cheese,
plus more for serving

1 garlic clove, shredded on
a Microplane zester

Kosher salt

1 pound spaghetti

2 tablespoons extra-virgin olive oil,
plus more for serving

1 pound ripe heirloom tomatoes,
seeded and coarsely chopped into
1-inch chunks

Finely grated zest of ½ lemon

¼ teaspoon hot red pepper flakes

8 ounces fresh leaf spinach,
stemmed, washed well,
and cut into ½-inch shreds

1 pound fresh mozzarella,
cut into ¾-inch dice

3 tablespoons Sicilian Bread Crumbs
(page 181, optional)

Balsamic glaze (page 34), or use
store-bought, for serving

1. Bring a large pot of salted water to a boil over high heat.

2. Meanwhile, mash the butter, 2 tablespoons of the basil, 2 tablespoons of the Parmigiano, and the garlic together in a small bowl. Season to taste with salt. Set the basil butter aside.

3. Add the spaghetti to the boiling water and cook according to the package instructions until al dente.

4. While the spaghetti is cooking, heat the oil in a large skillet over high heat. Add the tomatoes and cook, tossing occasionally in the skillet, until the skins shrink, 4 to 5 minutes. Remove from the heat and add the lemon zest and hot pepper flakes.

5. Drain the spaghetti and return to its cooking pot. Add the basil butter, tomato mixture, spinach, and mozzarella and toss until the spinach is wilted and the mozzarella is beginning to melt. Season to taste with salt. Transfer to a serving bowl and sprinkle with the bread crumbs, if using, and the remaining basil and Parmigiano. Drizzle with balsamic glaze and serve hot, with additional Parmigiano passed on the side.

Spaghettini *with* **Zucchini and Parsley Pesto**

MAKES

4 *to* 6

SERVINGS

This vibrant vegetarian pasta is definitive proof that you can skip the meat and not the flavor. As much as I like basil, the freshness of parsley and spinach in the pesto is unexpected and makes a terrific match for zucchini. Break into the fried egg on top and allow the rich, yellow yolk to add a decadent finish.

SICILIAN BREAD CRUMBS

1 garlic clove, finely chopped

3 cups cubed (1-inch) trimmed brioche, challah, or crusty Italian bread

2 tablespoons extra-virgin olive oil

2 tablespoons coarsely chopped fresh flat-leaf parsley

PARSLEY PESTO

1½ cups packed fresh flat-leaf parsley leaves

1 cup packed baby spinach

1 garlic clove, crushed under a knife and peeled

¼ cup pine nuts, toasted (see Note, page 183)

3 tablespoons freshly grated Parmigiano-Reggiano cheese

2 teaspoons fresh lemon juice

⅓ cup plus 1 tablespoon extra-virgin olive oil

Kosher salt and freshly ground black pepper

PASTA AND ZUCCHINI

1 pound spaghettini or thin spaghetti

2 tablespoons extra-virgin olive oil

1 garlic clove, finely chopped

1 pound zucchini, cut into julienne strips about 2 inches long and ¼ inch wide (use a mandoline, V-slicer, or large knife)

½ teaspoon hot red pepper flakes

1 tablespoon fresh lemon juice

EGGS

¼ cup extra-virgin olive oil

4 to 6 large eggs

Kosher salt and freshly ground black pepper

————————

½ cup freshly grated Parmigiano-Reggiano cheese, plus more for serving

Kosher salt and freshly ground black pepper

4 sprigs fresh flat-leaf parsley, for garnish (optional)

1. To make the bread crumbs: Position a rack in the center of the oven and preheat the oven to 350°F. With the machine running, drop the garlic through the tube of a food processor to mince the garlic. Add the bread cubes, oil, and parsley and pulse until the bread becomes coarse crumbs. Spread on an 18-by-13-inch half-sheet pan. Bake, stirring occasionally, until the crumbs are lightly toasted and smell garlicky, 7 to 10 minutes. Let cool. Makes 2 cups. Measure out 1 cup of the bread crumbs. (Reserve the remaining bread crumbs for another use; they can be frozen in an airtight container for up to 1 month.)

2. To make the pesto: Bring a medium saucepan of water to a boil over high heat. Add ¾ cup of the parsley and the spinach and cook just until the greens turn a darker shade of green, about 30 seconds. Drain in a wire sieve and rinse under cold running water to cool. Press the greens in the sieve to remove as much moisture as possible.

3. With the machine running, drop the garlic through the tube of a food processor to mince the garlic. Add 3 tablespoons of the bread crumbs, the reserved ¾ cup raw parsley, and the drained spinach mixture, pine nuts, Parmigiano, and lemon juice and pulse until finely chopped. With the machine running, gradually add the oil and process into a thick paste. Season the pesto to taste with
→

salt and pepper. (The pesto can be covered and stored at room temperature for up to 6 hours.)

4. To prepare the pasta: Bring a large pot of salted water to a boil over high heat. Add the pasta and cook according to the directions until al dente.

5. Meanwhile, to make the zucchini: Heat the oil and garlic together in a large skillet over medium-high heat until the garlic is fragrant but not browned, about 1 minute. Add the zucchini and hot pepper flakes and cook, stirring occasionally, until the zucchini is hot and barely wilted, about 2 minutes. Stir in the lemon juice. Set aside to keep warm.

6. Just before serving, cook the eggs: Heat the oil in a very large nonstick skillet over medium heat. (If making six servings, heat two medium to large skillets and increase the oil accordingly.) Crack the eggs into the oil and cover the skillet. Cook just until the egg whites are set, about 1½ minutes. The runny yolk becomes part of the sauce so it is very important to not overcook the eggs. Season the eggs to taste with salt and pepper. Set aside to keep warm.

7. Scoop out and reserve ½ cup of the pasta cooking water. Drain the pasta and return it to its cooking pot. Add ½ cup of the bread crumbs, the pesto, the zucchini mixture, and the Parmigiano and toss, adding enough of the reserved pasta water to loosen the pesto. Season to taste with salt and pepper.

8. Divide the pasta among 4 serving bowls. Top each with a sprinkle of the remaining bread crumbs, a fried egg, and a sprig of parsley, if desired. Serve immediately, with additional Parmigiano passed on the side.

Note: To toast pine nuts, heat a small skillet over medium heat. Add the pine nuts and cook, stirring occasionally, until toasted, about 3 minutes. Transfer the nuts to a plate and let cool completely.

RICOTTA
AND BASIL MANICOTTI

MAKES
16
MANICOTTI
6 TO 8
SERVINGS

Consider this special recipe for a holiday meal or when you need some hands-on cooking for a little kitchen therapy. Sure, you can buy pasta tubes for manicotti at the supermarket, but for a truly incredible dish, make delicate crepes to envelop the creamy ricotta filling. You can serve the Old-School Meatballs on page 142 with them, but they are delicious enough with just some marinara sauce.

MANICOTTI CREPES

1½ cups (210 grams) unbleached all-purpose flour

4 large eggs

½ cup whole milk

½ cup water

2 tablespoons unsalted butter, melted

½ teaspoon kosher salt

Vegetable oil, for cooking

RICOTTA FILLING

1 cup packed fresh basil leaves

2 tablespoons extra-virgin olive oil

2 cups whole-milk ricotta cheese, preferably fresh

1⅓ cups finely ground panko (processed in a food processor)

¼ cup (1 ounce) freshly grated Parmigiano-Reggiano cheese

1 large egg, beaten

2 tablespoons fresh lemon juice

1 teaspoon kosher salt

½ teaspoon hot red pepper flakes

———

Softened butter, for the dish

2 tablespoons unsalted butter, melted

Marinara Sauce (page 142), heated

Freshly grated Parmigiano-Reggiano cheese, for serving

1. To make the manicotti crepes: Whisk all of the ingredients except the oil together in a medium bowl. Cover and set aside for 30 minutes.

2. Select a nonstick skillet that measures 6 inches across the bottom and heat over medium-high heat. Oil the skillet with a folded paper towel dipped in vegetable oil. Pour about 3 tablespoons batter into the skillet and tilt the skillet to coat the bottom with the batter. Use dribbles of batter remaining in the measuring cup to fill in any empty spots. Cook until the top of the crepe looks set and the underside is browned, about 1 minute. Flip the crepe and brown the other side, about 1 minute more. Transfer to a plate. Continue with the remaining batter, oiling the skillet as needed, separating the crepes with pieces of parchment or waxed paper. (You will have more than the needed 16 crepes, but the extras could come in handy if you are not a practiced crepe-maker.) Let the crepes cool. (The crepes can be covered with plastic wrap and refrigerated for up to 1 day. Bring to room temperature before using.)

3. To make the ricotta filling: Bring a small saucepan of water to a boil over high heat. Add the basil leaves and cook just until they turn a brighter shade of green, about 30 seconds. Drain the basil in a sieve, rinse under cold running water, and squeeze the basil in your fist to extract excess water. Puree the basil with the oil in a mini–food processor or blender. Pour the basil oil into a medium bowl and add the ricotta, panko, Parmigiano, egg, lemon juice, salt, and hot pepper flakes, and mix well.

4. Lightly butter a large baking dish. For each manicotti, spoon about 2 heaping tablespoons of the filling in a strip on the bottom third of a crepe. Starting at the bottom, roll up the crepe and place, seam side down, in the baking dish. Cover the dish with aluminum foil. (The assembled manicotti can be refrigerated for up to 6 hours. Remove from the refrigerator 1 hour before baking.)

5. Position a rack in the center of the oven and preheat the oven to 350°F. Lightly brush the tops of the manicotti with melted butter. Cover again with the foil and bake until they are heated through, about 25 minutes.

6. Transfer the manicotti to shallow bowls and top each serving with some of the sauce. Serve immediately, with more Parmigiano passed on the side.

VEGETABLES & GRAINS

In another time and place, these might be called side dishes—a term that to many cooks suggests an unimportant add-on to the menu, something to round out the meal while the meat hogs the spotlight. Not here. These vegetable and grain recipes are designed to be standouts, and are seasoned with authority to make a statement. I am always happy when I serve my friends something as simple as the orange-and-chile Brussels sprouts (page 193), and they fight over the last sprout in the bowl. Also popular are my angry potatoes (page 202), with their crispy surface and tender interiors spiked with the sharp heat of pickled peppers. And while you certainly don't have to be a vegetarian to love these dishes, I keep them in mind when I want to serve a meat-free meal to friends, and offer up a selection to serve "tapas style."

GRILLED
Asparagus
with Cilantro-Lime
Mayonnaise

—

*SPICY
BROCCOLINI*
with **Soy and Garlic**

—

Orange and
Chile–Glazed
Brussels Sprouts

—

ROASTED
Cauliflower
Gratin *with*
Gremolata Crumbs

—

Twice-Cooked
EGGPLANT
with Cilantro-Sesame
Pesto

Crispy Hominy
with **Skillet Corn
and Cheese**

—

Miso-Glazed
MUSHROOMS

—

ANGRY
POTATOES
with **Cherry Peppers**

—

Harissa Pearl
COUSCOUS
*with Tahini
and Baby Spinach*

—

Creamy Mascarpone
Polenta

—

STICKY
Rice Cakes

GRILLED
Asparagus
with CILANTRO-LIME MAYONNAISE

MAKES

4

SERVINGS

Every chef has a pet ingredient. Mayonnaise (and its cousin aioli) might be mine—as long as it is a creamy, top-notch brand like Hellman's (called Best Foods west of the Mississippi) or the Japanese import Kewpie. This version of asparagus came to mind when I had the ingredients for Mexican-style corn... but no corn. If you don't want to grill the asparagus, roast it in the oven (see Note).

CILANTRO-LIME MAYONNAISE

½ cup mayonnaise

2 tablespoons minced fresh cilantro

2 tablespoons fresh lime juice

1 garlic clove, shredded on a Microplane zester

¼ teaspoon pure ground ancho chile

Salt and freshly ground black pepper

GRILLED ASPARAGUS

1 pound asparagus, woody stems discarded

Extra-virgin olive oil

Kosher salt and freshly ground black pepper

1 tablespoon cilantro leaves

¼ cup (1 ounce) grated Cotija cheese

1 lime, cut into eighths

1. Prepare an outdoor grill for direct cooking over medium heat (400°F).

2. Meanwhile, make the mayonnaise: Whisk all of the ingredients together in a large bowl, seasoning with salt and pepper to taste. Cover and set aside.

3. To grill the asparagus: Lightly brush the asparagus with oil and season with salt and pepper. Brush the cooking grate clean. Place the asparagus on the grill, perpendicular to the grate. Grill with the lid closed as much as possible, occasionally rolling the asparagus spears to turn them, until the asparagus is seared and barely tender, about 5 minutes (depending on the thickness of the spears).

4. Toss the warm asparagus in the mayonnaise dressing and finish with the cilantro, Cotija, and squeezes of juice from the lime wedges.

Note: To roasted the asparagus, toss the spears with oil on an 18-by-13-inch half-sheet pan to coat them lightly, then spread out on the sheet. Roast in a 425°F oven, turning the asparagus after 7 minutes, until crisp-tender, 10 to 15 minutes. Season to taste with salt and pepper.

SPICY BROCCOLINI
with SOY AND GARLIC

1 tablespoon Japanese
soy sauce

1 tablespoon Vietnamese or
Thai fish sauce

1 tablespoon unseasoned rice vinegar

1 tablespoon canola oil

1 garlic clove, minced

2 bunches broccolini,
about 12 ounces

1 cup Vegetable Stock
(this page) or reduced-sodium
chicken broth

2 teaspoons sambal oelek
or other Asian chili paste

Broccolini, a broccoli hybrid, is another vegetable that deserves to be on more dinner tables. This is a quick, easy, and spicy stir-fry that bursts with Asian flavor. While I typically serve it as a side dish, it is good enough to eat as a light meal over a bowl of rice. If your broccolini stalks are thicker than an inch, cut them in half lengthwise so they are all about the same size.

1. Mix the soy sauce, fish sauce, and rice vinegar together in a small bowl.

2. Heat the oil and garlic together in a large skillet over medium heat until the garlic begins to brown, about 2 minutes. Add the broccolini and mix well. Stir in the soy sauce mixture, stock, and sambal oelek and increase the heat to high. Cover and cook for 3 minutes. Uncover and cook, stirring occasionally, until the broccolini is barely tender and the sauce has reduced to a few tablespoons, about 2 minutes. Transfer to a serving bowl and serve hot.

VEGETABLE STOCK

Makes about 3 cups

While there are acceptable brands of canned chicken and beef broths, most store-bought vegetable broths have a harsh cabbage flavor. Here is a super-easy meatless broth to make with ingredients that you are likely to have on hand in reasonable amounts.

1 quart cold water

1 large celery rib, coarsely chopped

1 medium carrot, coarsely chopped

1 small yellow onion, coarsely chopped

½ teaspoon black peppercorns

½ small bay leaf

1. Combine all of the ingredients in a medium saucepan and bring to a boil over high heat. Reduce the heat and simmer until full-flavored, about 1 hour.

2. Strain the stock through a colander into a large bowl, pressing hard on the solids. Let cool. Transfer to covered containers and refrigerate for up to 3 days or freeze for up to 6 months.

ORANGE *and* CHILE-GLAZED
Brussels Sprouts

MAKES

4

SERVINGS

Brussels sprouts are a very versatile ingredient, and they readily absorb other flavors. This recipe relies on the age-old combination of sweet and salty flavors, utilizing a glaze made from reduced orange juice and soy sauce. Thai chile enliven the dish with a pop of heat—but you can remove the chile seeds for a milder result.

1 pound Brussels sprouts, ends trimmed, halved lengthwise

2 tablespoons vegetable or canola oil

1½ cups fresh orange juice

1 Thai or ½ serrano chile, minced

1 tablespoon reduced-sodium soy sauce

1 tablespoon water

1 teaspoon minced shallot

⅛ teaspoon kosher salt

Flaky sea salt, such as Maldon, for serving

1. Position a rack in the center of the oven and preheat the oven to 425°F.

2. Toss the Brussels sprouts and oil in a large bowl. Spread on an 18-by-13-inch half-sheet pan. Roast, stirring occasionally, until browned and tender, about 30 minutes.

3. Meanwhile, make the glaze: Boil the orange juice and chile in a small saucepan over medium heat until reduced to ⅓ cup, 10 to 15 minutes. Take care that the orange juice does not scorch. (The orange juice mixture can also be reduced in a microwave oven on high). Transfer to a small bowl and let cool slightly. Stir in the soy sauce, water, shallot, and salt. (The glaze can be stored at room temperature for up to 4 hours.)

4. Stir the glaze into the sprouts and roast until the glaze reduces slightly, about 3 minutes. Transfer to a serving bowl, sprinkle with the sea salt, and serve immediately.

ROASTED
CAULIFLOWER GRATIN
with GREMOLATA CRUMBS

MAKES

4 *to* 6

SERVINGS

If you are stumped for a holiday side dish, consider this warm gratin, featuring cauliflower, one of the best cold-weather vegetables. Most gratins use root vegetables (such as potatoes or celery root), but the hearty nature of cauliflower allows it to retain its notable texture in the cheesy cream sauce. The lemon- and garlic-accented bread crumbs balance the richness with a crisp, vibrant finish.

ROASTED CAULIFLOWER

1 head cauliflower, about
2¼ pounds, cut into florets

3 tablespoons extra-virgin olive oil

1 teaspoon finely chopped fresh thyme

½ teaspoon kosher salt

¼ teaspoon freshly ground
black pepper

CHEESE SAUCE

1 tablespoon cold water

1½ teaspoons cornstarch

1 tablespoon unsalted butter

2 tablespoons finely chopped shallot

¾ cup heavy cream

1 cup (4 ounces) freshly grated
Pecorino Romano cheese

1 cup (4 ounces) freshly grated
Parmigiano-Reggiano cheese

⅓ cup sour cream

½ teaspoon hot red pepper sauce,
such as Tabasco

Kosher salt

Softened butter, for the baking dish

GREMOLATA CRUMBS

1 teaspoon olive oil

¼ cup soft bread crumbs, made in
a blender from day-old crusty bread

2 tablespoons finely chopped
fresh flat-leaf parsley

Finely grated zest of ½ lemon

1 small garlic clove, minced

1. To roast the cauliflower: Position a rack in the center of the oven and preheat the oven to 400°F.

2. Toss the cauliflower, oil, thyme, salt, and pepper in a large bowl. Spread on an 18-by-13-inch half-sheet pan. Roast, stirring occasionally, until the cauliflower is lightly browned and just crisp-tender (it will bake further in the oven when sauced), 20 to 25 minutes. Remove the cauliflower from the oven and leave it on.

3. Meanwhile, make the cheese sauce: Pour the water into a ramekin or custard cup. Sprinkle in the cornstarch and stir to dissolve. Melt the butter in a large saucepan over medium heat. Add the shallot and cook, stirring occasionally, until tender but not browned, about 2 minutes. Add the cream and bring to a boil. Stir in the cornstarch mixture and cook until boiling and thickened. Remove from the heat. Whisk in the Romano and Parmigiano cheeses, the sour cream, and the hot sauce. Season to taste with salt, but not too much, as the cheeses are salty.

4. Lower your oven setting to 350°F. Lightly butter a 9-by-13-inch baking dish. Mix the cauliflower and the cheese sauce together in the baking dish. Bake until the sauce is bubbling and beginning to brown, about 20 minutes.

5. Meanwhile, make the gremolata crumbs: Heat the oil in a small skillet over medium heat. Add the bread crumbs and cook, stirring often, until they are toasted, 1 to 2 minutes. Transfer to a small bowl and let cool. Stir in the parsley, lemon zest, and garlic.

6. Sprinkle the gremolata crumbs over the gratin and serve hot.

TWICE-COOKED
EGGPLANT
with Cilantro-Sesame Pesto

MAKES

4

SERVINGS

When people say that they don't like eggplant, I tell them they just haven't tried my eggplant. Eggplant chunks are first roasted for a lightly caramelized flavor, then finished in a wok with a myriad of Asian flavors. Dark purple globe eggplant works well here, but the narrow Japanese variety is my preference because it is sweeter. If you wish, use the Asian Pesto on page 79 instead of the cilantro pesto below.

ROASTED EGGPLANT

1½ pounds Japanese eggplant, cut into 1-inch chunks

2 tablespoons canola or vegetable oil

Kosher salt and freshly ground black pepper

CILANTRO-SESAME PESTO

2 garlic cloves, crushed under a knife and peeled

2 cups packed fresh cilantro leaves

2 tablespoons fresh lemon juice

2 tablespoons Asian sesame oil

2 tablespoons sesame seeds, toasted (see Note)

½ cup extra-virgin olive oil

Kosher salt and freshly ground black pepper

SRIRACHA-ORANGE MAYONNAISE

2 tablespoons mayonnaise, preferably Kewpie (see Chef Talk, page 197)

1 teaspoon sriracha

1 teaspoon fresh orange juice

1 teaspoon Japanese soy sauce

———————

2 tablespoons canola or vegetable oil

2 tablespoons pine nuts, toasted (see Note)

2 tablespoons packed cilantro leaves

1 teaspoon sesame seeds, toasted (see Note)

1. To roast the eggplant: Position a rack in the center of the oven and preheat the oven to 425°F.

2. Toss the eggplant with the oil in a large bowl. Season with salt and pepper. Spread on an 18-by-13-inch half-sheet pan. Roast, stirring occasionally, until tender and lightly browned, about 15 minutes. Let cool completely. (The eggplant can be covered and stored at room temperature for up to 4 hours.)

3. To make the pesto: With the machine running, drop the garlic through the feed tube of a processor to mince it. Add the cilantro, lemon juice, sesame oil, and sesame seeds and process until pureed. With the machine running, pour the olive oil through the feed tube to make a smooth sauce. Season to taste with salt and pepper. (The pesto can be covered tightly and stored at room temperature for up to 4 hours.)

4. To make the mayonnaise: Whisk all of the ingredients together in a small bowl. Set aside for up to 1 hour.

5. To finish the eggplant: Heat a large wok or skillet over high heat. Add the oil and swirl the wok to coat the sides. Add the eggplant and spread it out in a single layer. Let cook until the underside is seared, about 1 minute. Stir-fry until hot, about 1 minute more. Remove the wok from the heat. Add 3 tablespoons of the pesto, the pine nuts, the cilantro leaves, and the sesame seeds. Transfer to a serving bowl, drizzle with the mayonnaise, and serve hot, with the remaining pesto passed on the side. (Leftover pesto is delicious stirred into plain steamed rice or used to flavor vinaigrette.)

Note: *To toast either sesame seeds or pine nuts, heat a small skillet over medium heat. Add the seeds (or pine nuts) and cook, stirring occasionally, until toasted, about 1 minute for the seeds or slightly longer for the pine nuts. Transfer to a plate and let cool completely.*

CHEF TALK

Kewpie Mayonnaise

Kewpie is a brand of Japanese mayonnaise with a creamy texture and less tangy taste than American mayo. It is sold at Asian markets and online.

CRISPY HOMINY

with SKILLET CORN AND CHEESE

MAKES

4

SERVINGS

Hominy is the only canned vegetable I would ever have in my pantry (besides canned chipotles in adobo). I love the chewy texture, and frying the hominy gives it the perfect crisp exterior. I add fresh, roasted corn to my hominy for its bright color and sweet taste. This treatment, reminiscent of the corn on the cob you might buy from a Mexican street vendor, gives this not-too-familiar ingredient a flair that everyone loves.

CRISPY HOMINY

Vegetable oil, for deep-frying

¼ cup white rice flour (not sticky, glutinous, or sweet rice flour)

¼ teaspoon pure ground chipotle

⅛ teaspoon kosher salt

1 (15-ounce) can hominy, drained, rinsed, and patted dry with paper towels

SKILLET CORN

1½ cups fresh corn kernels, cut from about 2 ears

1 tablespoon minced red onion

2 teaspoons minced fresh cilantro

Finely grated zest of 1 lime

Kosher Salt

Small hunk of freshly grated aged Cotija or Pecorino Romano cheese, for grating

Lime wedges, for serving

CHEF TALK

Cotija

Cotija is a Mexican cow's milk cheese that is sometimes sold fresh, but it can also be aged until it is hard enough to grate. If you can't find Cotija cheese, most supermarkets carry some form of queso fresco that you could use here. Feta cheese would also be a good substitute; just make sure that it is dry and not packaged in water.

1. To heat the oil for the hominy: Pour enough oil to come 2 inches up the sides of a large saucepan and heat over high heat until it reaches 350°F on a deep-frying thermometer. Line a rimmed baking sheet with paper towels.

2. Meanwhile, cook the corn: Heat a large heavy skillet, preferably cast iron, over high heat until the skillet is very hot, at least 3 minutes. Add the corn and cook, without stirring, until the underside is deeply browned, 2 to 3 minutes. Stir in the red onion, cilantro, and lime zest and mix well. Remove from the heat.

3. To fry the hominy: Mix the rice flour, chipotle, and salt together in a medium bowl. Toss the hominy in the rice flour mixture to coat, transfer to a wire sieve, and shake to remove the excess coating. Gradually add the hominy to the hot oil, taking care that it doesn't boil over. Deep-fry until the hominy is crispy, about 2 minutes. Using a wire spider or a slotted spoon, transfer the hominy to the paper towels to drain briefly.

4. Add the hominy to the corn mixture and mix. Season to taste with salt. Transfer to a serving bowl. Using a Microplane zester, shred a few tablespoons of Cotija cheese on top. Serve immediately, with the lime wedges.

Miso-Glazed
Mushrooms

MAKES

4 *to* 6

SERVINGS

Umami, that almost indescribable taste element that invokes depth of flavor, is found in both mushrooms and miso. So, even with relatively few ingredients, this dish is a palate-punching powerhouse. It should take about 10 minutes to make, from start to finish. Feel free to use the glaze on other vegetables—give it a try on broccolini, summer squash, or cauliflower.

2 tablespoons standard sake, such as Gekkeikan

2 tablespoons mirin

1 tablespoon Japanese soy sauce

1 tablespoon light brown sugar

2 tablespoons white (shiro) miso

2 tablespoons canola oil

1 pound white button mushrooms, quartered

1 tablespoon finely chopped fresh mint

1 scallion, white and green parts, finely chopped

1. Bring the sake, mirin, soy sauce, and brown sugar to a boil in a small saucepan over high heat, stirring to dissolve the sugar. Remove from the heat. Add the miso and whisk until smooth.

2. Heat a large skillet over medium-high heat until it is very hot. Add the oil and swirl the pan to coat the bottom with oil. Add the mushrooms and cook, stirring occasionally, until they are lightly browned but haven't given off their juices, about 3 minutes. Stir in the miso mixture and cook until it has reduced to a glaze, about 1 minute. Add the mint and half of the scallion and mix well.

3. Transfer to a serving dish, sprinkle with the remaining scallion, and serve hot.

Angry Potatoes
with CHERRY PEPPERS

MAKES

4 *to* 6

SERVINGS

Crusty and tender at the same time, these potatoes are "angry" from pickled cherry peppers and hot pepper flakes. The peppers are sold either sliced or whole, and are standard at East Coast supermarkets with an Italian American clientele, but they can be found at Italian delicatessens as well.

1½ pounds fingerling or small
Yukon Gold potatoes

Extra-virgin olive oil

2 garlic cloves, finely chopped

¼ teaspoon hot red pepper flakes

2 tablespoons chopped pickled
hot cherry peppers

2 tablespoons finely chopped
fresh flat-leaf parsley

Kosher salt

1. Position a rack in the center of the oven and preheat the oven to 400°F.

2. Pierce each potato with a fork. Place the potatoes on a large rimmed baking sheet and bake until tender, about 40 minutes. Let cool until easy to handle, at least 20 minutes.

3. Using the heel of your hand, press down on each warm potato until it is about ½ inch thick, keeping the potato as intact as possible. (The potatoes can be covered and stored at room temperature for up to 4 hours.)

4. Pour enough oil into a very large skillet to come about ⅛ inch up the sides—do not skimp on the oil. In batches without crowding, add the potatoes and cook, turning halfway through cooking, until crisp and golden brown, about 4 minutes. Transfer the potatoes to a serving bowl. Discard any oil left in the skillet.

5. Off heat (the skillet will be very hot), add 2 tablespoons fresh oil and the garlic and hot pepper flakes. Stir until the garlic softens, about 30 seconds. Be careful not to burn the garlic. Stir in the cherry peppers and parsley. Return the potatoes to the skillet and toss to combine. Season to taste with salt. Transfer to a serving bowl and serve hot.

Harissa Pearl
COUSCOUS
with **Tahini and Baby Spinach**

MAKES

4

SERVINGS

Pearl couscous has a very interesting history. It was developed in the late 1940s by the Israeli government to give the country an exportable product. The round balls of pasta easily absorb the flavors of harissa chili paste and tahini. While the recipe calls for baby spinach, red Swiss chard leaves would also be excellent.

2 tablespoons unsalted butter

3 tablespoons finely chopped shallots

1 garlic clove, minced

1½ teaspoons harissa paste

1 (6-ounce) box pearl (Israeli) couscous, about 1 generous cup

2½ cups reduced-sodium chicken broth

1 (3-inch) sprig fresh rosemary

½ teaspoon kosher salt

1 small bay leaf

3 cups coarsely chopped baby spinach, about 3 ounces

2 tablespoons well-stirred tahini

Sweet paprika, for serving

1. Melt the butter in a medium saucepan over medium heat. Add the shallots and garlic and cook, stirring occasionally, until they soften, about 2 minutes. Stir in the harissa and cook until it begins to toast on the bottom of the saucepan, about 1 minute. Add the couscous and stir well. Add the broth, rosemary, salt, and bay leaf and bring to a boil over high heat.

2. Reduce the heat to medium-low and cover tightly. Simmer until the couscous is tender and has absorbed most of the liquid, about 12 minutes. Remove the saucepan from the heat.

3. A handful at a time, stir in the spinach, letting the first batch wilt before adding more. Stir in the tahini. Discard the bay leaf. Transfer the couscous to a bowl, sprinkle with the paprika, and serve.

Creamy Mascarpone
POLENTA

MAKES

4 *to* 6

SERVINGS

Polenta is one of the most delicious ways to get your grains, especially when cheese is involved. This version is a bit creamier than others. If you like a firmer polenta, reduce the broth to 2½ cups. And if you don't have mascarpone, you can substitute extra cream, but I like the bit of tang that the cheese provides. I always serve this dish with the spatch-cocked chicken on page 87.

2 tablespoons unsalted butter

½ cup finely chopped yellow onion

1 garlic clove, minced

3 cups reduced-sodium chicken broth

1½ cups whole milk

1 cup yellow polenta (coarse-grind cornmeal, not instant polenta)

Kosher salt and freshly ground black pepper

½ cup (2 ounces) freshly grated Parmigiano-Reggiano cheese

⅓ cup mascarpone cheese or additional heavy cream

⅓ cup heavy cream

2 teaspoons finely chopped fresh chives

Pinch of hot red pepper flakes

1. Melt the butter in a heavy medium saucepan, preferably enameled cast iron, over medium heat. Add the onion and cook, stirring occasionally, until it is lightly browned, about 5 minutes. Stir in the garlic and cook until fragrant, about 1 minute.

2. Add the broth, milk, polenta, ½ teaspoon salt, and ¼ teaspoon pepper to the saucepan and whisk well. Bring to a boil over high heat, whisking often to avoid scorching. Reduce the heat to low and simmer, whisking well every 5 minutes or so, until the polenta is very tender and thick enough to support a standing spoon, 45 minutes to 1 hour.

3. Stir in the Parmigiano, mascarpone, cream, chives, and hot pepper flakes. Season to taste with additional salt and pepper. If the polenta is too thick (it should spread slightly when served in a bowl), whisk in more milk, a tablespoon at a time, to adjust its consistency. Serve hot.

STICKY
Rice Cakes

MAKES
18
RICE CAKES
8 SERVINGS

These golden brown rice cakes are an incredibly impressive way to vary any dish that is typically served over rice. While they were developed for the "Beef and Broccoli" on page 137, they make an outstanding base for tuna or steak tartare as well. Be sure to use short-grain sticky rice, as its extra starch will help hold the cakes together.

About 3 tablespoons canola oil, as needed, plus more for the baking dish

1⅓ cups short-grain sticky (sweet or glutinous) rice

2 tablespoons unseasoned rice vinegar

2⅔ cups water

1 teaspoon minced fresh ginger

1 teaspoon kosher salt

1 large egg, beaten

1 tablespoon cornstarch

1 garlic clove, minced

CHEF TALK

Rice Types

The size of the grain designates rice as long-, medium-, or short-grain. The amount of starch decreases with the length of the grain, so short-grain rice is quite starchy. Sushi rice is an example of short-grain rice. For this recipe, use short-grain sticky rice. It is also known as glutinous or sweet rice, and although the rice does not taste sugary, it is used to make some Asian desserts.

1. Heat 1 tablespoon of the oil in a medium heavy-bottomed saucepan over high heat. Add the rice and cook, stirring often, until lightly browned. Stir in the vinegar, followed by the water, ginger, and salt. Bring to a boil and reduce the heat to low. Cover tightly and simmer until the rice is tender and has absorbed the liquid, about 20 minutes. Transfer to a large bowl and let cool until tepid.

2. Lightly oil an 11-by-8-inch baking dish. Stir the egg, cornstarch, and garlic into the rice. Spread the rice mixture into the baking dish and smooth the top while pressing it in firmly. Let cool completely.

3. Invert the baking dish and unmold the rice slab onto a cutting board. Using a lightly oiled knife, cut the slab into 18 equal pieces. (The rice cakes can be covered with plastic wrap and refrigerated for up to 6 hours.)

4. Preheat the oven to 200°F. Line another rimmed baking sheet with paper towels. Heat the remaining 2 tablespoons oil in a large skillet over high heat. In batches, add the rice cakes and cook, turning once, until golden brown on both sides, about 6 minutes. Transfer to the paper towels and keep warm in the oven while cooking the remaining cakes, adding more oil to the skillet as needed.

DESSERTS

If you take a glance at this chapter's recipe list, you may feel that you've traveled back in time. While many chefs promote cutting-edge desserts, I am happiest when my dessert reminds me of a childhood favorite, especially if it has been elevated for a more refined, adult palate. Put an ice cream sundae with loads of peanut butter (page 237) in front of me, and I am in heaven. I could say the same for a slice of devil's food cake (with ultra-creamy mascarpone filling—page 210), a "Twinkie" (take your choice of peanut-butter-and-jelly or red-velvet versions on pages 224 and 226), or decadent butterscotch pudding (with a bottom layer of chocolate—page 232). Cheesecake, blondies, chocolate chip cookies— all of the American classics are here, Santos style.

Devil's Food Cake
with Vanilla
Mascarpone Filling

—

WARM
STOUT CAKES
with **Toffee Sauce**

—

**Pumpkin Pie
Cheesecake**
with Gingersnap Crust

—

APPLE TART
with Cheddar Streusel

—

CHOCOLATE
Bread Pudding

—

Peanut Butter
and Jelly
"Twinkies"

—

RED VELVET
"Twinkies"
with Crème Fraîche
Filling

WHITE CHOCOLATE
Blondies
with **Semisweet Chips**

—

Reverse
CHOCOLATE CHIP
COOKIES

—

CACAO NIB
Lace
Cookies

—

**Black-Bottomed
Butterscotch
*Pots de Crème***

—

**LIME AND
BLACKBERRY**
Semifreddo

—

PEANUT BUTTER
Ice Cream
Sundaes *with*
Hot Fudge and
Peanut Brittle

DEVIL'S FOOD CAKE
with VANILLA MASCARPONE FILLING

MAKES

8

SERVINGS

This showstopper of a triple-layer cake has so many things going for it. The batter is super easy. The thick layer of mascarpone filling is luxurious. The finished cake can be refrigerated for a couple of days without getting stale. And if you are the kind of person who can't choose between chocolate and vanilla, this cake is definitely for you. In fact, it reminds me of an outrageous Oreo—always a good thing in my opinion.

VANILLA SYRUP

⅔ cup sugar

⅓ cup water

1 teaspoon vanilla extract

3 tablespoons chocolate cream liqueur (preferably Godiva), or white or dark crème de cacao

DEVIL'S FOOD CAKE

Softened butter and flour, for the pans

1⅔ cups (235 grams) unbleached all-purpose flour

1 cup plus 3 tablespoons sugar

½ cup Dutch-process cocoa powder

1¼ teaspoons baking soda

¼ teaspoon fine sea salt

1 cup buttermilk

⅓ cup canola or vegetable oil

2 large eggs, at room temperature

1 teaspoon vanilla extract

5 tablespoons unsalted butter, melted and cooled to tepid

VANILLA MASCARPONE FILLING

½ cup heavy cream

½ cup sugar

½ teaspoon vanilla extract, or seeds from 1 split vanilla bean

1 (8.8-ounce) container mascarpone (1 generous cup)

CHOCOLATE ICING

¼ cup sugar

¼ cup Dutch-process cocoa powder

¼ cup water

¼ cup heavy cream

2 tablespoons light corn syrup

6 ounces bittersweet chocolate (about 70% cacao), finely chopped

2 tablespoons unsalted butter

———————

Milk Ice Cream (page 213) or store-bought vanilla ice cream, for serving

1. To make the syrup: Bring the sugar and water to a boil in a small saucepan over high heat, stirring to dissolve the sugar. Pour into a small bowl and stir in the vanilla. Let cool. Stir in the liqueur. (The syrup can be covered and refrigerated for up to 3 days.)

2. To make the cake: Position a rack in the center of the oven and preheat the oven to 350°F. Lightly butter an 8-by-3-inch springform pan and line the bottom with a round of parchment or waxed paper. Dust the inside with flour and tap out the excess flour.

3. Sift the flour, sugar, cocoa, baking soda, and salt through a wire sieve into the bowl of a standing heavy-duty mixer. Whisk the buttermilk, oil, eggs, and vanilla together in a medium bowl. Add to the flour mixture. Mix with the paddle attachment with the machine on low speed just until the batter is combined. Gradually add in the melted butter, letting the batter absorb the butter before adding more, and mix just until the batter is shiny and smooth. Spread the batter evenly in the pan.

4. Bake until a long cake tester or bamboo skewer inserted into the center of the cake comes out clean, about 50 minutes. Let the cake cool in the pan on a wire rack for 10 minutes. Run a knife around the inside of the pan to loosen the cake ➤

Making Ice Cream

Once you own an ice cream machine, there is no turning back. If you love making desserts, having the ability to make homemade ice cream to accompany your sweets is an excellent investment. There are many different models, including frozen canister, ice-cube-and-table-salt chilled, self-contained refrigeration, and even old-fashioned hand-cranked with rock salt. The frozen canister is the most efficient for the home cook—as long as you have the room in your freezer for an overnight chilling. Here are a few things to keep in mind when making ice cream at home:

• The ice cream base (usually a custard) must be thoroughly chilled before freezing. You could refrigerate the mixture overnight, but it is much quicker to place the bowl of custard in a larger bowl of ice water—it will be ready in about 30 minutes.

• Ice cream is never frozen to a firm scooping texture. Instead, it is semi-soft, like soft-serve ice cream. It must be transferred from the ice cream machine to a covered container and frozen for a few hours to be hard enough to scoop.

• Frozen food dulls the palate, so if you taste the ice cream base, it should always taste very sweet to overcompensate for the very cold eating temperature.

from the pan. Remove the pan sides. Invert the cake onto a wire rack, remove the pan bottom and paper, and turn right side up on the rack. Let the cake cool completely. Clean the pan and replace the sides.

5. To make the filling: In a chilled medium bowl, using a handheld electric mixer set on high speed, whip the cream, sugar, and vanilla until soft peaks form. With the mixer on low speed, gradually beat in the mascarpone in four or five additions to make a smooth filling.

6. Using a long serrated knife, trim any dome on the cake to level it. Using the serrated knife, cut the cake horizontally into thirds. Place the bottom layer in the clean, reassembled springform pan. Brush the cake with one-third of the vanilla syrup. Using a small offset metal spatula, spread with half of the filling. Repeat with the second layer, more syrup and remaining filling. Top with the third layer and brush with the remaining syrup. Loosely cover the cake and refrigerate until chilled (the icing works best on a chilled cake), at least 1 hour or up to 1 day.

7. To make the icing: Whisk the sugar and cocoa together in a medium saucepan. Gradually whisk in the water, followed by the heavy cream and corn syrup. Bring to a boil over high heat, stirring with a wooden spoon to dissolve the sugar. Remove from the heat. Add the chocolate and butter and whisk until they are melted and the icing is smooth. Cool slightly for 10 minutes. The icing will have the consistency of thick pudding but will firm when it comes into contact with the chilled cake.

8. Run a knife around the inside of the pan to loosen the cake. Remove the sides of the springform pan. Put the cake on a wire rack set over a large rimmed baking sheet. Using the knife, scrape off any excess filling from the sides of the cake. Using an offset metal icing spatula, spread the icing on the top of the cake, followed by the sides, reserving about one-quarter of the icing. Try not to smear the filling on the sides, but if you do, it can be corrected later. Refrigerate to firm the icing, about

15 minutes, leaving the reserved icing at room temperature. Spread the remaining icing on the sides of the cake to hide any smears. Refrigerate the cake, uncovered, to set the icing, at least 1 hour or up to 1 day.

9. Using a long, thin knife dipped in hot water, cut the cake into wedges. Serve on dessert plates, with the ice cream.

MILK ICE CREAM

Makes about 1½ quarts

Milk ice cream? Isn't that redundant? Most ice creams contain milk, but this recipe includes nonfat milk powder, which adds so much extra dairy flavor that the ice cream doesn't even need vanilla. Omitting eggs gives this unique "ice cream" a remarkably light consistency.

1 cup sugar

⅔ cup nonfat dry milk powder

1 teaspoon cornstarch

3⅓ cups whole milk

1 cup heavy cream

3 tablespoons light corn syrup

1. Whisk the sugar, milk powder, and cornstarch together in a large saucepan. Whisk in the milk, cream, and corn syrup. Heat over medium heat, stirring often to dissolve the sugar, until the mixture comes to a simmer.

2. Pour the milk mixture into a large heatproof bowl set in a larger bowl of ice water. Let it stand, stirring occasionally, until cold, about 30 minutes. Remove the bowl of custard from the ice water, cover with plastic wrap, and refrigerate until well chilled, at least 2 hours or up to 1 day.

3. Freeze the milk mixture in an ice cream machine according to the manufacturer's directions. (The ice cream will be semisoft at this stage.) Transfer the ice cream to a covered container. Freeze until the ice cream is firm enough to scoop, at least 4 hours or up to 2 days.

Warm Stout Cakes
with TOFFEE SAUCE

MAKES

6

SERVINGS

In this dessert inspired by the sinful flavors of British sticky toffee pudding (*pudding* means any kind of dessert in British English, not just our American soft ones), stout gives the cakes much more flavor than the typical classic version. For the best, "stickiest" texture, use fresh dates instead of dried—although either will work.

TOFFEE SAUCE

½ cup (1 stick) unsalted butter

1 cup packed dark brown sugar

3 tablespoons light corn syrup

½ vanilla bean, split lengthwise

1 cup heavy cream, heated to steaming

CAKES

Softened butter and flour, for the ramekins

⅓ cup plus 1 tablespoon stout, preferably Guinness

⅓ cup pitted and coarsely chopped fresh dates (preferably Medjool) or dried dates (see Note, page 216)

1 teaspoon baking soda

½ cup plus 1 tablespoon (1 stick plus 1 tablespoon) unsalted butter, at room temperature

⅔ cup packed dark brown sugar

3 large eggs, at room temperature

1½ teaspoons vanilla extract

¾ cup (105 grams) unbleached all-purpose flour

¼ teaspoon fine salt

———

Whipped cream, for serving

1. To make the sauce: Melt the butter in a tall, medium saucepan over medium heat. Add the brown sugar, corn syrup, and vanilla bean halves and cook, stirring often, until the brown sugar is melted and boiling. Gradually whisk in the cream, being sure that the mixture does not boil over, and return to a boil. Cook at a steady boil, stirring often, until the sauce has thickened to about 2 cups, about 10 minutes. Remove the sauce from the heat and let stand until warm. Remove the vanilla bean halves and use the tip of a small knife to scrape the seeds back into the sauce; discard the bean pods. (The cooled sauce can be refrigerated in a covered bowl for up to 1 day. Reheat the sauce in a medium saucepan over low heat, whisking often, until barely warm.)

2. To make the cakes: Position a rack in the center of the oven and preheat the oven to 350°F. Lightly butter and flour the insides of six 6-ounce ramekins, tapping out the excess flour.

3. Bring the stout and dates to a simmer in a medium saucepan over high heat. Remove from the heat, stir in the baking soda, and let stand for 5 minutes, until the dates are softened. Puree the date mixture in a blender. Transfer the puree to a small bowl to cool slightly.

4. Beat the butter in a medium bowl with an electric mixer set on high speed until creamy, about 1 minute. Gradually beat in the brown sugar and continue beating until the mixture is light in color and texture, about 2 minutes. One at a time, beat in the eggs, beating well after each addition, followed by the vanilla extract. Whisk the flour and salt together in a medium bowl. With the mixer on low speed, add the flour mixture in thirds, alternating with two equal additions of the date puree, mixing

➡

just until smooth and scraping down the sides of the bowl as needed. Divide the batter evenly among the ramekins and smooth the tops.

5. Place the ramekins on an 18-by-13-inch half-sheet pan. Bake until a wooden toothpick inserted in the center of a cake comes out clean, about 25 minutes. Let cool on the baking sheet for 5 to 10 minutes.

One at a time, protecting your hands with a kitchen towel, run a knife around the inside of the ramekins, being sure to free the cakes from the bottom. Invert and unmold each cake onto a dessert plate. (The cakes can be cooled, transferred to a baking dish, covered with aluminum foil, and stored at room temperature for up to 8 hours. Reheat in a 350°F oven until warm, about 10 minutes. When warm, use a metal spatula to transfer each to a dessert plate.) Top with a dollop of whipped cream. Spoon about ⅓ cup toffee sauce over the top. Serve immediately.

Note: *If you substitute chopped dried dates for the fresh Medjool dates, they will take about 5 minutes longer to soften in the warm stout mixture. Chop the dates yourself by hand, and skip the pre-chopped ones, as they are too dry and sweet.*

PUMPKIN PIE
Cheesecake
with Gingersnap Crust

MAKES

8 *to* 10

SERVINGS

Thanksgiving comes around and everyone's brain goes straight to pumpkin pie. I offer you this mildly spiced cheesecake with a spicy cinnamon sauce as a new way to feature the winter squash in a dessert. The gingersnap crust really sets the cheesecake apart, and the best part is that it can be refrigerated for a few days before serving—a huge plus when planning a busy holiday meal.

CRUST

2 tablespoons unsalted butter, melted

1⅓ cups finely crushed gingersnap cookies

¼ teaspoon ground ginger

⅛ teaspoon ground cinnamon

FILLING

1 (15-ounce) can solid-pack pumpkin, about 1¾ cups

3 large eggs

⅓ cup plus 1 tablespoon heavy cream

2 teaspoons vanilla extract

1 pound cream cheese, at room temperature

¾ cup packed dark brown sugar, rubbed through a wire sieve to remove lumps

¾ teaspoon ground cinnamon

½ teaspoon ground ginger

⅛ teaspoon ground cloves

Pinch of kosher salt

Pinch of freshly ground black pepper

A few gratings of fresh nutmeg

CINNAMON CARAMEL SAUCE

1 cup heavy cream

2 (3-inch) cinnamon sticks

1 cup granulated sugar

⅓ cup water

Pinch of ground cinnamon (optional)

1. To prepare the crust: Position a rack in the center of the oven and preheat the oven to 350°F. Lightly butter the inside of a 9-inch springform pan with some of the melted butter. Wrap the outside of the pan in two layers of heavy-duty aluminum foil.

2. Mix the crumbs, ginger, and cinnamon together. Stir in the remaining melted butter and mix until the crumbs are moistened. Press the mixture firmly and evenly onto the bottom of the pan. Place the pan on an 18-by-13-inch half-sheet pan. Bake until the crust smells toasty, about 10 minutes. Remove the pan and sheet from the oven.

3. Meanwhile, make the filling: Whisk the pumpkin, eggs, cream, and vanilla together in a medium bowl until combined. Beat the cream cheese, brown sugar, cinnamon, ginger, cloves, salt, pepper, and nutmeg together in a heavy-duty standing mixer set on medium speed with the paddle attachment just until the cheese is smooth. Reduce the mixer speed to low and gradually mix in the pumpkin mixture, just until combined. Do not overmix. Pour the filling into the springform pan and smooth the top.

4. Place the springform pan in a large roasting pan. Place the pan setup in the oven and pour in enough hot water to come about ½ inch up the sides. Bake just until the edge of the cheesecake is just beginning to brown and the filling moves as a unit when the pan is gently shaken, about 50 minutes.

5. Transfer the cheesecake in the pan to a wire cake rack set over a rimmed baking sheet (to catch the dripping water). Run a knife around the edge of the springform pan to loosen the

➡️

cheesecake. Let cool for 15 minutes. Remove the foil and completely cool the cheesecake. Remove the sides of the pan. Refrigerate, uncovered, until chilled, at least 4 hours or up to 2 days.

6. To make the sauce: Bring the cream and cinnamon sticks to a simmer in a small saucepan over medium heat. Remove from the heat and let stand for 15 minutes. Discard the cinnamon sticks.

7. Bring the granulated sugar and water to a boil in a medium saucepan over high heat, stirring constantly, until the sugar is dissolved and the syrup is boiling. Cook without stirring, occasionally swirling the saucepan by the handle and washing down any sugar crystals on the sides of the saucepan with a pastry brush dipped in cold water, until the caramel has turned the color of an old penny and gives off wisps of smoke, 5 to 7 minutes. Gradually and carefully stir the hot cream (it will bubble and splatter) into the caramel and stir until the mixture is smooth. Stir in the ground cinnamon, if using. Let cool. (The sauce can be covered and refrigerated for up to 1 day. Bring to room temperature before serving.)

8. Using a thin sharp knife dipped in hot water, cut the chilled cheesecake into slices. Transfer the slices to dessert plates. Spoon the caramel sauce around each slice and serve.

CHEF TALK

Perfect Cheesecake

Be sure that your cream cheese is good and soft before beating—let it stand at room temperature for at least 1 hour, and overnight is not too long, if the kitchen is relatively cool. Never overmix a cheesecake filling. Beating incorporates extra air into the eggs, which makes them "soufflé" and puff during baking, leading to shrinkage and cracking during cooling.

APPLE TART

with CHEDDAR STREUSEL

MAKES

8

SERVINGS

Naturally, fruit and cheese are a timeless combination, but I was surprised to learn that there are parts of the country where it is common to serve apple pie with a slice of sharp Cheddar cheese. My longtime pastry chef, Jaime Sudberg, educated me on this unique tradition by creating this apple tart topped with an intriguing, spectacular Cheddar streusel that is balanced by an orange shortbread crust.

ORANGE SHORTBREAD DOUGH

½ cup (1 stick) unsalted butter, at room temperature

2 tablespoons confectioners' sugar

Finely grated zest of ½ navel orange

1¼ cups (175 grams) unbleached all-purpose flour, plus more for rolling the dough

¼ teaspoon baking powder

⅛ teaspoon fine sea salt

FILLING

4 Granny Smith apples (see Note, page 222), about 1 pound, 10 ounces total

½ teaspoon ground cinnamon

⅛ teaspoon ground allspice

⅛ teaspoon freshly grated nutmeg

Pinch of fine sea salt

2 tablespoons granulated sugar

2 tablespoons cornstarch

⅓ cup water

CHEDDAR STREUSEL

⅔ cup (95 grams) unbleached all-purpose flour

3 tablespoons granulated sugar

1 tablespoon dark brown sugar

⅛ teaspoon ground cinnamon

⅛ teaspoon fine sea salt

½ cup (2 ounces) shredded sharp white Cheddar cheese, preferably Grafton Village

3 tablespoons unsalted butter, melted

───────────

Vanilla ice cream, for serving

1. To make the dough: Beat the butter, confectioners' sugar, and orange zest in a heavy-duty standing mixer fitted with the paddle attachment on medium-high speed until the butter is light in color, about 2 minutes. Whisk the flour, baking powder, and salt together in a small bowl. With the machine on low speed, gradually add the flour mixture and mix just until it clumps together. Gather up the dough into a thick disk. Wrap the dough in plastic wrap and refrigerate until chilled, about 1 hour. (The dough is easiest to use when it is chilled, but not rock hard. If chilled longer than 1 hour, let the dough stand at room temperature for 10 minutes or so to soften slightly before rolling out.)

2. Roll out the dough on a lightly floured work surface into a 12-inch round about ⅛ inch thick. Fit into a 9-inch tart pan with a removable bottom. The dough will crack, but just press it together, being sure that the dough is not too thick where the sides meet the bottom. Trim away the excess dough. Press the dough firmly against the sides of the pan so it rises about ¹⁄₁₆ inch above the pan rim. Freeze for 15 to 30 minutes.

3. Position a rack in the bottom third of the oven and preheat the oven to 375°F. Pierce the dough a few times with a fork. Line the pan with aluminum foil and fill the foil with pie weights or dried beans. Place the pan on a baking sheet. Bake until the dough looks set, 15 to 20 minutes. Remove the foil with the weights and continue baking until the dough is just beginning to brown, about 5 minutes more. Remove from the oven.

➤

4. To make the filling: Peel and core the apples and cut into ½-inch pieces. Combine the apples, cinnamon, allspice, nutmeg, and salt in a medium bowl. Whisk the granulated sugar and cornstarch together in a small microwave-safe bowl. Add the water and whisk well to dissolve. Microwave on high (100 percent) just until the mixture comes to a boil and thickens into a paste, about 30 seconds (or bring the cornstarch mixture to a simmer in a small saucepan over medium heat). Add the paste to the apple mixture and mix thoroughly but gently. Set aside while making the streusel.

5. To make the streusel: Using your fingers, mix the flour, granulated and brown sugars, cinnamon, and salt together in a medium bowl to break up the brown sugar. Add the cheese and mix to coat it. Add the melted butter and stir with a spoon until moistened. Press the streusel mixture into large clumps.

6. Reduce the oven temperature to 350°F. Mound the apple filling into the crust, arranging the pieces closely together (the filling will shrink during baking). Crumble the streusel evenly over the top and press it gently into the filling to adhere. Return the tart to the oven on the baking sheet and bake until the apples are tender and the streusel is golden brown, about 45 minutes. Let the tart cool in the pan on a wire cake rack for 10 minutes. Remove the sides of the pan and cool completely.

7. Cut the tart into wedges and serve with the ice cream.

__Note:__ I use Granny Smith apples here because they are sold everywhere, but ask your local apple source to suggest some baking apples. They must be a variety that holds its shape during baking. On the east coast, Golden Delicious are a good choice, but the same variety grown in west coast orchards isn't as flavorful.

CHOCOLATE
Bread Pudding

MAKES

8

SERVINGS

There is only one way to improve upon basic bread pudding, and that is to add chocolate (and lots of it, too). This is one of those desserts that always elicits a long "Oh... my... God..." from guests. If you really want to get fancy, add a cacao nib cookie to the top of each serving, as we do at the restaurants. However, trust me—this dessert is chocolate-y enough on it's own. Serve warm from the oven with vanilla ice cream or freshly whipped cream.

---

2 cups heavy cream

2 cups whole milk

3 (3-inch) cinnamon sticks

1 vanilla bean, split in half lengthwise

12 ounces bittersweet chocolate (about 70% cacao), finely chopped

¾ cup sugar

8 large egg yolks

12 ounces day-old brioche or challah bread, cut into 1-inch cubes, about 6 cups

Softened butter, for the baking dish

Vanilla ice cream or Whipped Cream (page 237), for serving

8 Cacao Nib Lace Cookies (page 231, optional)

---

1. Heat the cream, milk, cinnamon sticks, and vanilla bean halves together in a medium saucepan over medium heat, stirring occasionally, until tiny bubbles appear around the edge of the pan. Remove from the heat and let stand for 30 minutes. Discard the cinnamon sticks. Using the tip of a small knife, scrape the seeds from the vanilla bean into the liquid and discard the pod. Reheat the cream mixture until steaming.

2. Place the chocolate in a very large heatproof bowl. Pour in about half of the hot cream mixture and whisk until the chocolate is smooth and melted. Whisk in the remaining cream mixture. Whisk the sugar and egg yolks in a medium bowl until pale yellow. Gradually whisk in about 1 cup of the chocolate mixture, then whisk this back into the large bowl. Stir in the brioche cubes. Let the mixture stand, stirring occasionally, for 30 minutes for the bread to soak up some of the liquid.

3. Meanwhile, position a rack in the center of the oven and preheat the oven to 350ºF. Lightly butter a 9-by-13-inch baking dish.

4. Pour the bread mixture into the dish. Place the dish in a larger roasting pan. Pour enough hot water into the roasting pan to come about ½ inch up the sides. Transfer the pan setup to the oven and bake until the pudding has puffed evenly and a knife inserted in the center comes out clean, about 1¼ hours. Let cool until warm, about 20 minutes.

5. Cut the pudding into 8 equal portions. Transfer each to a dessert plate and top with a scoop of the ice cream. If desired, stick a cookie, standing up, in each ice cream scoop. Serve immediately.

PEANUT BUTTER
AND JELLY
"TWINKIES"

MAKES
18
TWINKIES

I love desserts that bring out the kid in me. This variation of the classic Twinkie combines submarine-shaped cakes with another childhood favorite, peanut butter and jelly. You will need silicone pans with log-shaped molds (sometimes called Christmas, buche, or yule log molds), which can be found online at bakedeco.com and amazon.com. The room-temperature cakes are easiest to fill with preserves that are chilled.

TWINKIE CAKES

Softened butter and flour,
for the molds

3 large eggs, at room temperature

1 cup plus 2 tablespoons sugar

1¼ cups (175 grams) unbleached
all-purpose flour

¾ teaspoon baking powder

¾ cup whole milk

½ cup smooth peanut butter

2 tablespoons unsalted butter,
thinly sliced

---

1 cup strawberry preserves

1 cup smooth peanut butter

½ cup finely crushed honey-roasted
peanuts

Special Equipment: 2 (9-cup) or
1 (24-cup) Christmas, buche, or yule
log silicone (sometimes called Flexipan)
baking pans, each mold measuring
about 3⁵⁄₁₆ by 1⅜ inches; round bristle
brush (optional); 2-ounce portion scoop
(optional); chopstick or mini–melon
baller; 2 small (12-inch) pastry bags;
2 (³⁄₁₆-inch) plain pastry tips, such
as Ateco #801

---

1. To make the cakes: Position a rack in the center of the oven and preheat the oven to 350°F. Butter and flour the insides of 18 log silicone molds, taking extra care not to leave any gaps (a round bristle brush works best); shake out the excess flour. Do not skip this step because the molds are flexible, but not actually nonstick. Place the pans on an 18-by-13-inch half-sheet pan.

2. Beat the eggs in the bowl of a standing heavy-duty mixer with the whisk attachment at medium-high speed until thickened. Gradually add the sugar and beat until the mixture is thick, fluffy, and tripled in volume, about 3 minutes.

3. Meanwhile, whisk together the flour and baking powder. Bring the milk, peanut butter, and butter to a simmer in a small saucepan, being sure the butter is melted. With the mixer on low speed, gradually beat the hot milk mixture into the egg mixture. Remove the bowl from the mixer. Add the flour mixture to the egg mixture and fold it in with a rubber spatula. Divide the batter evenly among the 18 molds, filling them about three-quarters full. (A 2-ounce-capacity portion scoop works best for transferring the batter.)

4. Bake until the cakes spring back when pressed gently with a fingertip, 20 to 25 minutes. Let the cakes cool *completely* in the pans. Do not rush this step. Run a dull knife around the inside of the molds, and carefully unmold the cakes.

5. Puree the preserves in a mini–food processor or blender, being sure to pulverize the chunks of fruit. Transfer to a small bowl and freeze until thickened but semi-fluid, at least 30 minutes.

6. Fit each of two small (12-inch) pastry bags with a ³⁄₁₆-inch plain pastry tip. Using a chopstick, poke a hole through the center of each cake. (A mini–melon baller also works very well to scoop out a tunnel for the filling.) Fill one end of the tunnel with preserves and the other side with peanut butter; reserve the remaining peanut butter and preserves. (The cakes can be loosely covered with plastic wrap and stored at room temperature for up to 8 hours.)

7. Put the Twinkies on a platter. Decorate the tops with the reserved peanut butter and preserves. Sprinkle with the peanuts and serve.

RED VELVET "TWINKIES"
with Crème Fraîche Filling

RED VELVET TWINKIE CAKES

Softened butter and flour, for the molds

1 cup plus 2 tablespoons (155 grams) unbleached all-purpose flour

2 tablespoons Dutch-process cocoa powder

1½ teaspoons baking powder

¼ teaspoon fine sea salt

2 tablespoons unsalted butter

½ cup whole milk

¼ teaspoon red food coloring gel or paste, plus more as needed

2 teaspoons vanilla extract

1 cup granulated sugar

2 large eggs and 1 large egg yolk, at room temperature

CRÈME FRAÎCHE FILLING

6 ounces cream cheese, at room temperature

½ cup confectioners' sugar

2 tablespoons crème fraîche or sour cream

¼ teaspoon vanilla extract

¼ teaspoon vanilla bean paste, or seeds scraped from ½ vanilla bean

---

Confectioners' sugar, for serving

Special Equipment: 2 (9-cup) or 1 (24-cup) Christmas, buche, or yule log silicone (also called Flexipan) baking pans, each mold measuring about 3⁵⁄₁₆ by 1⅜ inches; 2 medium pastry bags; round bristle brush (optional); 2-ounce-capacity portion scoop (optional); 1 large Bismarck tip (Ateco 230) or 1 (¼-inch) French star tip (Ateco 862); chopstick or mini–melon baller

Once you have the molds for the Peanut Butter and Jelly "Twinkies" on page 224, you'll be thinking of all the different flavors you can make. Red velvet cake used to be a Southern or Texas specialty, but now it's beloved all over the country—and perhaps nowhere more than in New York City. Here is my handheld Twinkie version of the classic. For the best color, use red food coloring gel or paste, not liquid.

1. To make the cakes: Position a rack in the center of the oven and preheat the oven to 350°F. Butter and flour the insides of 14 silicone log molds, taking extra care not to leave any gaps (a round bristle brush works best); shake out the excess flour. Do not skip this step because the molds are flexible, but not actually nonstick. Place the pans on an 18-by-13-inch half-sheet pan.

2. Sift the flour, cocoa, baking powder, and salt together. Melt the butter in a small saucepan over low heat. Add the milk and bring to a simmer. Remove from the heat, whisk in the food coloring and vanilla, and partially cover to keep warm.

3. Whip the granulated sugar, eggs, and egg yolk in the bowl of a heavy-duty standing mixer with the whisk attachment at medium-high speed until the mixture is pale yellow and forms a slowly dissolving, thick ribbon on the surface when the whisk is lifted, about 3 minutes. With the machine on medium-low speed, gradually pour the hot milk mixture into the mixer bowl. With the machine on low speed, gradually beat in the flour mixture and mix until smooth, scraping down the sides of the bowl as needed. If desired, tint the batter with additional red food coloring. Divide the batter evenly among the molds, filling them about three-quarters full. (A 2-ounce-capacity portion scoop works best for transferring the batter.)

4. Bake until the cakes spring back when pressed gently with a fingertip, 20 to 25 minutes. Let the cakes cool *completely* in the pans. Do not rush this step. Run a dull knife around the inside of the molds, and carefully unmold the cakes.

5. To make the filling: Mix the cream cheese and confectioners' sugar together in a medium bowl on medium speed until smooth. Add the crème fraîche, vanilla extract, and vanilla paste and mix on high speed until combined. Cover and refrigerate until chilled, at least 1 hour or up to 4 hours.

Transfer the filling to a pastry bag fitted with a ¼-inch star tip. (If you have it, a large Bismarck tip is made for filling long pastries and works best.) Using a chopstick, poke a tunnel through the center of each cake. (A mini–melon baller also works very well to scoop out a hole for the tunnel.) Working with one cake at a time, pipe the filling into both sides of the cake to fill the tunnel. Smooth the ends of the cake with your fingertip. Pipe an elongated swirl decoration onto the top of each cake.

6. Refrigerate the cakes to set the filling, about 10 minutes. Loosely cover the cakes and refrigerate until ready to serve, up to 8 hours. Sprinkle with confectioners' sugar and serve.

WHITE CHOCOLATE
BLONDIES
with SEMISWEET CHIPS

MAKES
12
LARGE BLONDIES

Everyone loves brownies, but for me, blondies are the way to go. Flavored with sweet and vanilla-y white chocolate, these moist and chewy squares are chock-full of semisweet chocolate chips as well. Be careful when purchasing white chocolate, as some inferior brands are made with palm oil, so check the ingredients to make sure that cacao butter is listed.

Softened butter and flour, for the pan

2 large eggs plus 1 large egg yolk, at room temperature

2 teaspoons vanilla extract

6 ounces white chocolate, finely chopped

¾ cup (1½ sticks) unsalted butter, cut up

1¼ cups sugar

2 cups unbleached all-purpose flour

¹⁄₁₆ teaspoon fine sea salt

1 cup semisweet chocolate chips

CHEF TALK

Quarter-Sheet Pans

Most home cooks are familiar with half-sheet pans, the workhorse of the professional kitchen. But check out quarter-sheet pans, measuring 9 by 13 by 1 inch. They also are very sturdy and handy for cooking smaller amounts of food—and they are the perfect pan for baking a batch of these blondies.

1. Position a rack in the center of the oven and preheat the oven to 350°F. Butter a 9-by-13-inch quarter-sheet pan, dust with flour, and tap out the excess flour. (If you'd like to use a standard 9-by-13-by-2-inch baking pan, butter the pan. Take an 18-inch-long piece of parchment paper and fold or cut it lengthwise so it is 9 inches wide. Fit it into the pan to line the bottom and two short sides, letting the excess paper hang over the sides as handles. Because the parchment paper is nonstick, buttering and flouring it is optional.)

2. Beat the eggs, yolk, and vanilla together in a small bowl. Put the white chocolate in the bowl of a standing heavy-duty mixer. Melt the butter in a medium saucepan over low heat. Pour over the white chocolate, let stand until softened, and whisk until smooth. Attach the bowl to the mixer and affix the paddle attachment. With the machine on medium-low speed, gradually beat in the sugar, followed by the egg mixture. Reduce the speed to low and mix in the flour and salt, followed by the chips. Spread the batter evenly in the pan.

3. Bake until the top is golden brown, about 25 minutes. Let cool completely in the pan on a wire cake rack. Run a dinner knife around the inside of the pan to loosen the blondie. (If using a standard baking pan, lift up on the paper handles to remove the blondie in one piece.) Cut the blondies into 12 equal pieces and serve. (The blondies can be individually wrapped in plastic wrap and stored in an airtight container at room temperature for up to 3 days.)

Reverse Chocolate Chip
Cookies

**MAKES
ABOUT**
28
COOKIES

You probably already have a favorite chocolate chip cookie recipe.
I'm here to share mine, which turns the tables by featuring a chocolate
dough studded with white chocolate chips. You'll get the deepest chocolate flavor from a bittersweet chocolate with 65% to 70% cacao content—
which is the amount listed on the wrappers of most top chocolates now.

3 tablespoons unsalted butter

9 ounces bittersweet chocolate
(about 70% cacao), finely chopped

3 ounces unsweetened chocolate,
finely chopped

⅓ cup plus 1 tablespoon (60 grams)
unbleached all-purpose flour

1 teaspoon fine sea salt

¾ teaspoon baking soda

1¼ cups sugar

3 large eggs, at room temperature

2 cups (12 ounces)
white chocolate chips

1. Position racks in the top third and center of the oven and
preheat the oven to 350°F. Line two 18-by-13-inch half-sheet
pans with parchment paper.

2. Bring about ½ inch of water to a simmer in a large skillet
over low heat. Put the butter in a large heatproof bowl, place the
bowl in the skillet, and melt the butter. Add the bittersweet and
unsweetened chocolate and heat, stirring occasionally with a
rubber spatula, until the mixture is smooth and the chocolate is
melted, about 5 minutes. Remove the bowl from the water
and let stand, stirring occasionally, until the mixture is tepid
and still liquid, 10 to 15 minutes.

3. Sift the flour, salt, and baking soda together. Combine the
sugar and eggs in the bowl of a heavy-duty standing mixer.
Beat on medium-high speed with the whisk attachment until the mixture is
pale yellow and has tripled in volume, about 2 minutes. With the mixer on low
speed, gradually mix in the chocolate mixture, followed by the flour mixture.
Mix in the chips.

4. Using about 2 tablespoons for each cookie (a 1-ounce food portion scoop
works well), scoop dough onto the baking sheets, spacing the cookies about
2 inches apart. Bake, switching the positions of the sheets from top to bottom
and front to back halfway through baking, until the cookies have a thin, shiny
crust and the edges feel set, 12 to 15 minutes. Let cool on the baking sheets
for 5 minutes. Transfer to wire cake racks to cool completely. (The cookies
can be stored in an airtight container at room temperature for up to 5 days.)

CACAO NIB
LACE COOKIES

3

Do not miss out on these delicate, almost transparent cookies with bittersweet cocoa flavor. They are surprisingly easy to make and keep for a few days. Stick one vertically into a scoop of ice cream and it will instantly add height and drama to the simple dessert. They are excellent with the chocolate bread pudding on page 223.

⅔ cup sugar

3 tablespoons light corn syrup or glucose

3 tablespoons whole milk

¼ cup (½ stick) unsalted butter, melted

¼ cup Dutch-processed cocoa powder

½ cup very coarsely crushed cacao nibs (see Chef Talk, this page)

CHEF TALK

Cacao Nibs

Cacao nibs are crushed cacao beans. They are unsweetened and bitter, so don't bite into one and expect the same flavor as a chocolate bar... but that lack of sweetness is what makes them so useful in desserts. (Some people like them as a replacement for chocolate in chocolate chip cookies.) They are sold at natural food stores.

1. Position a rack in the top third and center of the oven and preheat the oven to 350°F. Line two 18-by-13-inch half-sheet pans with silicone baking mats or parchment paper.

2. Bring the sugar, corn syrup, and milk to a simmer in a medium saucepan over medium-low heat, whisking constantly to dissolve the syrup. Remove from the heat and whisk in the melted butter, followed by the cocoa. Stir in the cacao nibs.

3. Using about 2 teaspoons for each cookie, spoon 4 mounds of the batter onto the silicone mats, spacing them well apart. (Because the cookies spread so much—even more than you might expect—it helps to do a test run to check the number of cookies that will fit on your baking sheet.) Bake the cookies until they spread into 3-inch rounds and look lacy with set edges, 7 to 10 minutes. Let the cookies cool and crisp on the baking sheet, about 5 minutes. Transfer the cookies to a wire rack to cool completely. Repeat with the remaining batter. Once you get the hang of it, you can bake two sheets of cookies at a time. (The cookies can be stored in an airtight container at room temperature for up to 5 days.)

BLACK-BOTTOMED
BUTTERSCOTCH
Pots de Crème

MAKES
6
SERVINGS

When it comes to dining, I love a good surprise. These layered butterscotch desserts feature a hidden chocolate base and an unexpected coconut-infused whipped cream topping. Make sure you instruct your guests to really dig down into the bottom of their glasses, as the best bites include all three elements. The butterscotch layer is thickened with egg yolks only, so be patient when cooking, as it takes time for the mixture to reach the thickening point.

CHOCOLATE BASE

⅔ cup heavy cream

3 tablespoons whole milk

3 large egg yolks

3 ounces bittersweet chocolate
(about 70% cacao), finely chopped

1½ ounces milk chocolate
(about 40% cacao), finely chopped

BUTTERSCOTCH CRÈME

3 cups heavy cream,
heated to steaming

½ vanilla bean, split lengthwise

⅔ cup packed dark brown sugar

¼ cup water

9 large egg yolks

2 tablespoons granulated sugar

¹⁄₁₆ teaspoon fine sea salt

WHIPPED COCONUT TOPPING

¼ cup plus 3 tablespoons
sweetened coconut flakes

⅔ cup heavy cream

2 teaspoons confectioners' sugar

½ teaspoon vanilla extract

Special Equipment: 6 (1-cup)
glasses or jars

1. To make the chocolate base: Heat the cream and milk together in a small heavy-bottomed saucepan over medium heat until steaming. Whisk the egg yolks well in a medium heatproof bowl. Gradually whisk in the hot cream mixture. Return this to the saucepan and reduce the heat to medium-low. Cook, stirring constantly with a wooden spoon, until the custard reaches 185°F on an instant-read thermometer and is thick enough to coat the spoon (a finger swiped through the custard on the spoon will cut a swath), about 3 minutes.

2. Combine the bittersweet and milk chocolates in a medium heatproof bowl, and place a wire sieve over the bowl. Strain the custard (to remove any bits of cooked egg) directly into the chocolates. Let the mixture stand for 1 minute. Whisk until the chocolate is smooth and melted. Divide the chocolate base equally among six 1-cup glasses or jars. Cover and refrigerate until the base is chilled and set, at least 1 hour.

3. To make the butterscotch layer: Bring the cream and vanilla bean to a simmer in a medium saucepan over medium heat. Remove from the heat and let stand for 15 minutes. Using the tip of a small knife, scrape the seeds from the bean into the cream and discard the bean.

4. Bring the brown sugar and water to a boil in a medium heavy-bottomed saucepan over high heat, stirring constantly, until the sugar is dissolved and the syrup is boiling. Cook without stirring, occasionally swirling the saucepan by the handle, until the syrup is very thick with large bubbles and reaches 270°F on a candy thermometer, about 5 minutes. Reduce the heat to low. Carefully ladle the hot cream mixture into the brown sugar syrup (it will splatter) and stir until well combined. Remove from the heat.

➡

5. Whisk the egg yolks and granulated sugar together in a medium heatproof bowl. Choose a wide saucepan large enough to nestle the bowl. Bring about 1 inch of water to a simmer in the saucepan over high heat. Reduce the heat to keep the water at a steady simmer.

6. Whisk the hot cream mixture into the egg yolks. Place the bowl over the simmering water (the bowl bottom should not touch the water). Cook, stirring almost constantly with a rubber spatula and scraping down any splashes on the side of the bowl, until the custard reaches at least 190°F on an instant-read thermometer and is thicker than the typical custard sauce, about 10 minutes. The idea is to cook the custard as much as possible without it coming to a simmer and curdling, which takes some time, so be patient.

7. Strain the custard through a wire sieve into another medium bowl to remove any bits of cooked egg. Add the salt. Using an immersion blender or hand mixer on low speed, beat the custard for 1 to 2 minutes to expel some of the steam and help cool it. Place the bowl in a larger bowl of ice water and let stand, stirring occasionally, until the custard is tepid, about 10 minutes. Divide the custard evenly over the chocolate bases in the glasses. Cover each glass with plastic wrap. Refrigerate until the pots de crème are chilled, at least 4 hours or up to 1 day.

8. To make the topping: Combine ¼ cup of the coconut with the heavy cream in a small saucepan and bring to a simmer over low heat. Remove from the heat and let infuse for 30 minutes. Strain the mixture through a wire sieve into a medium bowl, pressing hard on the coconut. Place the bowl in a larger bowl of ice water and let stand until chilled, about 30 minutes. Add the confectioners' sugar and vanilla. Whip with an electric mixer until the topping forms soft peaks. Cover and refrigerate until ready to serve, up to 4 hours.

9. Meanwhile, position a rack in the center of the oven and preheat the oven to 350°F. Spread the remaining 3 tablespoons coconut on a small baking sheet. Bake, stirring occasionally, until the coconut is lightly browned, 7 to 10 minutes. (This can also be done, very efficiently, in a toaster oven.) Let cool.

10. Top each pot de crème with a dollop of whipped topping and a sprinkling of the toasted coconut. Serve chilled.

LIME AND BLACKBERRY
SEMIFREDDO

For a refreshing summer dessert, try this cool *semifreddo*, a "half-frozen" dessert that does not require an ice cream maker. Similar to gelato, semifreddo has a creamy texture and a tangy flavor with purple layers of blackberries running through it. It is best made a day before serving so it has ample time to achieve the ideal firmness. It takes a few bowls to make, but you won't mind when you taste the end result.

MAKES

8 *to* 10

SERVINGS

LIME CURD

4 to 5 limes

3 large eggs plus 3 large egg yolks
(reserve the whites for the semifreddo)

⅓ cup plus 1 tablespoon sugar

½ cup (1 stick) unsalted butter,
cut into tablespoons,
at room temperature

BLACKBERRY PUREE

1 (6-ounce) container fresh
blackberries, about 1⅓ cups

½ cup sugar

1 tablespoon water

SEMIFREDDO

1 cup sugar

4 large egg whites, at room
temperature

1 cup heavy cream

1 lime, for serving

Additional blackberries,
for serving

1. To make the curd: Finely grate the zest from 3 of the limes into a small bowl and set aside. Juice the limes to get ½ cup. Whisk the eggs, yolks, and sugar together in a small nonreactive saucepan. Cook over medium-low heat, whisking constantly, until warm, about 2 minutes. Gradually whisk in the juice. Continue cooking, whisking constantly, until the mixture is very thick, steaming, and reaches 185°F on an instant-read thermometer, about 3 minutes. Do not let the mixture boil, or it will curdle and you'll have to start over. Strain through a wire sieve (to remove any cooked bits of egg white) into a medium bowl. Put the bowl in a larger bowl of ice water and let the curd cool, whisking occasionally, until tepid, about 10 minutes.

2. Using an immersion blender, add the butter to the lime mixture, one tablespoon at a time, and beat until smooth. (Or whisk in the butter, a tablespoon at a time.) Stir in the reserved zest. Cover and refrigerate until chilled and set, at least 1 hour or up to 3 days.

3. Meanwhile, make the blackberry puree: Combine the blackberries with the sugar and water in a medium nonreactive saucepan. Bring to a simmer over medium heat, crushing the berries to release juices and stirring to dissolve the sugar. Simmer until the juices form a light syrup, about 5 minutes. Rub the mixture through a wire sieve into a small bowl to remove the seeds; discard the solids. Transfer the bowl to the larger bowl of ice water (use fresh ice) and let it cool until chilled, about 10 minutes.

➤

4. To make the semifreddo: Whisk the sugar and egg whites together in the bowl of a standing heavy-duty mixer. Place the bowl over a saucepan of simmering water and whisk, being sure to scrape down any splashes on the sides of the bowl, until the sugar is completely dissolved and the mixture is very warm; do not overcook. Set the bowl in the mixer and whip with the whisk attachment on medium-high speed until the meringue is cool (feel the bowl bottom), shiny, and forms stiff peaks, about 5 minutes. Remove the bowl from the mixer. Using a rubber spatula, fold the cold curd into the meringue.

5. Whip the cream in a chilled medium bowl with an electric mixer set on high speed until it forms soft peaks. Fold the cream into the meringue mixture.

6. Line a 9-by-5-by-3-inch loaf pan with a large sheet of plastic wrap, letting the excess wrap hang over the sides. Fill the loaf with one-third of the lime mixture, and top with one half of the blackberry puree. Repeat, and finish with the remaining lime mixture. Smooth the top and cover with the wrap overhang. Freeze until frozen and set (it won't be as hard as ice cream), at least 6 hours or overnight.

7. Fold back the plastic wrap and unmold the semifreddo onto a platter, discarding the wrap. Using a thin sharp knife dipped in warm water, slice the semifreddo. Transfer each slice to a dessert plate and top with a few berries and some lime zest grated with a Microplane.

Peanut Butter
ICE CREAM SUNDAES
with HOT FUDGE AND PEANUT BRITTLE

MAKES
6
SERVINGS

I am seriously in love with peanut butter… but I'm a two-timer because I also have a crush on ice cream. When I want to indulge in both my passions, this is the dessert that scratches the itch. I suppose you could make it with stuff off the supermarket shelf, but it is more satisfying and tasty to make all the components yourself.

FUDGE SAUCE

¾ cup sugar

⅓ cup plus 1 tablespoon
Dutch-processed cocoa powder

¹⁄₁₆ teaspoon fine sea salt

½ cup water

⅓ cup light corn syrup

½ cup (1 stick) unsalted butter, cut up

4 ounces bittersweet chocolate
(about 70% cacao), finely chopped

½ teaspoon vanilla extract

PEANUT BRITTLE

1 cup sugar

½ cup light corn syrup

¼ cup water

⅛ teaspoon cream of tartar

1 cup roasted peanuts,
coarsely crushed

1 tablespoon unsalted butter

½ teaspoon ground cinnamon

½ teaspoon fine sea salt

½ teaspoon baking soda, sifted
to remove any lumps

PEANUT BUTTER CRUNCH

⅓ cup smooth peanut butter

1½ ounces white chocolate,
finely chopped

1 cup crispy rice cereal, such as
Rice Krispies or Cocoa Krispies

WHIPPED CREAM

1 cup heavy cream

2 tablespoons confectioners' sugar

½ teaspoon vanilla extract

———————

Peanut Butter Ice Cream (page 239)

———————

Special Equipment: Silicone
baking mat

1. To make the fudge sauce: Whisk the sugar, cocoa, and salt together in a medium saucepan. Gradually whisk in the water, followed by the corn syrup. Bring the mixture to a boil over high heat, whisking often to dissolve the sugar. Remove from the heat, add the butter and chocolate, and whisk until they are melted. Return to medium heat and return to a boil, whisking often. Remove from the heat and stir in the vanilla. Transfer the sauce to a heatproof bowl and let cool until tepid. You should have about 2¼ cups fudge sauce. (The sauce can be covered and refrigerated for up to 1 day. Reheat by placing the bowl in a skillet of lightly simmering water, or in a microwave oven.)

2. To make the peanut brittle: Line a large rimmed baking sheet with a silicone baking mat. Bring the sugar, corn syrup, water, and cream of tartar to a boil in a medium saucepan over high heat, stirring constantly, until the sugar is dissolved and the syrup is boiling. Cook without stirring, occasionally swirling the saucepan by the handle and washing down any sugar crystals on the sides of the saucepan with a pastry brush dipped in cold water, until the caramel has turned the color of an old penny, about 5 minutes. Remove from the heat. Add the peanuts, butter, cinnamon, and salt and stir to combine. Stir in the baking soda (the brittle will foam up) and immediately pour out onto the baking mat. Let cool completely. Coarsely break the brittle into pieces about 2 inches square. (The brittle can be stored in an ■→→

airtight container at room temperature for up to 2 days.)

3. To make the crunch: Line a small baking sheet with parchment paper. In the top part of a double boiler over barely simmering water, heat the peanut butter until it softens. Add the white chocolate and heat, stirring often, until the mixture is smooth. Stir in the cereal. Pour the crunch onto the baking sheet. Refrigerate until the crunch is set (it will not be hard), about 30 minutes. Coarsely chop the crunch.

4. To whip the cream: Whip the cream, confectioners' sugar, and vanilla in chilled medium bowl with an electric hand mixer at high speed until stiff. (The whipped cream can be covered and refrigerated for up to 4 hours.)

5. To serve, scoop equal amounts of the ice cream into 6 large ice cream dishes or bowls, preferably glass. Divide the hot fudge sauce, peanut brittle, and peanut butter crunch among the bowls, and top with the whipped cream. Serve immediately.

PEANUT BUTTER ICE CREAM

Makes about 5 cups

Infused with intense peanut flavor, this is bound to become a favorite if you love peanut butter as much as I do.

1½ cups heavy cream

1½ cups whole milk

¾ cup coarsely crushed roasted unsalted peanuts

5 large egg yolks

⅔ cup sugar

⅓ cup plus 1 tablespoon creamy peanut butter

Pinch of fine sea salt

1. Heat the cream, milk, and peanuts together in a medium saucepan over medium heat, stirring occasionally, until tiny bubbles appear around the edges of the liquid. Remove from the heat and let stand for 30 minutes.

2. Whisk the yolks and sugar together in a medium heat-proof bowl until the mixture is pale yellow. Gradually whisk in the hot cream mixture. Return this mixture to the saucepan. Cook over medium-low heat, stirring constantly, until the custard registers 185°F on an instant-read thermometer and coats the spoon (a finger swiped through the custard on the spoon will cut a swath), 3 to 5 minutes. Strain the custard into a clean medium bowl discarding the solids in the sieve. Add the peanut butter and whisk until smooth.

3. Place the bowl in a larger bowl of ice water and let stand, stirring often, until the custard is cold, about 30 minutes. Stir in the salt. Remove the bowl of custard from the ice water, cover with plastic wrap, and refrigerate until well chilled, at least 2 hours or up to 1 day.

4. Freeze the custard in an ice cream machine according to the manufacturer's directions. (The frozen ice cream will be semisoft.) Transfer the ice cream to a covered container. Freeze until the ice cream is firm enough to scoop, at least 4 hours or up to 2 days.

BRUNCH

Brunch is the perfect meal for entertaining. On a weekend afternoon, guests are more relaxed because they aren't rushing in after a day of work, and the cook often has a bit of extra time to prepare the meal. Since the weekends are meant for bending the rules, I like my brunch spreads to be a little richer and more indulgent than the rest of the week (pancakes, waffles, and French toast—I'm talking to you). So, here are my best brunch dishes, offering something for everyone, from the people who must have eggs to start the day to the ones who love sweets with (or without) their coffee.

SLOW-BAKED
Tomato Bruschetta
with Eggs and Parmesan

—

Triple-Decker
CROQUE
MONSIEURS

—

BAKED EGGS *with*
SERRANO HAM *and*
Manchego "Grits"

—

Fried Chicken
with **Cheddar Waffles and Spicy Butter**

—

HUEVOS RANCHEROS
Soft Tacos *with*
Avocado Pico de Gallo

—

POTATO LATKES
with Sour Cream and
Fresh Applesauce

—

JUICY LUCY
Sausage Biscuits

OREO PANCAKES
with
Vanilla Crème Icing

—

Lemon Berry
Pancakes
with Whipped Citrus Ricotta

—

FRENCH TOAST
Bread Pudding
with **Pumpkin Maple Syrup**

—

Orange-Bourbon
Pull-Apart Bread

—

DOUGHNUTS
with Cinnamon Sugar and Berry Sauce

—

Red Velvet
WAFFLES
with Cream Cheese Sauce

Slow-Baked
Tomato Bruschetta
with EGGS and PARMESAN

MAKES

18

BRUSCHETTA

4 SERVINGS

A variation on the eggs-and-toast theme, this is especially easy to pull off if you marinate the tomatoes overnight—a step that not only saves time on Sunday morning, but also deepens their flavor. When scrambling the eggs, be sure to keep them very soft, as they will continue to cook and firm from crossover heat.

MARINATED TOMATOES

9 Roma (plum) tomatoes, cored and halved lengthwise

Extra-virgin olive oil

Kosher salt and freshly ground black pepper

Finely grated zest of 1 lemon

2 tablespoons fresh lemon juice

2 teaspoons finely chopped fresh basil

½ teaspoon finely chopped fresh thyme (optional)

1 small garlic clove, minced

⅛ teaspoon hot pepper flakes

———

18 (¼ inch) slices baguette, cut on a diagonal

2 tablespoons unsalted butter

9 large eggs

½ teaspoon kosher salt

¼ teaspoon freshly ground black pepper

3 tablespoons freshly grated Parmigiano-Reggiano cheese

1. To bake the tomatoes: Position a rack in the center of the oven and preheat the oven to 300°F. Line a large rimmed baking sheet with parchment paper.

2. Arrange the tomatoes, cut sides up, on the baking sheet and brush lightly with oil. Season to taste with salt and pepper. Bake until the tomatoes look shrunken and are beginning to brown around the edges, about 2½ hours. Let cool until warm. Keeping the tomatoes as intact as possible, slip off and discard the skins.

3. Whisk ¼ cup olive oil with the lemon zest and juice, basil, thyme, if using, garlic, and hot pepper flakes in a small bowl. Add the tomatoes, cover, and marinate at room temperature for at least 1 hour. (If you have the time, refrigerate the tomatoes for at least 4 hours or up to 3 days. Bring to room temperature before using.)

4. Position the broiler rack 4 inches from the source of heat and preheat the broiler on high. Toast the bread slices in the broiler, turning them once, about 2 minutes. Arrange the bread on a platter.

5. Melt the butter in a medium nonstick skillet over medium heat. Whisk the eggs, salt, and pepper together in a medium bowl. Add to the skillet and cook, stirring often with a heat-proof silicone spatula, until the eggs are set, but moist—do not overcook. Remove from the heat.

6. For each bruschetta, top a bread slice with a tomato half, followed by some egg. Sprinkle with Parmigiano. Drizzle some of the tomato-flavored oil from the marinated tomatoes over the bruschetta and serve immediately.

Triple-Decker
CROQUE
MONSIEURS

MAKES

4 *to* 6

SERVINGS

The French version of grilled cheese, known as a *croque monsieur*, is simply the ultimate. To double the decadence, I build a second layer of ham and cheese on the first. Slathered with a mustard-infused béchamel and griddled until golden brown, these triangular bites are made for sharing.

MUSTARD BÉCHAMEL SAUCE

¾ cup plus 2 tablespoons whole milk

⅓ cup heavy cream

¼ cup chopped yellow onion

½ teaspoon yellow mustard seed

¼ teaspoon freshly grated nutmeg

½ bay leaf

2 points star anise

2 cloves

3 tablespoons unsalted butter

3 tablespoons unbleached all-purpose flour

2 tablespoons Dijon mustard

Kosher salt

---

12 slices brioche loaf or challah (see Note, page 246)

1 cup (4 ounces) shredded Gruyère cheese

16 wide slices Black Forest ham (about 8 ounces), trimmed to fit the bread

8 wide slices domestic Muenster cheese (about 6 ounces), trimmed to fit the bread

---

Special Equipment: 16 bamboo or wooden skewers, for serving

1. To make the sauce: Bring the milk, cream, onion, mustard seed, nutmeg, bay leaf, star anise, and cloves to a simmer in a medium heavy-bottomed saucepan over medium heat, taking care that the mixture does not boil over. Reduce the heat to low and heat to steep without reducing the liquid, about 10 minutes. Strain the mixture through a wire sieve into a bowl. Press hard on the solids, then discard them. Wash the saucepan.

2. Melt the butter in the saucepan over medium heat. Whisk in the flour and let bubble without browning for 1 minute. Gradually whisk in the hot milk mixture and bring to a simmer. Reduce the heat to medium-low and simmer, whisking often, until no raw flour taste remains, about 5 minutes. Remove from the heat and stir in the Dijon mustard. Season to taste with salt. Transfer the sauce to a medium bowl, cover with plastic wrap pressed onto the surface, and let cool completely. (The sauce can be refrigerated for up to 1 day.)

3. To make four triple-decker sandwiches: For each sandwich, spread a bread slice with about 1 tablespoon of the warm sauce, followed by 2 tablespoons of shredded Gruyère, 2 slices of ham, and 1 slice of Muenster. Repeat with a second bread slice, sauce, Gruyère, ham, and Muenster. Top with a third slice of bread. Cover the remaining sauce with the saucepan lid and set aside. (The sandwiches can be wrapped in plastic wrap and stored at room temperature, with the sauce, for up to 2 hours.)

4. Heat a griddle over high heat. Reduce the heat to medium-low. Place the sandwiches onto the griddle. Cook, adjusting the heat as needed so the sandwiches don't brown too quickly but the bread has time to toast, until the undersides are golden brown, about 5 minutes. Flip them over to brown the other sides

➡

and heat the sandwiches through, about 5 minutes more. Transfer the sandwiches to a chopping board.

5. Cut each sandwich into quarters with a sharp, serrated knife to avoid pressing the sandwich. Serve warm with any remaining sauce.

Note: Rectangular loaves of brioche bread are sold at many specialty bakeries and natural food superstores. Challah is similar to brioche, but it is usually braided and makes irregularly shaped slices. Although egg-enriched bread is my personal favorite, any good-tasting sandwich bread will do for this recipe. The proportions of the filling may change slightly with the size of the bread slices, so be flexible with the amounts.

BAKED EGGS

with SERRANO HAM

AND MANCHEGO "GRITS"

MAKES

4

SERVINGS

One of the most comforting brunch dishes I know, this never fails to make an impression when the skillet, dotted with baked eggs, arrives at the table. Be flexible with the cheese, as Gruyère, sharp Cheddar, and Fontina are all good options. You could also turn this into a vegetarian dish by substituting sautéed mushrooms for the ham and vegetable broth for the chicken broth.

MANCHEGO "GRITS"

1¼ cups whole milk

1¼ cups reduced-sodium chicken broth

½ cup heavy cream

¼ cup (½ stick) unsalted butter

½ teaspoon dried oregano

½ teaspoon kosher salt

¼ teaspoon freshly ground black pepper

1 cup yellow masa arepa (see Note, page 97)

1 cup (4 ounces) shredded Manchego cheese

2 tablespoons finely chopped fresh chives

———————

4 ounces thinly sliced Serrano ham or prosciutto

⅓ cup (1½ ounces) shredded Manchego cheese

6 large eggs

Kosher salt and freshly ground black pepper, for serving

Finely chopped fresh chives, for garnish

1. To make the Manchego "grits": Bring the milk, broth, cream, butter, oregano, salt, and pepper to a simmer in a medium saucepan over medium heat. Whisk in the masa arepa and return to a simmer. Cook, whisking often, until the mixture thickens, about 3 minutes. Remove from the heat and whisk in the Manchego and chives.

2. Meanwhile, position a rack in the center of the oven and preheat the oven to 350°F.

3. Line a large heavy ovenproof skillet (about 12 inches in diameter), preferably cast iron, with three-quarters of the ham. Spread the masa mixture in the skillet and sprinkle with the cheese. Using the back of an oiled soup spoon, make 4 indentations in the masa mixture, spaced equally apart and large enough to hold a single egg. Crack an egg into each indentation. Bake just until the egg whites are set but the yolks are sunny side up, 20 to 25 minutes.

4. Cut the remaining ham into ½-inch strips. Cook in a small skillet over medium heat until lightly browned. Season the eggs with salt and pepper. Sprinkle with the ham, followed by the chives. Serve immediately.

Fried Chicken
with CHEDDAR WAFFLES
and Spicy Butter

MAKES ABOUT

12

(4-INCH) WAFFLES

4 TO 6 SERVINGS

Supposedly, chicken and waffles were popularized by jazz clubs in Chicago and Harlem—the musicians jammed so late that at mealtime, the chef had to offer a meal that served as both dinner *and* breakfast! These fresh, hot waffles are topped with crisp fried chicken, spiced up with piquant butter, and doused with maple syrup for a sweet-hot counterpoint that is truly irresistible.

SPICY BUTTER

½ cup (1 stick) unsalted butter, at room temperature

1 teaspoon hot red pepper sauce, preferably ½ teaspoon mellow sauce (such as Frank's RedHot) plus ½ teaspoon sharp sauce (such as Tabasco)

¼ teaspoon fine sea salt

Pinch of cayenne pepper

BREADED CHICKEN

2 large skinless, boneless chicken breast halves, each about 8 ounces

⅓ cup unbleached all-purpose flour

¼ teaspoon kosher salt

¼ teaspoon freshly ground black pepper

1 large egg

⅔ cup panko (Japanese bread crumbs)

CHEDDAR WAFFLES

2 large eggs

1½ cups whole milk

½ cup buttermilk

2 tablespoons unsalted butter, melted

2 cups (280 grams) unbleached all-purpose flour

⅓ cup yellow cornmeal, preferably stone-ground

1½ tablespoons sugar

4 teaspoons baking powder

½ teaspoon salt

1 cup (4 ounces) shredded sharp white Cheddar cheese

½ cup canola or vegetable oil, plus more for the waffle iron

1½ cups pure maple syrup, warmed, for serving

Special Equipment: Nonstick waffle iron

1. To make the spicy butter: Beat the butter in a medium bowl with an electric mixer on medium speed until fluffy. Add the mild and sharp hot sauces, salt, and cayenne, and beat until combined. Transfer to a small serving bowl and set aside at room temperature.

2. To bread the chicken: One at a time, place each chicken breast half between two sheets of plastic wrap. Using a flat meat pounder or rolling pin, pound the chicken to ¾-inch thickness.

3. Mix the flour, salt, and pepper in a wide shallow bowl. Beat the egg well in a second wide bowl, and spread the panko in a third bowl. Line a baking sheet with waxed paper. One at a time, use one hand to coat a piece of chicken in the flour. Use your other hand to dip the chicken in the eggs, shaking off the excess eggs. Go back to your dry hand to coat the chicken in the panko, patting to adhere the panko. Transfer the chicken to the waxed paper and let stand for 10 minutes.

4. Meanwhile, begin making the waffles: Position racks in the top third and center of the oven and preheat the oven to 200°F. Line a large rimmed baking sheet with a wire rack for the chicken. Preheat a nonstick waffle iron according to the manufacturer's directions.

5. Whisk the eggs together in a large bowl until combined. Add the milk, buttermilk, and ➤

melted butter and whisk to combine. In another bowl, whisk the flour, cornmeal, sugar, baking powder, and salt together. Add the Cheddar and toss to coat with the flour mixture. Add to the milk mixture and stir with a wooden spoon just until combined.

6. Lightly oil the waffle iron. Using about ⅔ cup of batter for each waffle, spoon the batter into the waffle iron and cook according to the manufacturer's instructions until golden brown. Transfer the waffle to directly on the oven rack (do not use a baking sheet) to keep warm. Repeat with the remaining batter.

7. Meanwhile, cook the chicken: Heat the ½ cup canola oil in a very large skillet over medium-high heat until the oil is shimmering but not smoking. Add the chicken and reduce the heat to medium. Cook until the undersides are golden brown, about 3½ minutes. Flip the chicken and cook until the other sides are crisp and the chicken feels firm when pressed on top in its center, about 3 minutes more. Adjust the heat as needed so the chicken cooks steadily without burning the panko. Using a slotted spatula, transfer the chicken to the wire rack on the baking sheet and keep warm in the oven while finishing the waffles.

8. Cut the waffles apart (usually into four individual waffles) and overlap them on a platter. Transfer the chicken to a chopping board and cut into 12 relatively equal pieces. Top each waffle with a piece of chicken, a teaspoon-sized dollop of the spicy butter, and a drizzle of warm maple syrup. Serve immediately, with the remaining maple syrup and spicy butter passed on the side.

HUEVOS RANCHEROS
SOFT TACOS with
AVOCADO PICO DE GALLO

MAKES
12
TACOS
4 TO 6
SERVINGS

I am all for my guests to go DIY at brunch, and self-serve tacos are the perfect way to do so. Huevos rancheros is a great brunch dish, but it needs some tweaking to serve to a group, so I've broken down the elements. Scramble your eggs with chorizo, and they're ready to tuck into warm tortillas, with toppings like pico de gallo, black beans, and chile crema. If you have a chafing dish or fondue pot, you could use it to keep the scrambled eggs warm during serving.

AVOCADO PICO DE GALLO

1 ripe beefsteak tomato, seeded and cut into ½-inch dice

2 tablespoons minced red onion

1 tablespoon minced fresh cilantro

1 tablespoon minced seeded jalapeño

1 tablespoon fresh lime juice

1 teaspoon adobo sauce from canned chipotles

1 ripe Hass avocado, pitted, peeled, and cut into ½-inch dice

Kosher salt and freshly ground black pepper

BLACK BEANS

1 tablespoon extra-virgin olive oil

½ cup chopped white onion

1 garlic clove, minced

1 (15-ounce) can black beans, rinsed and drained

½ cup Vegetable Stock (page 190) or reduced-sodium chicken broth

1 canned chipotle in adobo, minced to a puree

½ cup (2 ounces) shredded sharp white Cheddar cheese

2 tablespoons chopped fresh cilantro

Kosher salt and freshly ground black pepper

CHILE CREMA

½ cup sour cream

1 chipotle chile in adobo, minced

EGGS

4 ounces smoked Spanish-style chorizo, cut into ¼-inch dice

2 tablespoons unsalted butter

10 large eggs

Kosher salt and freshly ground black pepper

1 cup (4 ounces) shredded sharp white Cheddar cheese

————————

12 soft-taco flour tortillas

Lime wedges, for serving

1. To make the pico de gallo: Mix the tomato, onion, cilantro, jalapeño, lime juice, and adobo in a medium bowl. Add the avocado and fold it in gently without mashing. Season to taste with salt and pepper. Cover with plastic wrap and set aside. (The pico de gallo can be stored at room temperature for up to 4 hours.)

2. To make the black beans: Heat the oil in a medium saucepan over medium heat. Add the onion and garlic and cook, stirring occasionally, until the onion is translucent, about 4 minutes. Add the beans, stock, and chipotle and bring to a simmer. Adjust the heat to medium-low and cook at a brisk simmer, stirring occasionally, until the beans are hot and the stock has reduced by about half, about 10 minutes. Remove from the heat. Add the cheese and cilantro. Using an immersion blender, process in the saucepan into a chunky sauce. (Or mash the mixture with a potato masher.) Season to taste with salt and pepper. Reduce the heat to very low, cover, and keep warm. (The beans can be cooled, covered, and refrigerated for up to 1 day. Reheat in the saucepan.)

3. To make the crema: Mix the sour cream and chipotle together in a small serving bowl. Set aside at room temperature for 30 minutes to lose its chill.
➡

4. To scramble the eggs: Cook the chorizo in a large skillet, preferably nonstick, over medium heat, stirring occasionally, until the chorizo is browned, 3 to 5 minutes. Using a slotted spoon, transfer the chorizo to paper towels to drain. Pour off the fat in the skillet.

5. Melt the butter in the skillet over medium heat. Using a handheld blender or a large whisk, whip the eggs with ½ teaspoon salt and ¼ teaspoon pepper in a large bowl. Pour into the skillet and add the chorizo. Cook, stirring occasionally, just until the eggs are softly scrambled, about 5 minutes. Remove from the heat and fold in the cheese. Season to taste with salt and pepper. Transfer to a serving bowl.

6. Heat the tortillas according to the package directions. Place the tortillas in a napkin-lined basket to keep warm.

7. Transfer the black beans to a serving bowl. Serve the scrambled eggs, black beans, pico de gallo, crema, warm tortillas, and limes, allowing guests to make their own tacos.

POTATO LATKES

with **SOUR CREAM** AND **FRESH APPLESAUCE**

MAKES
16
LATKES
4 SERVINGS

I've spent a couple of decades working on Manhattan's Lower East Side, the hub of traditional Jewish culture in New York, and subsequently learned how to make a mean latke. Most recipes start with grated raw potatoes, which need to be squeezed to remove the excess juice. Instead, I use baked potatoes, and they work perfectly. Another important tip: Don't skimp on the cooking oil or the pancakes won't develop that crispy, golden brown that latke lovers crave. Applesauce is the traditional sweet-sour accompaniment.

APPLESAUCE

4 Granny Smith apples, cored, peeled, and coarsely chopped

⅓ cup sugar

½ cup water

LATKES

4 large baking potatoes, such as russets, about 2½ pounds total

2 scallions, white and green parts, finely chopped

1 large egg, beaten

1 teaspoon kosher salt

½ teaspoon freshly ground black pepper

A few gratings of fresh nutmeg

Vegetable oil, for frying

---

1 scallion, white and green parts, finely chopped, for garnish (optional)

½ cup sour cream, for serving

Special Equipment: 2½-inch round cookie cutter

1. To make the applesauce: Bring the apples, sugar, and water to a boil in a medium heavy-bottomed saucepan, stirring often to dissolve the sugar. Reduce the heat to medium-low and simmer, uncovered, stirring occasionally, until the apples are very tender and the water has evaporated, about 20 minutes. Puree the apple mixture in the saucepan with an immersion blender (or in batches in a standing blender with the lid ajar). Transfer to a small bowl and let cool. (The applesauce can be made up to 3 days ahead. Bring to room temperature before serving.)

2. To make the latkes: Position a rack in the center of the oven and preheat the oven to 375°F. Pierce each potato a few times with a dinner fork. Place the potatoes on a baking sheet and bake until tender, about 40 minutes. Let the potatoes cool until they can be handled but are still warm, about 15 minutes. Peel the potatoes. Shred the potatoes on the large holes of a box grater into a large bowl. Add the scallions, egg, salt, pepper, and nutmeg and mix well.

3. Line a large rimmed baking sheet with parchment paper. Using a 2½-inch cookie cutter as a mold, shape 16 latkes directly on the baking sheet. Let stand for 15 to 30 minutes. (The uncooked latkes can be covered with plastic wrap and refrigerated for up to 4 hours.)

4. Position a rack in the center of the oven and preheat the oven to 200°F. Line a large baking sheet with paper towels. Pour enough oil to come ½ inch up the sides of a large deep skillet and heat over medium-high heat until the oil is very hot but not smoking. In batches without crowding, fry the latkes until the undersides are golden brown, about 3 minutes, adjusting the heat as needed so the latkes don't brown too quickly. Turn and cook the other side, 2 to 3 minutes more. Using a slotted spatula, transfer the latkes to the paper towels and keep warm in the oven while frying the remainder.

5. Transfer the latkes to a large serving platter and sprinkle with the scallion, if desired. Serve hot, with the sour cream and apple-sauce passed on the side.

JUICY LUCY

SAUSAGE BISCUITS

MAKES

8

BISCUITS

4 SERVINGS

These miniature sandwich biscuits are a perfect trifecta: herbaceous sausage patties, filled with homemade pimiento cheese, served in tender biscuits. When you bite into the sandwich, the cheese can ooze out, so warn your tablemates. Serve some scrambled eggs on the side, and maybe a simple cherry tomato and shaved celery vinaigrette salad, and you have a truly great brunch.

PIMIENTO CHEESE

3 tablespoons heavy cream, heated to boiling

1 cup (4 ounces) shredded domestic Fontina cheese

⅓ cup (1½ ounces) shredded sharp yellow Cheddar cheese

¼ teaspoon granulated onion or onion powder (see Chef Talk, page 257)

¼ teaspoon granulated garlic or garlic powder (see Chef Talk, page 257)

Pinch of kosher salt

2 tablespoons (¼-inch) diced piquillo or jarred pimiento peppers

Vegetable oil, for the ramekin

SAUSAGE

1¼ pounds ground pork

1 tablespoon molasses (not blackstrap)

1 tablespoon dried parsley flakes

1 tablespoon ground sage

¾ teaspoon ground coriander

¼ teaspoon ground thyme

1¼ teaspoons kosher salt

½ teaspoon freshly ground black pepper

¼ teaspoon hot red pepper flakes

1 tablespoon vegetable oil

BISCUITS

2 cups (240 grams) unbleached all-purpose flour

1½ teaspoons baking powder

¾ teaspoon kosher salt

¼ teaspoon baking soda

¼ teaspoon freshly ground black pepper

¼ cup (½ stick) unsalted butter, frozen

⅓ cup (1½ ounces) sharp Cheddar cheese, preferably white Cheddar

⅔ cup buttermilk

⅓ cup half-and-half

———

½ cup vegetable oil

1. To make the pimento cheese: Bring the cream to a boil in a small saucepan over medium heat. Reduce the heat to very low. Add the Fontina, Cheddar, granulated onion, granulated garlic, and salt and heat, stirring almost constantly, until the mixture is smooth and melted. Remove from the heat. Stir in the piquillo peppers. Lightly oil a 1-cup ramekin or dry measuring cup. Pour in the cheese mixture and let cool for 15 minutes. Cover with plastic wrap and refrigerate until chilled, semi-firm, and malleable, at least 1 hour or up to 1 day.

2. To prepare the sausage: Mix the pork, molasses, parsley, sage, coriander, thyme, salt, black pepper, and red pepper flakes together until combined.

3. Using a tablespoon, scoop out 8 equal portions of the cheese mixture. On a sheet of plastic wrap on the work surface, flatten each portion under the heel of your hand into a 2-inch-diameter disk.

4. Divide the pork mixture into eight equal meatballs. One at a time, flatten each into a 4-inch patty. Place a cheese disk in the center of one, and bring up the sides of the patty to completely cover the cheese. Do not allow any cheese to peek out of the patty or it will melt into the skillet during cooking. Repeat to make 8 patties. (The patties can be covered and refrigerated for up to 12 hours.)

5. To make the biscuits: Position a rack in the center of the oven and preheat the oven to 375°F. Line a large rimmed baking sheet with parchment paper.

6. Whisk the flour, baking powder, salt, baking soda, and pepper together in a medium bowl. Working on the large holes of a box shredder, shred the frozen butter directly into the flour. Add the Cheddar and mix until it is coated. Whisk the buttermilk and half-and-half together, pour into the flour mixture, and stir just until it forms a soft dough.

7. Turn the dough out onto a lightly floured work surface and knead one or two times just to smooth out the dough. Pat the dough into a rectangle about 1 inch thick. Cut the dough into eight equal portions. (This technique eliminates the scraps that occur when the dough is punched out with a biscuit cutter.) Transfer to the baking sheet and bake until the biscuits are golden brown, 20 to 25 minutes. Let the biscuits cool until warm or to room temperature.

8. To serve, heat the oil in a very large skillet, preferably nonstick, over medium heat. Add the sausage patties and cook, turning once, adjusting the heat as needed so they don't brown too quickly, until they are browned and feel firm when pressed with a fingertip, about 10 minutes. (The patties must be cooked long enough for the heat to reach the center and melt the pimiento cheese, so moderate heat works best.)

9. Slice each biscuit in half horizontally. Sandwich a sausage patty on each biscuit and serve.

CHEF TALK

Granulated Onion and Garlic

There are times when you want the flavor of garlic or onion, but not the texture of the fresh version. That's where granulated garlic and granulated onion come in. These are simply dehydrated versions of the vegetables that have been very finely ground into a coarse powder. Granulated garlic and onion seem to have a fresher, cleaner taste than the old-fashioned, finely processed powder. There are even some brands of powder that are actually granulated. So, while granulated is preferred, the powders can be substituted.

Oreo Pancakes
with VANILLA CRÈME ICING

MAKES ABOUT

14

PANCAKES

4 SERVINGS

Oreo lovers rejoice, you finally have an excuse to eat cookies for breakfast. And if you are the type of person who goes straight for the filling in the sandwich cookie, you might as well just earmark this page for the crème icing recipe. While I always have maple syrup on hand for these pancakes, the crème icing is really all you need.

VANILLA CRÈME ICING

1 cup vegetable shortening

¼ cup (½ stick) unsalted butter, at room temperature

1 teaspoon vanilla extract

3 cups confectioners' sugar

¼ cup finely crushed chocolate sandwich cookies, such as Oreo

PANCAKE BATTER

2 cups (280 grams) unbleached all-purpose flour

3 tablespoons granulated sugar

1 tablespoon baking powder

½ teaspoon fine sea or table salt

1¼ cups whole milk, plus more as needed

1 cup buttermilk

2 large eggs

3 tablespoons unsalted butter, melted and cooled to tepid

1½ teaspoons vanilla extract

1 cup finely crushed chocolate sandwich cookies, such as Oreo

---

Vegetable oil, for the griddle

½ cup coarsely crushed chocolate sandwich cookies, such as Oreo, for serving

Confectioners' sugar, for serving (optional)

1. To make the icing: Beat the shortening, butter, and vanilla together in the bowl of a standing heavy-duty mixer with the paddle attachment on low speed until combined. Gradually beat in the confectioners' sugar. Increase the mixer speed to medium-high and beat until fluffy, about 1 minute. Mix in the crushed cookies. Transfer to a bowl, cover, and store at room temperature for up to 1 day.

2. To make the batter: Sift the flour, granulated sugar, baking powder, and salt together into a large bowl. Whisk the milk, buttermilk, eggs, unsalted butter, and vanilla together in another bowl. Pour into the flour mixture. Whisk just until combined. Stir in the crushed cookies.

3. Position a rack in the center of the oven and preheat the oven to 200°F. Heat a large griddle or two skillets over medium heat until a splash of water skitters on the surface. Lightly oil the griddle. Using about ⅓ cup for each pancake, pour the batter onto the griddle. Cook until bubbles appear on the pancake surface and the bubbles burst, about 2 minutes. Flip the pancakes and cook until the undersides are golden brown, about 1 minute more. Transfer to the oven rack to keep warm while cooking the remaining pancakes. If the batter thickens upon standing, thin with a little more milk.

4. Spread each pancake with a dollop of the icing. Stack the pancakes in tall stacks, and top each stack with additional icing and a generous sprinkle of crushed cookies and confectioners' sugar, if desired. Serve immediately with the remaining icing passed on the side.

LEMON BERRY
Pancakes
with **Whipped Citrus Ricotta**

MAKES ABOUT

12

PANCAKES

4 SERVINGS

Adding citrus is a great way of lightening up even the heaviest of dishes. These lemony flapjacks are served with juicy berries and topped with a whipped ricotta flavored with even more citrus. Use your favorite sweet berries (raspberries may be a bit too tart), and wow your table with these gorgeous griddlecakes.

WHIPPED CITRUS RICOTTA

2 tablespoons honey

Finely grated zest of 1 lemon

1 tablespoon fresh lemon juice

Finely grated zest of ½ navel orange

1 tablespoon fresh orange juice

Pinch of kosher salt

2 cups whole-milk ricotta, preferably fresh

PANCAKES

2 large eggs

1 cup buttermilk

1 cup whole milk

3 tablespoons unsalted butter, melted

½ teaspoon lemon oil or finely grated zest of 1 large lemon

2 cups (280 grams) unbleached all-purpose flour

3 tablespoons granulated sugar

1 tablespoon baking powder

½ teaspoon fine table salt

Vegetable oil, for the griddle

Honey, for serving (optional)

2 (6-ounce) containers (2⅔ cups total) blackberries, for serving

---

1. To make the ricotta: Whisk the honey, lemon zest and juice, orange zest and juice, and salt together in a medium bowl to dissolve the honey. Add the ricotta and whisk well. Set aside and let stand at room temperature for about 1 hour to lose its chill.

2. To make the pancakes: Whisk the eggs in a large bowl. Add the buttermilk, milk, butter, and lemon oil and whisk again. Whisk the flour, granulated sugar, baking powder, and salt together into a large bowl. Add the dry ingredients to the egg mixture and whisk just until combined. Do not overmix.

3. Position a rack in the center of the oven and preheat the oven to 200°F. Heat a large griddle or two skillets over medium heat until a splash of water skitters on the surface.

4. Lightly oil the griddle. Using about ¼ cup for each pancake, pour the batter onto the griddle. Cook until bubbles appear on the pancake surface and the bubbles burst, about 2 minutes. Flip the pancakes and cook until the undersides are golden brown, about 1 minute more. Transfer to the oven rack to keep warm while cooking the remaining pancakes.

5. Shingle the pancakes on a large platter. Serve immediately with the whipped ricotta, honey, if desired, and blackberries on the side.

FRENCH TOAST
BREAD PUDDING
with **Pumpkin Maple Syrup**

MAKES

8 *to* 10

SERVINGS

Soaking bread in custard makes the best French toast, so it made perfect sense to transform everyone's favorite breakfast into a communal confection. There are zillions of bread pudding recipes, but this one has a perfect proportion of bread to custard, and the pumpkin maple syrup makes this a damn near perfect autumn brunch dish.

SPICED CRÈME FRAÎCHE

½ cup crème fraîche or sour cream

2 tablespoons confectioners' sugar

¼ teaspoon pumpkin pie spice
(see Note)

BREAD PUDDING

Soft butter, for the baking dish

5 large eggs

1¼ cups granulated sugar

2 cups heavy cream

2 cups whole milk

1 teaspoon ground cinnamon

8 cups (1-inch) cubes rich bread,
such as challah or brioche loaf,
preferably slightly stale,
about 10 ounces

PUMPKIN MAPLE SYRUP

1 cup pure maple syrup

⅔ cup solid-pack pumpkin puree

¼ cup heavy cream

¼ teaspoon pumpkin pie spice
(see Note)

1. To make the crème fraîche: Whisk all of the ingredients together in a small bowl. Cover and let stand at room temperature for at least 1 hour. (If you have the time, refrigerate the crème fraîche mixture overnight. Let stand at room temperature for 1 hour before serving.)

2. To make the bread pudding: Position a rack in the center of the oven and preheat the oven to 350°F. Lightly butter a 9-by-13-inch baking dish. Have ready a large roasting pan to hold the baking dish.

3. Whisk the eggs and sugar well in a large bowl. Whisk in the cream, milk, and cinnamon. Add the bread cubes and mix well. Let stand 5 minutes for the bread to soak up some of the liquid. Pour into the baking dish. Cover tightly with aluminum foil.

4. Place the baking dish in the roasting pan. Put the pan on the oven rack, and carefully pour enough boiling water into the roasting pan to come about ½ inch up the sides of the dish. Bake for 30 minutes. Uncover and bake until the pudding is barely browned and feels set when pressed gently in the center, about 30 minutes more. Remove from the roasting pan and let stand for 5 minutes.

5. Meanwhile, make the syrup: Whisk all of the ingredients together in a medium saucepan. Bring to a simmer over medium heat. Remove from the heat and keep warm.

6. Spoon the pudding into individual bowls and top with dollops of the spiced crème fraîche. Serve immediately, with the warm pumpkin syrup passed on the side.

Note: If you don't have pumpkin pie spice, mix 1 teaspoon ground cinnamon, ½ teaspoon ground ginger, ¼ teaspoon freshly grated nutmeg, and a large pinch of ground cloves.

ORANGE-BOURBON
Pull-Apart Bread

MAKES

8 *to* 10

SERVINGS

Nothing makes a brunch more special than a freshly baked sweet bread, its spicy aroma filling the entire house. This delicious example is a member of the monkey bread family, with chunks of dough baked with sugar and toffee sauce in bite-sized portions that are pulled from the main loaf. Start the dough the night before and you will be ahead of the game when you get up to bake the next morning.

DOUGH

1 (¼-ounce) package active dry yeast, 2¼ teaspoons

1 cup warm (105°F to 115°F) water

½ cup (1 stick) unsalted butter, melted and cooled to tepid

3½ cups (490 grams) unbleached all-purpose flour, as needed

2 tablespoons granulated sugar

Finely grated zest of ½ large orange

½ teaspoon fine sea salt

Softened butter, for the bowl

BOURBON TOFFEE SAUCE

1 cup (2 sticks) unsalted butter, thinly sliced

2 cups packed light brown sugar

¼ cup heavy cream

¼ cup bourbon

2 teaspoons vanilla extract

———

5 tablespoons unsalted butter, softened

⅓ cup granulated sugar

1½ teaspoons ground cinnamon

Finely grated zest of ½ large orange

1. To make the dough: Sprinkle the yeast over the warm water in the bowl of a heavy-duty standing mixer. Let stand until the mixture looks creamy, about 5 minutes. Stir well to dissolve the yeast. Stir in the melted butter, followed by 3 cups of the flour, the granulated sugar, orange zest, and salt.

2. Affix the bowl to the mixer and fit with the paddle attachment. With the machine on medium-low speed, gradually add enough of the remaining flour to make a shaggy dough. Remove the paddle attachment, cover the bowl with a kitchen towel, and let stand for 10 minutes. Attach the dough hook. Knead on low speed, adding enough flour as needed to make a soft dough that just cleans the sides of the bowl. Continue kneading, occasionally stopping to pull the climbing dough off the hook, until the dough is pillowy and smooth, but slightly sticky, 6 to 8 minutes. This is a soft dough—do not add too much flour.

3. Lightly butter a large bowl with softened butter. Shape the dough into a ball and transfer to the buttered bowl. Turn the dough to coat with butter. Let stand in a warm place until doubled in volume, about 1¼ hours. (The dough can also be refrigerated for 12 to 18 hours. Let stand at room temperature for about 2 hours before baking to lose its chill.)

4. Meanwhile, make the toffee sauce: Melt the butter in a small saucepan over medium heat. Add the brown sugar and heavy cream and stir constantly until the mixture comes to a boil. Reduce the heat to medium-low and continue stirring until the sugar is completely dissolved, about 2 minutes. Remove from the heat and stir in the bourbon and vanilla. Let the sauce cool until tepid.

➡

5. Butter the inside of a 12-cup nonstick fluted tube pan (also called a bundt pan) with 1 tablespoon of the softened butter. Turn out the dough onto an unfloured work surface—the buttery dough will not stick. Stretch and pat the dough into a 13-by-9-inch rectangle. Spread the remaining 4 tablespoons softened butter over the dough. Mix the granulated sugar, cinnamon, and orange zest together in a small bowl. Sprinkle the cinnamon sugar evenly over the butter. Cut the dough lengthwise into 6 strips, and then crosswise into 7 strips to make 42 pieces. Layer half of the pieces in the tube pan and drizzle with about one-third of the sauce. Repeat with the remaining dough and another third of the sauce. Sprinkle any cinnamon sugar on the work surface over the dough. Reserve the remaining sauce.

6. Loosely cover the pan with plastic wrap and let stand in a warm place until the dough looks puffy, 15 to 30 minutes. (The warm toffee sauce will decrease the rising time.)

7. Meanwhile, position a rack in the center of the oven and preheat the oven to 350°F.

8. Bake the bread until the top is golden brown, 35 to 45 minutes (if the top browns too quickly, tent the pan with aluminum foil). If you are using a dark tube pan, use the shorter baking time. Place a platter over the pan. Using a kitchen towel, hold and invert them together, but do not remove the pan yet. Let stand for 10 minutes. Lift off the pan to unmold the bread, being careful of the hot toffee sauce. Let the bread cool for 10 minutes more. Reheat the remaining sauce. Serve the bread warm or cooled to room temperature with the toffee sauce.

Doughnuts

with Cinnamon Sugar and Berry Sauce

MAKES

2 Dozen

DOUGHNUT HOLES

There is no way that people will stay in bed if you promise that there will be fresh doughnuts on the brunch table. The addition of potato makes these doughnuts (actually doughnut holes, which are much easier to dip) impressively light and airy. Enveloped as they are in a coating of cinnamon and sugar, one dip in the berry sauce and the delicious gems will give your favorite jelly-filled doughnut a run for its money. You'll find a couple of alternative sauces on page 271. Or, if you wish, serve all three options.

DOUGHNUT DOUGH

1 small baking potato, peeled and cut into ½-inch dice

2 tablespoons vegetable shortening, coarsely chopped, plus more for the bowl

⅔ cup whole milk

2 tablespoons sugar

2 tablespoons warm (105°F to 115°F) water

¾ teaspoon active dry yeast

1 large egg yolk

½ teaspoon vanilla extract

¼ teaspoon baking powder

¼ teaspoon fine sea salt

About 2¼ cups (315 grams) unbleached all-purpose flour, as needed

BERRY SAUCE

1 (6-ounce) container blackberries or blueberries (or a combination), about 1⅓ cups

2 tablespoons sugar, or more as needed

2 tablespoons water

―――――――

Vegetable oil, for deep-frying

⅓ cup granulated sugar

½ teaspoon ground cinnamon

1. To make the dough: Put the diced potato in a small saucepan, add enough cold water to cover, and bring to a boil over high heat. Reduce the heat to medium-low and cover with the lid ajar. Simmer until the potato is tender, 15 to 20 minutes. Drain the potato, transfer to a bowl, and mash well with a fork. Measure 2 tablespoons mashed potato and discard the remainder.

2. Melt the shortening in a small saucepan over medium heat. Add the mashed potato, milk, and sugar and remove from the heat. Stir to dissolve the sugar. Transfer the mixture to the mixing bowl of a standing heavy-duty mixer and set aside until tepid, about 10 minutes.

3. Meanwhile, pour the warm water into a custard cup or ramekin and sprinkle the yeast on top. Let stand until the yeast softens, about 5 minutes. Stir well to dissolve the yeast.

4. Add the yeast mixture to the milk mixture, then the egg yolk, vanilla, baking powder, and salt. Affix the paddle attachment to the mixer. With the machine on medium-low, gradually add enough of the flour (you may not need all of it) to make a sticky, soft dough. Continue beating until the dough is smooth, shiny, and tacky, about 5 minutes.

5. Lightly grease a medium bowl with shortening. Scrape the dough into the bowl and turn to coat the dough with the shortening. Cover the bowl with plastic wrap and let stand in a warm place until doubled in volume, about 1¼ hours. (The dough can also be made the night before, covered, and allowed

➡

to rise in the refrigerator. Let the dough stand at room temperature for about 1½ hours to lose its chill before proceeding.)

6. To make the berry sauce: Bring the blackberries, sugar, and water to a boil, stirring often, in a small saucepan over medium-high heat. Reduce the heat to medium-low and simmer, stirring often, until the berries are soft and the mixture is juicy, about 5 minutes. Taste and adjust the sweetness with sugar, if needed. Remove from the heat. Using a handheld blender, puree the sauce in the saucepan. (Or let the sauce cool until tepid, and puree in a standard blender.) Rub the sauce through a fine wire sieve into a small bowl; discard the seeds. Let cool. (The sauce can be covered and refrigerated for up to 5 days. Bring to room temperature before serving.)

7. To fry the doughnuts: Line a large rimmed baking sheet with waxed paper, and a second sheet with paper towels. Pour enough oil to come 2 inches up the sides of a large, deep saucepan and heat over high heat to 350°F on a deep-frying thermometer. Using about 2 tablespoons for each, shape the dough into 24 equal balls and transfer to the sheet with the waxed paper. In batches without crowding, deep-fry the dough balls, turning them over if needed, until golden brown, about 3 minutes. Using a wire spider or slotted spoon, transfer the doughnut holes to the sheet with the paper towels.

8. To coat the doughnuts: Whisk the granulated sugar and cinnamon together in a medium bowl. A few at a time, add the warm doughnuts and toss to coat them with the sugar mixture. Transfer to a platter.

9. Serve the doughnuts warm with the sauce for dipping.

MORE DOUGHNUT SAUCES

I actually have *three* favorite dipping sauces for warm doughnuts—the berry one in the recipe, and these two—chocolate and caramel. So, rather than decide, I very often just make them all. They all keep well in the fridge to serve at other meals as dessert toppings, so it's worth the extra few minutes.

Chocolate Sauce

Makes 1½ cups

1 cup whole milk

1 tablespoon light brown sugar

2 teaspoons cornstarch

Pinch of ground cinnamon

3 ounces bittersweet chocolate (about 65% cacao), finely chopped

Whisk the milk, brown sugar, cornstarch, and cinnamon together in a small saucepan. Cook over medium heat, whisking often, until the mixture is thickened and boiling. Remove from the heat. Add the chocolate and whisk until it is melted and the sauce is smooth. Set the sauce aside. (The sauce can be covered and refrigerated for up to 1 day. Warm slightly before serving.)

Salted Caramel Sauce

Makes ¾ cup

The slightly bitter sweetness of caramel makes you keep coming back for more. To give the sauce the right dipping consistency, warm it slightly before serving.

1 cup sugar

⅓ cup water

½ cup heavy cream, heated to steaming

¼ teaspoon kosher salt

Bring the sugar and water to a boil in a medium saucepan over high heat, stirring constantly, until the sugar is dissolved and the syrup is boiling. Cook without stirring, occasionally swirling the saucepan by the handle and washing down any sugar crystals on the sides of the saucepan with a pastry brush dipped in cold water, until the caramel has turned the color of an old penny and gives off wisps of smoke, 5 to 7 minutes. Gradually and carefully stir in the hot cream (it will bubble and splatter) and stir until the mixture is smooth. Remove from the heat and stir in the salt. Let cool until warm. (The sauce can be covered and refrigerated for up to 1 day. Warm slightly before serving.)

Red Velvet Waffles
with CREAM CHEESE SAUCE

MAKES ABOUT

12

4-INCH WAFFLES

4 SERVINGS

As I mentioned before in the Red Velvet "Twinkies" on page 226, red velvet cake is understandably everywhere with its brilliant red color and subtle chocolate flavor. Instead of having to make an entire cake, you can make these red velvet waffles, which offer the same flavor, in a fraction of the time. The cream cheese sauce is a sweet alternative to maple syrup.

CREAM CHEESE SAUCE

4 ounces cream cheese, at room temperature

¼ cup (½ stick) unsalted butter, at room temperature

1½ cups confectioners' sugar

1 teaspoon vanilla extract

About 2 tablespoons whole milk, as needed

RED VELVET WAFFLES

2 cups (280 grams) unbleached all-purpose flour

⅓ cup Dutch-processed cocoa powder

⅔ cup confectioners' sugar

2 tablespoons granulated sugar

4 teaspoons baking powder

½ teaspoon fine sea or table salt

1 cup whole milk

¾ cup buttermilk

2 large eggs

3 tablespoons unsalted butter, melted

2 teaspoons red food coloring paste

1 teaspoon vanilla extract

1 teaspoon distilled vinegar

Vegetable oil, for the waffle iron

Special Equipment: Nonstick waffle iron

1. To make the sauce: Using a handheld mixer on medium speed, beat the cream cheese and butter together in a large bowl until the mixture is light in color, about 1 minute. Reduce the mixer speed to low and beat in the confectioners' sugar and vanilla. Beat in enough of the milk to make a smooth, opaque sauce with a drizzling consistency—the sauce should not be thin or transparent. Set aside at room temperature.

2. To make the waffles: Preheat a waffle iron according to the manufacturer's directions. Position a rack in the center of the oven and preheat the oven to 200°F.

3. Sift the flour, cocoa powder, confectioners' sugar, granulated sugar, baking powder, and salt together into a medium bowl. Whisk the milk, buttermilk, eggs, butter, food coloring, vanilla, and vinegar together in another bowl, being sure to dissolve the food coloring. Pour into the dry mixture and whisk just until smooth. Do not overmix.

4. Lightly oil the waffle iron grids. Spoon the recommended amount of batter into the waffle iron, close the lid, and cook according to the manufacturer's directions. Transfer the waffle to an oven rack (not a baking sheet) and keep warm in the oven while making the remaining waffles.

5. Cut the waffles along their grid lines into individual portions. Transfer to a platter and drizzle with some of the sauce. Serve immediately, with the remaining sauce passed on the side.

ACKNOWLEDGMENTS

I have worked with incredible people over the years. Of all the things I've done in my life, I am proudest of the collaborative nature and sense of family that I have built with this amazing group. On the following pages you will find 16 selfies of those individuals who have directly helped shape the recipes in this book through constant collaboration, creativity, and lots of hard work. While not all of those pictured work in my kitchens, everyone acknowledged here has made me a better chef, and most importantly, all of them have become my closest friends.

Derrick Prince, Chef de Cuisine at The Stanton Social: When I found Derrick, one of my young guns, he was a computer programmer spending his day off cooking at a hot sauce festival. I could sense his creativity from day one. I knew if I could convince him to trade computers for pots and pans that he would become an excellent chef, and he is well on his way.

Jaime Sudberg, Executive Pastry Chef at Vandal: Jaime was the opening pastry chef at The Stanton Social in 2005 and has been by my side ever since. Jaime is, in fact, the first and only pastry chef I have ever hired, and she has collaborated with me on almost every project that I have done. It's been over a decade that we've worked together and I hope to spend the rest of my career bouncing ideas off of my charmingly grouchy sugar queen.

Jonathan Kavourakis, Executive Chef/Partner at Vandal: Considering that Jonathan is the first chef who has become a partner in one of my restaurants, he has come an incredibly long way from almost getting fired for being too cocky in the early days of his employment. But in all serious-ness, I am glad that I stuck with him, because while this boisterous Greek chef has an ego, he also has the talent and work ethic to back it up. They don't call him "Big Sexy" for nothing,

Juan Borjas, Chef de Cuisine at Beauty & Essex: Part of the process of applying to be a part of my team is preparing a tasting for the management. I was immediately impressed by Juan's steady, confident approach to all of the dishes he presented. He is always focused and not one to pat himself on the back. He is just super talented, creative, and humble—except when it comes to his game with the ladies.

Kyle Kingrey, Executive Chef at Beauty & Essex Los Angeles: I first met Kyle, as talented a chef as I've ever known, while we were working together in Las Vegas many years ago, and I was lucky enough to recruit him for the opening of Beauty & Essex in New York City. I lost Kyle briefly to the sandy beaches and blue waters of Turks and Caicos, but I have once again lured him back to run our West Coast kitchens. This time I'm not letting him go.

Ryan Angulo, former Executive Chef at The Stanton Social: Ryan was our opening chef at The Stanton Social, and like me, a Rhode Island boy, which also means we are friends for life. Ryan has moved on to open other restaurants, where he has had great success. Even though we haven't worked together in years, his thumbprints are still on The Stanton Social menu ten years later, and in this book. He helped put Stanton on the map and for that I will always be grateful.

Neil Howell, former Executive Chef at The Stanton Social: Replacing Ryan at The Stanton Social proved to be a daunting task until this affable British chef walked through my doors. Neil effortlessly collaborated with me from our first day in the kitchen until his last. Not only is Neil a terrific chef, but he is one of the nicest guys you'll ever meet. Plus, I've always been a sucker for an English accent.

Paul LeFebvre, Executive Production Chef at Beauty & Essex: Every kitchen team needs a driving force, and for Beauty & Essex that force is Paul. It's funny to see him smiling in his selfie since I am used to him grunting, "Get out my way, I'm busy!" A seasonally driven chef, Paul is our go-to guy when the weather is changing, and his fresh contributions to our menu never cease to amaze.

Peder Hollinghurst, Executive Sous Chef at Beauty & Essex: Peder started with me as an underappreciated intern of sorts at The Stanton Social and slowly and steadily worked his way up the ladder. Peder, more than any of my other chefs, has a unique cooking style and is deeply prideful of his cooking. The result is that Peder's dishes are always as charmingly quirky as he is.

Sarah Nelson, Executive Chef at Beauty & Essex and The Stanton Social: After we lost Kyle, along came Sarah. Sarah now runs two of my restaurants in New York, which means that she has mastered much more than just cooking. She is truly the rarest of chefs: assertive yet easygoing, able to command a kitchen with her quiet confidence day in and day out.

Seth Coburn, Executive Production Chef at Vandal: Seth was my first sous chef, period. Within a few days of working together we almost got into a fistfight in the kitchen. The next day we became best friends. After many decades of being very best friends, we recently reunited professionally and I am happy to report there haven't been any fights—just good food and good times.

Timothy Peterson, Executive Culinary Assistant: Timothy has been my secret weapon since 1996. Always by my side, Timmy has literally been a part of every restaurant I have ever opened and almost every dish that we have served. He is the culinary yin to my yang, and, as far as I'm concerned, the hardest working man in show business. He is my brother and his loyalty knows no bounds.

Tommy Gillespie, Director of Purchasing: I call Tommy my consigliere, as I bounce every idea off of him before executing. Technically speaking, Tommy was actually my boss when I first moved to New York City, and he taught me the ropes. Now, many years later, I am proud to call him my partner as well as one of the greatest drinking buddies I have ever known.

Richard Wolf, Partner and Co-Founder of The Stanton Social, Beauty & Essex, and Vandal: Rich has been my business partner for over a decade and has opened more doors than I could ever have asked for. More importantly, he challenges me daily to be a better chef, leader, and friend to our enormous family of employees. In short, he has been the greatest mentor and someone to whom I will always be grateful. In addition he throws one hell of a party.

Erica Beth Koffler, Cookbook Assistant, Life Coach: Erica worked tirelessly on this book, but prior to that was my first full-time assistant, something I never dreamed I would ever need. Over five years, Erica not only showed me that I in fact *did* need a bright, motivated individual to keep me organized and on point daily while juggling multiple projects, but also that I could take on and accomplish so much more with an "Assistant-Partner" pushing me each day. Part-time cheerleader, part-time therapist, part-time recipe tester, Erica was and will always be full-time family to me.

Amy Landsman, Executive Assistant: Amy has accrued many nicknames as my assistant, such as "Ray of Sunshine" or "Button" (as in cute as a button), but I prefer to call her "The Little Engine That Could." She is willing and able to take on any project big or small and if she doesn't know how, she figures it out and fast. Better still, when I don't know how, she figures it out and fast! Like a little sister and mini-CEO of All Things

Related to Me, Amy is a superhero—which is fitting since she is a comic book nerd, too.

In addition, there are a few other people I would like to acknowledge. Foremost, a general thank-you and shout-out to my entire family: My brothers **Jay** and **Mark**, my sister **Ginny**, and my closest friends for their general understanding for all of the special occasions I had to miss in order to pursue my dreams.

A BIG THANK-YOU–

To **Enda Mullen**, wherever he may roam, the very first chef I worked for at the age of 13. You actually inspired me on that very first day to be what I am today.

To **Jared Boles** and **Jen Rucker**, my managing partners, who guide the restaurants with a steady hand. They run a tight ship, and I am forever grateful for their amazing dedication.

To **Chad Harris**, you made the White House West Wing kitchen like a second home to me and my staff. That was an incredible honor, and I am even more grateful to have made such great friends along the way.

To **Joe Torkomian**, an amazing chef I first met in culinary school and had the pleasure to work with in Massachusetts. Over time, Joe became my best friend, and like family, he has been instrumental in keeping my confidence and drive up when times get tough. Thank you, Joe!

To **Cliff Rigano** and the Jägermeister Family, for bringing me and my food all over the country so that I could connect with fellow music and food lovers across America.

To Grand Central book editor **Karen Murgolo**, co-author **Rick Rodgers**, and photographer **Quentin Bacon**, who made what I thought was going to be a difficult task in writing this book amazingly easy and actually fun. Copyeditor **Deri Reed** was exacting and her work made the book even better. Also to **Gary Tooth** of Empire Design Studio for giving the book its visual appeal. And to my various agents: **Ashley Eyzengart**, **Ken Slotnick**, and **David Vigliano**, who found a home for this book. Thank you so much for all of your hard work.

Finally, thank you to **Cynthia** and **Tyson**, who were there every step of the way.

ROGUES' GALLERY

Derrick Prince

Jaime Sudberg

Jonathan Kavourakis

Juan Borjas

Peder Hollinghurst

Rich Wolf

Ryan Angulo

Sarah Nelson

Kyle Kingrey

Amy Landsman

Neil Howell

Paul LeFebvre

Seth Coburn

Timothy Peterson

Tommy Gillespie

Erica Beth Koffler

INDEX

INDEX

A

Achiote Oil, Arroz con Pollo with, 89

aioli. *See also* House Aioli

    Lamb Souvlaki with Tzatziki and Lime-Harissa Aioli, 161

allspice dram

    about, 23

    in The Woodsman, 23

ancho chiles

    about, 6

    in Chile Relleno Empanadas, 41

    Pork Tenderloin with Ancho-Caramel Glaze and BBQ Beans, 147

Angry Potatoes with Cherry Peppers, 202

Angulo, Ryan, 48

annatto seeds

    about, 90

    in Arroz con Pollo with Achiote Oil, 89

Aperol

    in The Coronado, 16

    in Sherry-Citrus Punch, 30

appetizers

    about, 32

    Avocado, Lemon, and Espelette Focaccia, 47

    Chicken Liver Focaccia with Braised Shallot-Rioja Marmalade, 44

    Chile Relleno Empanadas, 41

    Citrus-Pickled Vegetables, 61

    Crab Corn Dogs with Old Bay Aioli, 48

    The Famous French Onion Soup Dumplings, 39

    Grilled and Chilled Haricots Verts, 63

    "Grilled Cheese" Dumplings in Tomato Soup, 36

    Nori-Spiced Tuna Poke Crisps, 51

    Pizza Bianca, 43

    Potato and Goat Cheese Pierogi with Caramelized Onions, 52

    Salt-and-Pepper Shrimp with Thai Papaya Salad, 121

    Spicy Wok-Seared Edamame, 58

    Tomato "Tartare" on Brioche Crostini, 55

    Warm Stuffed Piquillo Pepper Bruschetta, 35

apples

    Apple Tart with Cheddar Streusel, 221

    Kale, Apple, and Pancetta Salad, 73

    Potato Latkes with Sour Cream and Fresh Applesauce, 254

Apple-Cider Mussels with Roasted Fall Vegetables and Mustard Butter, 123

Apple Cider Vinaigrette, in Kale, Apple, and Pancetta Salad, 73

Apple Tart with Cheddar Streusel, 221

Arepas with Salsa Verde, Open-Faced Chicken, 96

Arroz con Pollo with Achiote Oil, 89

arugula. *See* baby arugula

Asian Braised Short Ribs with Broccoli Puree ("Beef and Broccoli"), 137

Asian Noodles with Shrimp, Miso Butter, and Spicy Peanuts, 174

Asian pantry ingredients, 5

Asian Pesto, 79

    in Soba Noodle and Beet Salad, 77

asparagus

    Asparagus Ribbon and Spring Pea Salad with Lemon Ricotta, 67

    Grilled Asparagus with Cilantro-Lime Mayonnaise, 189

Asparagus Ribbon and Spring Pea Salad with Lemon Ricotta, 67

avocados

    Avocado, Lemon, and Espelette Focaccia, 47

    in Chicken Taquitos with Guacamole Puree, 101

    Cobb Salad Bites with Avocado Vinaigrette, 68

    Huevos Rancheros Soft Tacos with Avocado Pico de Gallo, 251

    in Nori-Spiced Tuna Poke Crisps, 51

    in Open-Faced Chicken Arepas with Salsa Verde, 96

    in Red Snapper Mini-Tacos with Mango Salsa and Guacamole, 110

Avocado, Lemon, and Espelette Focaccia, 47

Avocado Crema, in Pork Belly BLT Tacos with Charred-Lime Vinaigrette, 153

B

baby arugula

    in My House Salad with Carrot Harissa Vinaigrette, 70

    in Olive Oil-Poached Cod with Beet, Orange, and Tangerine Salad, 106

Baby Back Ribs with Jägermeister-Black Cherry Cola Glaze, 151

baby greens

    in Asparagus Ribbon and Spring Pea Salad with Lemon Ricotta, 67

    in My House Salad with Carrot Harissa Vinaigrette, 70

    in Panzanella with Tomato Vinaigrette and Blue Cheese, 75

baby spinach. *See* spinach

bacon

    Cajun Bacon Risotto, 154

    in Cobb Salad Bites with Avocado Vinaigrette, 68

    Grilled Cheddar and Jalapeño Bacon Sandwiches, 156

    in "Grilled Cheese" Dumplings in Tomato Soup, 36

    in Pork Tenderloin with Ancho-Caramel Glaze and BBQ Beans, 147

    in Sexy Sliders with Fancy Sauce and Cola Onions, 139

baguettes

    in Panzanella with Tomato Vinaigrette and Blue Cheese, 75

in Slow-Baked Tomato Bruschetta with Eggs and Parmesan, 243

in Warm Stuffed Piquillo Pepper Bruschetta, 35

Baked Eggs with Serrano Ham and Manchego "Grits," 247

baking dishes and gratins, 10

Balsamic Glaze, 34

Balsamic Sauce, Brined Pork Milanese with Tomato-, 149

bamboo skewers on the grill, 88

Barbecue Sauce

    Baby Back Ribs with Jägermeister-Black Cherry Cola Glaze, 151

    in Smoky Rubbed Chicken Wings with Honey, Bourbon, and Molasses Sauce, 94

bar drinks

    about, 12

    bar essentials, 18

    Beauty Elixir, 14

    The Best Bloody Mary, 26

    The Coronado, 16

    Emerald Gimlet, 17

    Garnet Gimlet, 27

    Ginger Rogers, 19

    La Presa, 21

    Pink Grapefruit-Mint Martini, 20

    Red Tequila Sangria, 24

    Ruby Red Punch, 29

    Sherry-Citrus Punch, 30

    White Sangria with Cranberry and Cucumber, 28

    The Woodsman, 23

bar essentials, 18

bar spoons, 18

basil. See also Thai basil

    frying leaves, 47

    in Asian Pesto, 79

    in Avocado, Lemon, and Espelette Focaccia, 47

    in Emerald Gimlet, 17

    in Garnet Gimlet, 27

    Ricotta and Basil Manicotti, 184

BBQ Beans, Pork Tenderloin with Ancho-Caramel Glaze and, 147

Beauty Elixir, 14

Beauty & Essex, 14, 142

beef

    about, 126

    "Beef and Broccoli" (Asian Braised Short Ribs with Broccoli Puree), 137

    Hanger Steak with Red Pepper and Olive Chimichurri, 129

    Individual Beef Wellingtons, 130

    Korean Short Rib Tacos with Kimchi, 145

    Old-School Meatballs with Marinara Sauce, 142

    Ribeye Steak with Garlic-Butter Baste and Mustard-Bourbon Sauce, 133

    Sexy Sliders with Fancy Sauce and Cola Onions, 139

"Beef and Broccoli" (Asian Braised Short Ribs with Broccoli Puree), 137

Beef Wellingtons, Individual, 130

beets

    roasting tip, 79

    Olive Oil-Poached Cod with Beet, Orange, and Tangerine Salad, 106

    Soba Noodle and Beet Salad, 77

bell peppers

    roasting tip, 42

    Chouriço and Pepper Sloppy Joes, 158

    Citrus-Pickled Vegetables, 61

    Hanger Steak with Red Pepper and Olive Chimichurri, 129

    Orecchiette with Sausage, Leeks, Mushrooms, and Red Peppers, 167

    in Soba Noodle and Beet Salad, 77

    in Thai Marinated Papaya Salad, 76

Best Bloody Mary, The, 26

Biscuits, Juicy Lucy Sausage, 256

black beans

    in Huevos Rancheros Soft Tacos with Avocado Pico de Gallo, 251

    in Pork Tenderloin with Ancho-Caramel Glaze and BBQ Beans, 147

Blackberry and Lime Semifreddo, 235

Black-Bottomed Butterscotch Pots de Crème, 232

Black Rice and Spicy Miso Sauce, Seared Tuna with Fried, 112

Blondies with Semisweet Chips, White Chocolate, 229

Bloody Mary, The Best, 26

blue cheese

    in Cobb Salad Bites with Avocado Vinaigrette, 68

    Panzanella with Tomato Vinaigrette and Blue Cheese, 75

Bolognese, Pasta with Spicy Veal and Lamb, 170

Bordelaise Sauce, in Individual Beef Wellingtons, 130

Borjas, Juan, 89

Boston shakers, 18

bourbon

    Orange-Bourbon Pull-Apart Bread, 264

    in Red Tequila Sangria, 24

    Smoky Rubbed Chicken Wings with Honey, Bourbon, and Molasses Sauce, 94

    in The Woodsman, 23

bowls, 7, 10

breads. See also bruschetta; focaccia

    Orange-Bourbon Pull-Apart Bread, 264

    Panzanella with Tomato Vinaigrette and Blue Cheese, 75

bread pudding

    Chocolate Bread Pudding, 223

    French Toast Bread Pudding with Pumpkin Maple Syrup, 263

Brined Pork Milanese with Tomato-Balsamic Sauce, 149

brining, about, 6, 149

"Broccoli, Beef and" (Asian Braised Short Ribs with Broccoli Puree), 137

broccolini

    in Creamy Orzo with Pancetta and Vegetables, 176

    Spicy Broccolini with Soy and Garlic, 190

Brown Butter, Rigatoni with Merguez, Ricotta Salata, and, 173

brunch

about, 240

Baked Eggs with Serrano Ham and Manchego "Grits," 247

Doughnuts with Cinnamon Sugar and Chocolate Sauce, 268

French Toast Bread Pudding with Pumpkin Maple Syrup, 263

Fried Chicken with Cheddar Waffles and Spicy Butter, 249

Huevos Rancheros Soft Tacos with Avocado Pico de Gallo, 251

Juicy Lucy Sausage Biscuits, 256

Lemon Berry Pancakes with Whipped Citrus Ricotta, 260

Orange-Bourbon Pull-Apart Bread, 264

Oreo Pancakes with Vanilla Crème Icing, 259

Potato Latkes with Sour Cream and Fresh Applesauce, 254

Red Velvet Waffles with Cream Cheese Sauce, 272

Slow-Baked Tomato Bruschetta with Eggs and Parmesan, 243

Triple-Decker Croque Monsieurs, 244

bruschetta. See also crostini

Slow-Baked Tomato Bruschetta with Eggs and Parmesan, 243

Warm Stuffed Piquillo Pepper Bruschetta, 35

Brussels sprouts

in Cobb Salad Bites with Avocado Vinaigrette, 68

Orange and Chile-Glazed Brussels Sprouts, 193

burgers, Sexy Sliders with Fancy Sauce and Cola Onions, 139

butternut squash, in Creamy Orzo with Pancetta and Vegetables, 176

Butterscotch Pots de Crème, Black-Bottomed, 232

C

cabbage, in Korean Short Rib Tacos with Kimchi, 145

Cacao Nib Lace Cookies, 231

Cajun Bacon Risotto, 154

cakes

Devil's Food Cake with Vanilla Mascarpone Filling, 210

Warm Stout Cakes with Toffee Sauce, 214

cake stands, 9

Carbonara, Pork Belly, 164

carrots

Citrus-Pickled Vegetables, 61

My House Salad with Carrot Harissa Vinaigrette, 70

Seared-Squid Lettuce Wraps with Spicy Carrot Slaw, 124

in Soba Noodle and Beet Salad, 77

cashews

in Asian Pesto, 79

in Soba Noodle and Beet Salad, 77

Spinach Salad with Goat Cheese, Spicy Cashews, and Corn Vinaigrette, 80

cauliflower

in Apple-Cider Mussels with Roasted Fall Vegetables and Mustard Butter, 123

Roasted Cauliflower Gratin with Gremolata Crumbs, 195

Charred-Lime Vinaigrette, Pork Belly BLT Tacos with, 153

cheddar cheese

Apple Tart with Cheddar Streusel, 221

Fried Chicken with Cheddar Waffles and Spicy Butter, 249

Grilled Cheddar and Jalapeño Bacon Sandwiches, 156

"Grilled Cheese" Dumplings in Tomato Soup, 36

in Huevos Rancheros Soft Tacos with Avocado Pico de Gallo, 251

Mac 'n' Cheese with Chorizo and Poblanos, 169

cheese. See also specific types of cheese

grating, about, 6

shredding soft, 72

"Grilled Cheese" Dumplings in Tomato Soup, 36

Mac 'n' Cheese with Chorizo and Poblanos, 169

Triple-Decker Croque Monsieurs, 244

Cheesecake with Gingersnap Crust, Pumpkin Pie, 217

Cheesy "Grits" with Smoky Red Pepper Sauce, Shrimp and, 119

Cherry Peppers, Angry Potatoes with, 202

chicken

about, 84

Arroz con Pollo with Achiote Oil, 89

Chicken Liver Focaccia with Braised Shallot-Rioja Marmalade, 44

Chicken Meatballs in Creamy Mushroom Sauce with Whipped Ricotta, 91

Chicken Taquitos with Guacamole Puree, 101

Chilaquiles Verdes with Chipotle Chicken, 99

Fried Chicken with Cheddar Waffles and Spicy Butter, 249

Open-Faced Chicken Arepas with Salsa Verde, 96

Orange-Marinated Chicken Satay with Peanut Sauce, 88

Orecchiette with Sausage, Leeks, Mushrooms, and Red Peppers, 167

Smoky Rubbed Chicken Wings with Honey, Bourbon, and Molasses Sauce, 94

Spatchcocked Roast Chicken with Citrus Rub, 87

Chicken Liver Focaccia with Braised Shallot-Rioja Marmalade, 44

Chicken Meatballs in Creamy Mushroom Sauce with Whipped Ricotta, 91

Chicken Taquitos with Guacamole Puree, 101

chickpeas, in My House Salad with Carrot Harissa Vinaigrette, 70

Chilaquiles Verdes with Chipotle Chicken, 99

Chile Crema, in Huevos Rancheros Soft Tacos with Avocado Pico de Gallo, 251

Chile Relleno Empanadas, 41

chiles. *See also specific types of chiles*

    roasting tip, 42

Chimichurri, Hanger Steak with Red Pepper and Olive, 129

chipotles (canned, in adobo)

    about, 6

    Chilaquiles Verdes with Chipotle Chicken, 99

    Grilled Chipotle Shrimp with Tomatillo, Roasted Corn, and Feta Salsa, 116

    in Huevos Rancheros Soft Tacos with Avocado Pico de Gallo, 251

    in Open-Faced Chicken Arepas with Salsa Verde, 96

chocolate

    in Black-Bottomed Butterscotch Pots de Crème, 232

    Chocolate Bread Pudding, 223

    in Devil's Food Cake with Vanilla Mascarpone Filling, 210

    Doughnuts with Cinnamon Sugar and Chocolate Sauce, 268

    Reverse Chocolate Chip Cookies, 230

    White Chocolate Blondies with Semisweet Chips, 229

Chocolate Bread Pudding, 223

Chopped (TV show), 6

chorizo

    in Huevos Rancheros Soft Tacos with Avocado Pico de Gallo, 251

    Mac 'n' Cheese with Chorizo and Poblanos, 169

Chouriço and Pepper Sloppy Joes, 158

chunjang

    about, 5, 146

    Korean Short Rib Tacos with Kimchi, 145

Cilantro-Lime Mayonnaise, Grilled Asparagus with, 189

Cilantro-Sesame Pesto, Twice-Cooked Eggplant with, 196

Cinnamon-Pear Syrup, 24

Citrus Chips, Dried, 15

Citrus-Pickled Vegetables, 61

Citrus Ricotta, Lemon Berry Pancakes with Whipped, 260

Citrus Rub, Spatchcocked Roast Chicken with, 87

Citrus Twists, 30

Cobb Salad Bites with Avocado Vinaigrette, 68

cocktail napkins, 9

cocktails

    about, 12

    bar essentials, 18

    Beauty Elixir, 14

    The Best Bloody Mary, 26

    The Coronado, 16

    Emerald Gimlet, 17

    Garnet Gimlet, 27

    Ginger Rogers, 19

    La Presa, 21

    Pink Grapefruit-Mint Martini, 20

    Red Tequila Sangria, 24

    Ruby Red Punch, 29

    Sherry-Citrus Punch, 30

    White Sangria with Cranberry and Cucumber, 28

    The Woodsman, 23

cocktail shakers, 18

cocktail syrups, 24

coconut, in Black-Bottomed Butterscotch Pots de Crème, 232

coconut milk, in Thai Marinated Papaya Salad, 76

coconut water, in The Coronado, 16

Cod, Olive Oil-Poached, with Beet, Orange, and Tangerine Salad, 106

Cola Onions, Sexy Sliders with Fancy Sauce and, 139

cookies

    Cacao Nib Lace Cookies, 231

Reverse Chocolate Chip Cookies, 230

corn

    roasting tip, 81

    Crispy Hominy with Skillet Corn and Cheese, 199

    Grilled Chipotle Shrimp with Tomatillo, Roasted Corn, and Feta Salsa, 116

    Spinach Salad with Goat Cheese, Spicy Cashews, and Corn Vinaigrette, 80

Corn Dogs, Crab, with Old Bay Aioli, 48

Coronado, The, 16

cotija

    about, 199

    in Crispy Hominy with Skillet Corn and Cheese, 199

course progression, 4

Couscous with Tahini and Baby Spinach, Harissa Pearl, 204

Crab Corn Dogs with Old Bay Aioli, 48

cranberry juice

    in Garnet Gimlet, 27

    in White Sangria with Cranberry and Cucumber, 28

cream cheese, in Pumpkin Pie Cheesecake with Gingersnap Crust, 217

Cream Cheese Sauce, Red Velvet Waffles with, 272

Cream of Tomato Soup, 83

    "Grilled Cheese" Dumplings in Tomato Soup, 36

Creamy Mascarpone Polenta, 206

Creamy Orzo with Pancetta and Vegetables, 176

Crème Fraîche Filling, Red Velvet "Twinkies" with, 226

Crispy Hominy with Skillet Corn and Cheese, 100

Croque Monsieurs, Triple-Decker, 244

crostini

    Chicken Liver Focaccia with Braised Shallot-Rioja Marmalade, 44

    Tomato "Tartare" on Brioche Crostini, 55

cucumbers

Citrus-Pickled Vegetables, 61

in Lamb Souvlaki with Tzatziki and Lime-Harissa Aioli, 161

White Sangria with Cranberry and Cucumber, 28

D

Demi-Glace, 132

desserts

about, 208

Apple Tart with Cheddar Streusel, 221

Black-Bottomed Butterscotch Pots de Crème, 232

Cacao Nib Lace Cookies, 231

Chocolate Bread Pudding, 223

Devil's Food Cake with Vanilla Mascarpone Filling, 210

Lime and Blackberry Semifreddo, 235

Peanut Butter and Jelly "Twinkies," 224

Peanut Butter Ice Cream Sundaes with Hot Fudge and Peanut Brittle, 237

Pumpkin Pie Cheesecake with Gingersnap Crust, 217

Red Velvet "Twinkies" with Crème Fraîche Filling, 226

Reverse Chocolate Chip Cookies, 230

Warm Stout Cakes with Toffee Sauce, 214

White Chocolate Blondies with Semisweet Chips, 229

Devil's Food Cake with Vanilla Mascarpone Filling, 210

doughnut sauces, 271

Doughnuts with Cinnamon Sugar and Chocolate Sauce, 268

Dried Citrus Chips, 15

drinks. See cocktails

duck fat

about, 45

in Chicken Liver Focaccia with Braised Shallot-Rioja Marmalade, 44

dumplings

The Famous French Onion Soup Dumplings, 39

"Grilled Cheese" Dumplings in Tomato Soup, 36

E

Edamame, Spicy Wok-Seared, 58

Eggplant, Twice-Cooked, with Cilantro-Sesame Pesto, 196

eggs

Baked Eggs with Serrano Ham and Manchego "Grits," 247

in Cobb Salad Bites with Avocado Vinaigrette, 68

Huevos Rancheros Soft Tacos with Avocado Pico de Gallo, 251

Slow-Baked Tomato Bruschetta with Eggs and Parmesan, 243

Emerald Gimlet, 17

Empanadas, Chile Relleno, 41

endive, in Panzanella with Tomato Vinaigrette and Blue Cheese, 75

ethnic markets, 5, 6

etiquette, 2

evaporated milk, about, 169

F

Famous French Onion Soup Dumplings, The, 39

fennel, in Apple-Cider Mussels with Roasted Fall Vegetables and Mustard Butter, 123

Feta Salsa, Grilled Chipotle Shrimp with Tomatillo, Roasted Corn, and, 116

fish. See seafood

fish sauce, about, 5

flour, measuring tip, 42

focaccia

Avocado, Lemon, and Espelette Focaccia, 47

Chicken Liver Focaccia with Braised Shallot-Rioja Marmalade, 44

Pizza Bianca, 43

fontina cheese

in Chile Relleno Empanadas, 41

in "Grilled Cheese" Dumplings in Tomato Soup, 36

in Juicy Lucy Sausage Biscuits, 256

French Onion Soup Dumplings, The Famous, 39

French Toast Bread Pudding with Pumpkin Maple Syrup, 263

Fried Black Rice, Seared Tuna with Spicy Miso Sauce and, 112

Fried Chicken with Cheddar Waffles and Spicy Butter, 249

furikake. See also katsuo fumi furikake; nori fumi furikake

about, 5

G

garlic

Ribeye Steak with Garlic-Butter Baste and Mustard-Bourbon Sauce, 133

Roasted Garlic, 134

Spicy Broccolini with Soy and Garlic, 190

Garlic-Butter Baste, Ribeye Steak with, and Mustard-Bourbon Sauce, 133

Garnet Gimlet, 27

Germon, George, 147

gin, in Beauty Elixir, 14

ginger juice

extraction tip, 58

in Soba Noodle and Beet Salad, 77

in Spicy Wok-Seared Edamame, 58

Ginger Rogers, 19

Gingersnap Crust, Pumpkin Pie Cheesecake with, 217

glassware, 9

goat cheese

in "Grilled Cheese" Dumplings in Tomato Soup, 36

Potato and Goat Cheese Pierogi with Caramelized Onions, 52

Spinach Salad with Goat Cheese, Spicy Cashews, and Corn Vinaigrette, 80

in Warm Stuffed Piquillo Pepper Bruschetta, 35

gochujang

about, 5, 146

in Korean Short Rib Tacos with Kimchi, 145

grains

about, 186

Creamy Mascarpone Polenta, 206

Harissa Pearl Couscous with Tahini and Baby Spinach, 204

Sticky Rice Cakes, 207

granulated garlic, 257

granulated onion, 257

grapefruit juice, in Sherry-Citrus Punch, 30

Grapefruit-Mint Martini, Pink, 20

grating cheeses, about, 6

green beans, Grilled and Chilled Haricots Verts, 63

green papayas

about, 5

Salt-and-Pepper Shrimp with Thai Papaya Salad, 121

Thai Marinated Papaya Salad, 76

Gremolata Crumbs, Roasted Cauliflower Gratin with, 195

Grilled and Chilled Haricots Verts, 63

Grilled Asparagus with Cilantro-Lime Mayonnaise, 189

Grilled Cheddar and Jalapeño Bacon Sandwiches, 156

"Grilled Cheese" Dumplings in Tomato Soup, 36

Grilled Chipotle Shrimp with Tomatillo, Roasted Corn, and Feta Salsa, 116

grits

Baked Eggs with Serrano Ham and Manchego "Grits," 247

Shrimp and Cheesy "Grits" with Smoky Red Pepper Sauce, 119

Gruyère cheese

in The Famous French Onion Soup Dumplings, 39

in Mac 'n' Cheese with Chorizo and Poblanos, 169

in Triple-Decker Croque Monsieurs, 244

Guacamole, Red Snapper Mini-Tacos with Mango Salsa and, 110

Guacamole Puree, Chicken Taquitos with, 101

Guajillo Sauce, 103

in Chicken Taquitos with Guacamole Puree, 101

in Pork Belly BLT Tacos with Charred-Lime Vinaigrette, 153

H

ham

Baked Eggs with Serrano Ham and Manchego "Grits," 247

in Triple-Decker Croque Monsieurs, 244

Hanger Steak with Red Pepper and Olive Chimichurri, 129

Haricots Verts, Grilled and Chilled, 63

harissa

about, 6

Harissa Pearl Couscous with Tahini and Baby Spinach, 204

Lamb Souvlaki with Tzatziki and Lime-Harissa Aioli, 161

My House Salad with Carrot Harissa Vinaigrette, 70

Harissa Pearl Couscous with Tahini and Baby Spinach, 204

Hawthorne strainers, 18

hazelnuts, in Olive Oil-Poached Cod with Beet, Orange, and Tangerine Salad, 106

Hominy with Skillet Corn and Cheese, Crispy, 199

Hot Fudge, Peanut Butter Ice Cream Sundaes with Peanut Brittle and, 237

House Aioli, 50

in Crab Corn Dogs with Old Bay Aioli, 48

in Korean Short Rib Tacos with Kimchi, 145

Huevos Rancheros Soft Tacos with Avocado Pico de Gallo, 251

I

ice cream

making, 212

Milk Ice Cream, 213

Peanut Butter Ice Cream, 239

ice cream machines, 212

Ice Cream Sundaes, Peanut Butter, with Hot Fudge and Peanut Brittle, 237

Individual Beef Wellingtons, 130

J

Jägermeister, in La Presa, 21

Jägermeister-Black Cherry Cola Glaze, Baby Back Ribs with, 151

Jalapeño Lime Crema, in Chile Relleno Empanadas, 41

Jalapeños, Pickled, 157

Jalapeño Soy Sauce, in Seared-Squid Lettuce Wraps with Spicy Carrot Slaw, 124

Jicama-Peanut Slaw, Tuna Sushi Satays with, 115

jiggers, 18

Juicy Lucy Sausage Biscuits, 256

julep strainers, 18

K

Kale, Apple, and Pancetta Salad, 73

katsuo fumi furikake

about, 121

in Salt-and-Pepper Shrimp with Thai Papaya Salad, 121

Kavourakis, Jonathan, 129

Kewpie mayonnaise, about, 197

Kimchi, Korean Short Rib Tacos with, 145

Kingrey, Kyle, 73

kitchen essentials, 10

Korean Short Rib Tacos with Kimchi, 145

L

lamb. *See also* merguez

Lamb Souvlaki with Tzatziki and Lime-Harissa Aioli, 161

Pasta with Spicy Veal and Lamb Bolognese, 170

Lamb Souvlaki with Tzatziki and Lime-Harissa Aioli, 161

La Presa, 21

Latino pantry ingredients, 6

Latkes, Potato, with Sour Cream and Fresh Applesauce, 254

lemons

Asparagus Ribbon and Spring Pea Salad with Lemon Ricotta, 67

Avocado, Lemon, and Espelette Focaccia, 47

Dried Citrus Chips, 15

Lemon Berry Pancakes with Whipped Citrus Ricotta, 260

Lemon Simple Syrup, 24

Lemon Berry Pancakes with Whipped Citrus Ricotta, 260

lemongrass

in Asian Noodles with Shrimp, Miso Butter, and Spicy Peanuts, 174

in Thai Marinated Papaya Salad, 76

Lettuce Wraps with Spicy Carrot Slaw, Seared-Squid, 124

Lime and Blackberry Semifreddo, 235

Lime-Harissa Aioli, Lamb Souvlaki with Tzatziki and, 161

M

Mac 'n' Cheese with Chorizo and Poblanos, 169

Maggi seasoning

about, 26

in The Best Bloody Mary, 26

make-ahead techniques, 6–7

Manchego cheese

in Baked Eggs with Serrano Ham and Manchego "Grits," 247

in Chile Relleno Empanadas, 41

in My House Salad with Carrot Harissa Vinaigrette, 70

in Open-Faced Chicken Arepas with Salsa Verde, 96

mandolines, 71

Mango Salsa, Red Snapper Mini-Tacos with Guacamole and, 110

Manicotti, Ricotta and Basil, 184

Marinara Sauce, Old-School Meatballs with, 142

marinating tip, 6

Martini, Pink Grapefruit-Mint, 20

Mascarpone Polenta, Creamy, 206

measuring cups, 18

meat. *See* beef; lamb; pork

meatballs

Chicken Meatballs in Creamy Mushroom Sauce with Whipped Ricotta, 91

Old-School Meatballs with Marinara Sauce, 142

menu planning, 4, 7

merguez

about, 6, 173

Rigatoni with Merguez, Ricotta Salata, and Brown Butter, 173

mescal, in La Presa, 21

Midori Vinaigrette, in Thai Marinated Papaya Salad, 76

Milk Ice Cream, 213

in Devil's Food Cake with Vanilla Mascarpone Filling, 210

mise en place, 6

miso

about, 5

Asian Noodles with Shrimp, Miso Butter, and Spicy Peanuts, 174

Miso-Glazed Mushrooms, 201

Seared Tuna with Fried Black Rice and Spicy Miso Sauce, 112

Miso-Glazed Mushrooms, 201

Miso Mayonnaise, in Seared-Squid Lettuce Wraps with Spicy Carrot Slaw, 124

Mixed Berry Sauce, 271

Mozzarella, Spaghetti Caprese with Tomatoes, Spinach, and, 178

muddlers, 18

mushrooms

Chicken Meatballs in Creamy Mushroom Sauce with Whipped Ricotta, 91

in Individual Beef Wellingtons, 130

Miso-Glazed Mushrooms, 201

Orecchiette with Sausage, Leeks, Mushrooms, and Red Peppers, 167

Pasta with Mushroom Ragout, Walnuts, and Pecorino, 175

music playlists, 7

Mussels, Apple-Cider, with Roasted Fall Vegetables and Mustard Butter, 123

Mustard Béchamel Sauce, in Triple-Decker Croque Monsieurs, 244

Mustard-Bourbon Sauce, Ribeye Steak with Garlic-Butter Baste and, 133

Mustard Butter, Apple-Cider Mussels with Roasted Fall Vegetables and, 123

My House Salad with Carrot Harissa Vinaigrette, 70

N

napa cabbage, in Korean Short Rib Tacos with Kimchi, 145

napkins, 9

Nelson, Sarah, 70

nori fumi furikake

about, 51

Nori-Spiced Tuna Poke Crisps, 51

Nori-Spiced Tuna Poke Crisps, 51

O

Old Bay Aioli, Crab Corn Dogs with, 48

Old-School Meatballs with Marinara Sauce, 142

Olive and Red Pepper Chimichurri, Hanger Steak with, 129

Olive Oil-Poached Cod with Beet, Orange, and Tangerine Salad, 106

onions
The Famous French Onion Soup Dumplings, 39
Sexy Sliders with Fancy Sauce and Cola Onions, 139

Open-Faced Chicken Arepas with Salsa Verde, 96

oranges
Dried Citrus Chips, 15
Olive Oil-Poached Cod with Beet, Orange, and Tangerine Salad, 106
Orange and Chile-Glazed Brussels Sprouts, 193
Orange-Marinated Chicken Satay with Peanut Sauce, 88

Orange and Chile-Glazed Brussels Sprouts, 193

Orange-Bourbon Pull-Apart Bread, 264

orange juice, in Red Tequila Sangria, 24

Orange-Marinated Chicken Satay with Peanut Sauce, 88

Orecchiette with Sausage, Leeks, Mushrooms, and Red Peppers, 167

Oreo Pancakes with Vanilla Crème Icing, 259

Orzo with Pancetta and Vegetables, Creamy, 176

P

pancakes
Lemon Berry Pancakes with Whipped Citrus Ricotta, 260
Oreo Pancakes with Vanilla Crème Icing, 259

pancetta
Creamy Orzo with Pancetta and Vegetables, 176
Kale, Apple, and Pancetta Salad, 73
in Pasta with Spicy Veal and Lamb Bolognese, 170

pantry stocking, 5

Panzanella with Tomato Vinaigrette and Blue Cheese, 75

papayas. See green papayas

Parmigiano-Reggiano
about, 6
in Creamy Mascarpone Polenta, 206
in Creamy Orzo with Pancetta and Vegetables, 176
in Old-School Meatballs with Marinara Sauce, 142
in Roasted Cauliflower Gratin with Gremolata Crumbs, 195
Slow-Baked Tomato Bruschetta with Eggs and Parmesan, 243
in Tomato "Tartare" on Brioche Crostini, 55

Parmigiano rinds
about, 171
in Pasta with Spicy Veal and Lamb Bolognese, 170

party planning, 9–10
music playlists, 7

pasta
about, 162
Creamy Orzo with Pancetta and Vegetables, 176
Mac 'n' Cheese with Chorizo and Poblanos, 169
Orecchiette with Sausage, Leeks, Mushrooms, and Red Peppers, 167
Pasta with Mushroom Ragout, Walnuts, and Pecorino, 175
Pasta with Spicy Veal and Lamb Bolognese, 170
Pork Belly Carbonara, 164
Ricotta and Basil Manicotti, 184
Rigatoni with Merguez, Ricotta Salata, and Brown Butter, 173
Spaghetti Caprese with Tomatoes, Mozzarella, and Spinach, 178
Spaghettini with Zucchini and Parsley Pesto, 181

Pasta with Mushroom Ragout, Walnuts, and Pecorino, 175

Pasta with Spicy Veal and Lamb Bolognese, 170

Peanut Butter and Jelly "Twinkies," 224

Peanut Butter Ice Cream, 239

Peanut Butter Ice Cream Sundaes with Hot Fudge and Peanut Brittle, 237

Peanut Sauce, Orange-Marinated Chicken Satay with, 88

pears, in The Woodsman, 23

Pea Salad with Lemon Ricotta, Asparagus Ribbon and Spring, 67

Pecorino Romano
about, 6
Pasta with Mushroom Ragout, Walnuts, and Pecorino, 175
in Pork Belly Carbonara, 164
in Roasted Cauliflower Gratin with Gremolata Crumbs, 195

Peterson, Timothy, 123

Pickled Carrots, 70

Pickled Jalapeños, 157

Pickled Red Onions, 100

Pickled Vegetables, Citrus-, 61

Pierogi, Potato and Goat Cheese, with Caramelized Onions, 52

pierogi parties, 54

Piment d'Espelette
about, 47
Avocado, Lemon, and Espelette Focaccia, 47

Pimiento Cheese, in Juicy Lucy Sausage Biscuits, 256

pineapple juice
making, 29
Ruby Red Punch, 29

Pink Grapefruit-Mint Martini, 20

piquillo peppers
about, 35
Warm Stuffed Piquillo Pepper Bruschetta, 35

Pizza Bianca, 43
in Avocado, Lemon, and Espelette Focaccia, 47
in Chicken Liver Focaccia with Braised Shallot-Rioja Marmalade, 44

plates, 9

platters, 10

poblano chiles

roasting tip, 42

in Chile Relleno Empanadas, 41

Mac 'n' Cheese with Chorizo and Poblanos, 169

Poke Crisps, Nori-Spiced Tuna, 51

Polenta, Creamy Mascarpone, 206

pork. *See also* bacon; ham

about, 126

Baby Back Ribs with Jägermeister-Black Cherry Cola Glaze, 151

Brined Pork Milanese with Tomato-Balsamic Sauce, 149

Chouriço and Pepper Sloppy Joes, 158

Juicy Lucy Sausage Biscuits, 256

Old-School Meatballs with Marinara Sauce, 142

Pork Belly BLT Tacos with Charred-Lime Vinaigrette, 153

Pork Belly Carbonara, 164

Pork Tenderloin with Ancho-Caramel Glaze and BBQ Beans, 147

Pork Belly BLT Tacos with Charred-Lime Vinaigrette, 153

Pork Belly Carbonara, 164

Pork Tenderloin with Ancho-Caramel Glaze and BBQ Beans, 147

potatoes

Angry Potatoes with Cherry Peppers, 202

Potato and Goat Cheese Pierogi with Caramelized Onions, 52

Potato Latkes with Sour Cream and Fresh Applesauce, 254

Potato and Goat Cheese Pierogi with Caramelized Onions, 52

Potato Latkes with Sour Cream and Fresh Applesauce, 254

pots and pans, 10

Pots de Crème, Black-Bottomed Butterscotch, 232

prepping ingredients, 6–7

Prince, Derrick, 137

puff pastry

about, 132

in Individual Beef Wellingtons, 130

Pull-Apart Bread, Orange-Bourbon, 264

Pumpkin Maple Syrup, French Toast Bread Pudding with, 263

Pumpkin Pie Cheesecake with Gingersnap Crust, 217

punches

Ruby Red Punch, 29

Sherry-Citrus Punch, 30

Q

quarter sheet pans, 10, 229

R

radicchio, in Kale, Apple, and Pancetta Salad, 73

radishes

in Asparagus Ribbon and Spring Pea Salad with Lemon Ricotta, 67

in My House Salad with Carrot Harissa Vinaigrette, 70

Red Onions, Pickled, 100

Red Snapper Mini-Tacos with Mango Salsa and Guacamole, 110

Red Tequila Sangria, 24

Red Velvet "Twinkies" with Crème Fraîche Filling, 226

Red Velvet Waffles with Cream Cheese Sauce, 272

Reverse Chocolate Chip Cookies, 230

Ribeye Steak with Garlic-Butter Baste and Mustard-Bourbon Sauce, 133

rice

types of, 207

Arroz con Pollo with Achiote Oil, 89

Seared Tuna with Fried Black Rice and Spicy Miso Sauce, 112

Sticky Rice Cakes, 207

ricotta

Asparagus Ribbon and Spring Pea Salad with Lemon Ricotta, 67

Chicken Meatballs in Creamy Mushroom Sauce with Whipped Ricotta, 91

Lemon Berry Pancakes with Whipped Citrus Ricotta, 260

Ricotta and Basil Manicotti, 184

Ricotta and Basil Manicotti, 184

Ricotta Salata, Rigatoni with Merguez, Brown Butter, and, 173

Rigatoni with Merguez, Ricotta Salata, and Brown Butter, 173

Risotto, Cajun Bacon, 154

Roast Chicken with Citrus Rub, Spatchcocked, 87

Roasted Cauliflower Gratin with Gremolata Crumbs, 195

Roasted Fall Vegetables and Mustard Butter, Apple-Cider Mussels with, 123

Roasted Garlic, 134

roasting peppers and chiles, 42

rock music, 3

Ruby Red Punch, 29

S

sake

about, 58

in Spicy Wok-Seared Edamame, 58

salads

about, 64

Asparagus Ribbon and Spring Pea Salad with Lemon Ricotta, 67

Cobb Salad Bites with Avocado Vinaigrette, 68

Kale, Apple, and Pancetta Salad, 73

My House Salad with Carrot Harissa Vinaigrette, 70

Olive Oil-Poached Cod with Beet, Orange, and Tangerine Salad, 106

Panzanella with Tomato Vinaigrette and Blue Cheese, 75

Soba Noodle and Beet Salad, 77

Spinach Salad with Goat Cheese, Spicy Cashews, and Corn Vinaigrette, 80

Thai Marinated Papaya Salad, 76

Salmon, Wasabi Pea-Crusted, with Soba Noodle and Beet Salad, 109

Salsa Verde, 97
   Open-Faced Chicken Arepas with, 96
Salt-and-Pepper Shrimp with Thai Papaya Salad, 121
Salted Caramel Sauce, 271
sambal oelek, about, 5
sangria
   Red Tequila Sangria, 24
   White Sangria with Cranberry and Cucumber, 28
satays
   Orange-Marinated Chicken Satay with Peanut Sauce, 88
   Tuna Sushi Satays with Jicama-Peanut Slaw, 115
seafood
   about, 104
   Apple-Cider Mussels with Roasted Fall Vegetables and Mustard Butter, 123
   Grilled Chipotle Shrimp with Tomatillo, Roasted Corn, and Feta Salsa, 116
   Olive Oil-Poached Cod with Beet, Orange, and Tangerine Salad, 106
   Red Snapper Mini-Tacos with Mango Salsa and Guacamole, 110
   Salt-and-Pepper Shrimp with Thai Papaya Salad, 121
   Seared-Squid Lettuce Wraps with Spicy Carrot Slaw, 124
   Seared Tuna with Fried Black Rice and Spicy Miso Sauce, 112
   Shrimp and Cheesy "Grits" with Smoky Red Pepper Sauce, 119
   Tuna Sushi Satays with Jicama-Peanut Slaw, 115
   Wasabi Pea-Crusted Salmon with Soba Noodle and Beet Salad, 109
Seared-Squid Lettuce Wraps with Spicy Carrot Slaw, 124
Seared Tuna with Fried Black Rice and Spicy Miso Sauce, 112
Semifreddo, Lime and Blackberry, 235
serrano chiles, in Orange and Chile-Glazed Brussels Sprouts, 193

serving utensils, 9
Sexy Sliders with Fancy Sauce and Cola Onions, 139
Shallot-Rioja Marmalade, Chicken Liver Focaccia with Braised, 44
sheet pans, 10, 229
Sherry-Citrus Punch, 30
shredding soft cheese, 72
shrimp
   Asian Noodles with Shrimp, Miso Butter, and Spicy Peanuts, 174
   Grilled Chipotle Shrimp with Tomatillo, Roasted Corn, and Feta Salsa, 116
   Salt-and-Pepper Shrimp with Thai Papaya Salad, 121
   Shrimp and Cheesy "Grits" with Smoky Red Pepper Sauce, 119
Shrimp and Cheesy "Grits" with Smoky Red Pepper Sauce, 119
Simple Syrup, 24
skillets, 10
Sliders with Fancy Sauce and Cola Onions, Sexy, 139
Slow-Baked Tomato Bruschetta with Eggs and Parmesan, 243
smoked paprika, about, 6
smoked peppercorns, about, 6
Smoky Red Pepper Sauce, Shrimp and Cheesy "Grits" with, 119
Smoky Rubbed Chicken Wings with Honey, Bourbon, and Molasses Sauce, 94
Soba Noodle and Beet Salad, 77
   Wasabi Pea-Crusted Salmon with, 109
soft cheese, shredding tip, 72
soups
   about, 64
   Cream of Tomato Soup, 83
   The Famous French Onion Soup Dumplings, 39
   "Grilled Cheese" Dumplings in Tomato Soup, 36
Souvlaki, Lamb, with Tzatziki and Lime-Harissa Aioli, 161
soy sauce

about, 5
   Spicy Broccolini with Soy and Garlic, 190
Spaghetti Caprese with Tomatoes, Mozzarella, and Spinach, 178
Spaghettini with Zucchini and Parsley Pesto, 181
Spatchcocked Roast Chicken with Citrus Rub, 87
Spiced Crème Fraîche, in French Toast Bread Pudding with Pumpkin Maple Syrup, 263
Spicy Broccolini with Soy and Garlic, 190
Spicy Carrot Slaw, Seared-Squid Lettuce Wraps with, 124
Spicy Miso Sauce, Seared Tuna with Fried Black Rice and, 112
Spicy Veal and Lamb Bolognese, Pasta with, 170
Spicy Wok-Seared Edamame, 58
spinach
   Harissa Pearl Couscous with Tahini and Baby Spinach, 204
   in Kale, Apple, and Pancetta Salad, 73
   Spaghetti Caprese with Tomatoes, Mozzarella, and Spinach, 178
   Spinach Salad with Goat Cheese, Spicy Cashews, and Corn Vinaigrette, 80
Spinach Salad with Goat Cheese, Spicy Cashews, and Corn Vinaigrette, 80
Spring Pea Salad with Lemon Ricotta, Asparagus Ribbon and, 67
Squid Lettuce Wraps with Spicy Carrot Slaw, Seared-, 124
sriracha, about, 5
Sriracha-Orange Mayonnaise, in Twice-Cooked Eggplant with Cilantro-Sesame Pesto, 196
starters
   about, 32
   Avocado, Lemon, and Espelette Focaccia, 47
   Chicken Liver Focaccia with Braised Shallot-Rioja Marmalade, 44

Chile Relleno Empanadas, 41

Citrus-Pickled Vegetables, 61

Crab Corn Dogs with Old Bay Aioli, 48

The Famous French Onion Soup Dumplings, 39

Grilled and Chilled Haricots Verts, 63

"Grilled Cheese" Dumplings in Tomato Soup, 36

Nori-Spiced Tuna Poke Crisps, 51

Pizza Bianca, 43

Potato and Goat Cheese Pierogi with Caramelized Onions, 52

Salt-and-Pepper Shrimp with Thai Papaya Salad, 121

Spicy Wok-Seared Edamame, 58

Tomato "Tartare" on Brioche Crostini, 55

Warm Stuffed Piquillo Pepper Bruschetta, 35

Sticky Rice Cakes, 207

in "Beef and Broccoli," 137

Stock, Vegetable, 190

Stout Cakes with Toffee Sauce, Warm, 214

strawberry preserves, in Peanut Butter and Jelly "Twinkies," 224

strawberry puree

in Beauty Elixir, 14

in Garnet Gimlet, 27

Sudberg, Jaime, 221

T

tablecloths, 9

tacos

Huevos Rancheros Soft Tacos with Avocado Pico de Gallo, 251

Korean Short Rib Tacos with Kimchi, 145

Pork Belly BLT Tacos with Charred-Lime Vinaigrette, 153

Red Snapper Mini-Tacos with Mango Salsa and Guacamole, 110

Tahini and Baby Spinach, Harissa Pearl Couscous with, 204

Taquitos, Chicken, with Guacamole Puree, 101

Tart, Apple, with Cheddar Streusel, 221

"Tartare" on Brioche Crostini, Tomato, 55

tequila

in The Coronado, 16

in Red Tequila Sangria, 24

Thai basil

about, 5

in Asian Noodles with Shrimp, Miso Butter, and Spicy Peanuts, 174

in Asian Pesto, 79

in Thai Marinated Papaya Salad, 76

Thai Marinated Papaya Salad, 76

Salt-and-Pepper Shrimp with, 121

Toffee Sauce, Warm Stout Cakes with, 214

togarashi

about, 113

in Seared Tuna with Fried Black Rice and Spicy Miso Sauce, 112

tomatillos

in Chilaquiles Verdes with Chipotle Chicken, 99

in Grilled Cheddar and Jalapeño Bacon Sandwiches, 156

Grilled Chipotle Shrimp with Tomatillo, Roasted Corn, and Feta Salsa, 116

in Salsa Verde, 97

tomatoes

Cream of Tomato Soup, 83

"Grilled Cheese" Dumplings in Tomato Soup, 36

Old-School Meatballs with Marinara Sauce, 142

Slow-Baked Tomato Bruschetta with Eggs and Parmesan, 243

Spaghetti Caprese with Tomatoes, Mozzarella, and Spinach, 178

Tomato "Tartare" on Brioche Crostini, 55

Tomato-Balsamic Sauce, Brined Pork Milanese with, 149

Tomato-Guajillo Sauce, in Pork Belly BLT Tacos with Charred-Lime Vinaigrette, 153

tomato juice, in The Best Bloody Mary, 26

Tomato "Tartare" on Brioche Crostini, 55

Tomato Vinaigrette and Blue Cheese, Panzanella with, 75

Triple-Decker Croque Monsieurs, 244

Truffle Crème Fraîche, in Potato and Goat Cheese Pierogi with Caramelized Onions, 52

tuna

Nori-Spiced Tuna Poke Crisps, 51

Seared Tuna with Fried Black Rice and Spicy Miso Sauce, 112

Tuna Sushi Satays with Jicama-Peanut Slaw, 115

Tuna Sushi Satays with Jicama-Peanut Slaw, 115

Twice-Cooked Eggplant with Cilantro-Sesame Pesto, 196

"Twinkies"

Peanut Butter and Jelly, 224

Red Velvet, with Crème Fraîche Filling, 226

Tzatziki, Lamb Souvlaki with Lime-Harissa Aioli and, 161

U

umami, 5, 201

V

Vanilla Crème Icing, Oreo Pancakes with, 259

Vanilla Mascarpone Filling, Devil's Food Cake with, 210

Veal and Lamb Bolognese, Pasta with Spicy, 170

vegetables. *See also specific vegetables*

about, 186

Citrus-Pickled Vegetables, 61

Vegetable Stock, 190

vinaigrettes

Apple Cider Vinaigrette, 73

Asian Dressing, 77

Avocado Vinaigrette, 68

Carrot Harissa Vinaigrette, 70

Charred-Lime Vinaigrette, 153

Corn Vinaigrette, 80

Dijon Vinaigrette, 67

Midori Vinaigrette, 76

Tangerines and Sherry Vinaigrette, 106

Tomato Vinaigrette, 75

vinegars, about, 6

vodka

in The Best Bloody Mary, 26

in Emerald Gimlet, 17

in Ginger Rogers, 19

in Pink Grapefruit-Mint Martini, 20

W

waffles

Fried Chicken with Cheddar Waffles and Spicy Butter, 249

Red Velvet Waffles with Cream Cheese Sauce, 272

Warm Stout Cakes with Toffee Sauce, 214

Warm Stuffed Piquillo Pepper Bruschetta, 35

Wasabi Pea-Crusted Salmon with Soba Noodle and Beet Salad, 109

Whipped Citrus Ricotta, Lemon Berry Pancakes with, 260

Whipped Coconut Topping, in Black-Bottomed Butterscotch Pots de Crème, 232

White Chocolate Blondies with Semisweet Chips, 229

White Sangria with Cranberry and Cucumber, 28

white truffle oil, about, 6

wonton wrappers

in The Famous French Onion Soup Dumplings, 39

in Nori-Spiced Tuna Poke Crisps, 51

Woodsman, The, 23

Z

Zucchini and Parsley Pesto, Spaghettini with, 181

ABOUT THE AUTHORS

Chris Santos is executive chef at three of the hottest and most iconic restaurants in New York City: Vandal, Beauty & Essex, and The Stanton Social, all on Manhattan's Lower East Side, and has recently created new venues in Las Vegas and Los Angeles. He is also a longtime resident judge on *Chopped*, the Food Network's most popular series, and has appeared on many other national television shows, including *The Rachael Ray Show* and *Today*. His website is santoscooks.com.

Rick Rodgers is the author of over forty cookbooks on subjects ranging from Viennese cafés to Thanksgiving. He is also an award-winning culinary teacher and has worked behind the scenes on cookbook projects for many celebrities and corporations. His website is rickrodgers.com.